Toward a Caring Society

3-20-12

TOWARD A CARING SOCIETY

Ideas into Action

Pearl M. Oliner and Samuel P. Oliner

PRAEGER

Westport, Connecticut
London

Library of Congress Cataloging-in-Publication Data

Oliner, Pearl M.
Toward a caring society : ideas into action / Pearl M. Oliner
and Samuel P. Oliner.
p.   cm.
Includes bibliographical references (p.   ) and index.
ISBN 0–275–95198–7 (acid-free paper).—ISBN 0–275–95453–6 (pbk.)
1. Altruism. 2. Caring. 3. Helping behavior. I. Oliner, Samuel
P. II. Title.
BJ1474.039 1995
171'.8—dc20   95–3339

British Library Cataloguing in Publication Data is available.

Library of Congress Catalog Card Number: 95–3339
ISBN: 0–275–95198–7
     0–275–95453–6 (pbk.)

First published in 1995

Praeger Publishers, 88 Post Road West, Westport, CT 06881
An imprint of Greenwood Publishing Group, Inc.

Printed in the United States of America

The paper used in this book complies with the
Permanent Paper Standard issued by the National
Information Standards Organization (Z39.48–1984).

10 9 8 7 6 5 4 3 2 1

Contents

Preface

In 1988 we completed a study which had a significant impact on our lives. The people we studied were non-Jews who, without benefit of any external rewards, had risked their lives, and often those of their families, to help some Jews survive the Nazi Holocaust. Rescuers, as they are commonly called, constituted less than one-half of one percent of the total population under German occupation. Hence they were extraordinary by virtue of their altruistic behavior as well as their numbers. By the time we concluded our work, we felt we understood some of the personality and situational factors which distinguished them so markedly from others.[1]

Following the study's publication, we were invited to address varied audiences both in the United States and abroad. These audiences often included people whose interest in the topic was more practical than academic. What they wanted to know above all were the pragmatic implications of our study. "What importance does this study have for our lives today?" was a typical question.

We found this question challenging and compelling. As we interpreted it, what people wanted to know was how to make our society a more caring one. This book is our attempt to answer this question.

Care in our view represents one of the primary moral challenges we face as a society. Care is the quality which promotes hope and a sense of investment in a society's future. Along with many other social critics, we believe that our society is out of balance: competition, individualism, and market relationships dominate our social lives. While we would argue that all these forms of social relationships are important in meeting individual and societal needs, we believe they need to be supplemented by care. Without a sense of being cared for or caring about others, people will have little reason to feel themselves part of a community or bound by notions of solidarity or group norms.

Like many contemporary social scientists, we find human behavior very complex and are painfully aware of the limitations of research, including our own. We believe that although more is known today than ever before about the conditions which promote care, much of this information has yet to reach a wide audience. This book is our attempt to disseminate this new knowledge, but in a way that will give readers ideas for action.

Our purpose here is to provide some pragmatic guidelines for individuals and groups who would like to enhance the caring quality of their private and public lives. We thus intend this book for educators, business people, professional and occupational groups, religious leaders and parishioners, parents, community activists, and generalists who want to consider their own and others' behaviors in the context of the organizations and institutions in which they routinely live their lives with the view of making them more caring. We believe it will be particularly useful for administrators and leaders who are seeking organizational changes that can enhance a sense of community as well as productivity, including administrators in business, education, social work, health occupations, and related fields. Because it is concerned with a primary moral issue, it should also be of interest to those who are concerned with moral action. Since a theoretical view of how change occurs and the forms it needs to take in order to realize a better society underlies all that follows, the book should also interest those concerned with the process of social change, the culture and structures of societal institutions, and community development.

In order to make our points, we give many examples. We make extensive use of published autobiographical and biographical materials, case studies, and interviews. Our primary consideration was their illustrative power, but we also tried to choose materials that were well written and richly allusive. Because we also wanted to suggest the broad applicability of the concepts we discuss, we chose materials that reflect a wide diversity of social contexts. Finally, we chose materials because we found them inspirational: they spoke movingly to us of human power and passion in the service of the "good." We hope the reader will find them similarly so.

NOTE

1. Samuel P. Oliner and Pearl M. Oliner, *The Altruistic Personality: Rescuers of Jews in Nazi Europe* (New York: Free Press, 1988).

Acknowledgments

We are most grateful to Eli Evans and the Charles H. Revson Foundation whose generous financial support made this project possible. We also want to express our deep appreciation to our colleagues who read the manuscript and provided us with many valuable suggestions—most notably among them Michelle McKeegan, Professors Susan Frances and Janusz Reykowski, and Dr. Marianne Pennekamp. We also want to thank Dean Lee Bowker of the College of Behavioral and Social Sciences at Humboldt State University and Linda Hall-Martin for their help in preparing the manuscript for publication.

Toward a Caring Society

CHAPTER 1

In Pursuit of Care

Some ten years ago, historian Irving Bernstein wrote a book bearing a title strikingly similar to our own but reflecting a very different meaning and social context. Called *A Caring Society*, Bernstein's book deals with the Great Depression in the United States—the years between 1929 and 1941—when savage unemployment made the lives of the majority desperate. The "caring society" Bernstein describes was the government's creation: it was the welfare state the New Deal under Franklin Delano Roosevelt designed to address unemployment through such measures as unemployment relief, welfare programs, the protection of the right of workers to organize and bargain collectively, and old age pensions.[1]

In today's context, the problems of the thirties seem almost simple and the very notion that government could create a caring society highly disputable. The major problem of the thirties was material; today's problems are both material and something more difficult to name. Sometimes described as a malaise of the soul, it includes a sense of loss of place and people, a breakdown of personal commitments, and a retreat from moral norms which define and hold communities together. The character of our contemporary society seems better captured by hostility than social glue: contentiousness has become increasingly common between men and women, parents and children, ethnic and racial groups, homosexuals and heterosexuals, those in authority and those over whom they might claim authority.

If the problems are different, they share at least one theme common to that implied by Bernstein. As in the thirties, far too many people feel uncared for and even more feel little responsibility to care for others. Without care, hope and a sense of investment in a society's future vanish.

But, as we see it, no government can resolve today's non-care problems, nor can any political program or structural change eliminate them, although they can help facilitate solutions. Change, we believe, needs to come primarily from the "inside out"—that is, from individuals finding, nurturing, and creating the conditions that promote care within the social institutions in which they routinely live their lives. A caring society, we believe, depends on just this very process.

A caring society, as we conceive it, is one in which care penetrates all major social institutions, including the family, schools, the workplace and religious institutions. Penetrating means to be present in some important degree, but it does not mean expunging or replacing all other modes of social relationships or goals. Educational institutions whose primary goal may be individual accomplishment, for example, can nonetheless accommodate and integrate care; the same can be said of businesses whose primary goal is profit. Competition and individualism appear to be basic human needs, and society benefits from them. But they need to be tempered and balanced by care.

Our purpose here is to provide some guidelines for individuals and groups who would like to enhance the caring quality of their private and public lives. We have distilled these guidelines from a wide variety of empirical, theoretical, and philosophical sources, including but not limited to sources in social psychology, management and communication theory, and feminist, ethnic, ecological, and peace studies. We have attempted to make these guidelines concrete and widely applicable, as relevant to the work place as to families, to schools as to religious institutions. In short, we hope they can be useful for all people who want to consider their own and others' behaviors in the context of the organizations and institutions in which they routinely live their lives, with the view of making them more caring.

We have organized our guidelines around a schematic framework which reflects our conception of care. Care, as we define it, means assuming personal responsibility for others' welfare. To assume personal responsibility for others' welfare means to acknowledge others' needs and to act responsively. The "others" we have in mind are a broad constituency: they include not only other humans in our immediate surroundings and those in more remote environments and communities, but also other living organisms and non-living things. Caring as we use the term is thus particularistic and planetary, national and global, encompassing humans and non-humans, the hemisphere and the ecosphere.

The scope of our framework reflects this particularity and generality. Care restricted to particular others threatens the welfare of generalized others; similarly, care confined to generalized others alone threatens particular others' welfare. To best illustrate this critical point, we offer some concrete examples.

Our first example, a very dramatic one, is the story of Horst Mahler, cofounder of and major theoretician for "The Red Army Faction," a notorious German terrorist group. Our account is based on an article by psychiatrist Otto Billig.

On October 9, 1970, Mahler was arrested. Subsequently tried and found guilty of armed robbery and conspiring to form a criminal organization, he was sentenced to twelve years imprisonment. A young and promising lawyer of conservative appearance, he evolved from member of a right-wing dueling fraternity at the Free University of Berlin to moderate Social Democrat (SPD) and finally to urban guerrilla—a classic illustration of the potential destructiveness of an ideologist run amok. Intent on saving the world and self-defined as a "moral rigorist," he wound up defending violence not only toward the very masses whose champion he was, but also toward his comrades in the struggle.[2]

Only eight years old when the Nazi regime collapsed, Mahler was deeply influenced by events of that period. Although his father, a dentist, remained an unrepentant Nazi, Mahler regarded him as a "good man." But he was deeply troubled by the role his parents had played in the Holocaust. The real culprit, he came to believe, was the State. In Nazi times, as well as currently, the State was the "absolute enemy . . . the world's evil, guilty of daily and unending suffering, murder, and manslaughter."[3] Because it threatened civilization by its abuse of modern technology and science, the State, along with the capitalistic system it supported, needed to be destroyed.

Concerned at first with injuries to human life, Mahler limited his initial activities to leading demonstrations and riots. Although he intended no harm to people, injuries to policemen as well as participants and bystanders occurred. When an elderly employee of the Berlin library was shot and severely injured during a complicated caper to free Andreas Baader from prison (a fellow conspirator who later became the head of the Baader-Meinhof gang), Mahler defended the action as an unfortunate unplanned by-product. Following his return to Germany from Jordan, however, where he and several colleagues had learned guerilla tactics at a Palestine Liberation Organization (PLO) camp, his tactics became increasingly violent. To obtain the money and weapons they needed for their forthcoming armed battle against the State, the conspirators planned several bank robberies and attacks on army installations.

To inure themselves against any lingering sensitivities toward harming others, Mahler and his associates developed an appropriate dehumanizing language. Those who opposed them or did not rally to their cause, they called "pigs" and "bulls"; those who sympathized or struggled with them were "comrades." The line between saviors and oppressors became increasingly blurred; eventually, any dissenter, even from within the group itself, was also labeled a "pig."

Revolution demanded courage and independence, said Mahler: the courage not only to face the enemy but also to face one's friend. Friendship was dangerous; it imposed obligations, bound one to the group's ideas, and impeded asking difficult questions as well as thinking in innovative ways. As he explained in a subsequent interview, it was not only "honorable to overcome cowardice in the face of the enemy," but also honorable to overcome the cowardice that "confronts us when meeting a friend."[4] Transforming society thus required severing all personal ties. Innocent victims, including one's friends and families, might suffer—a small price to pay for the salvation of the world's innocents.

What does Mahler's story tell us? Like many young Germans, he felt deeply repelled by his country's past. Like them, he found it difficult to reconcile his affection for his parents with his knowledge of their involvement in the Holocaust. Mahler found it particularly difficult in light of his father's unrepentant Nazi stance. Rather than confront his father directly, Mahler resorted to a common strategy; he exonerated his father by externalizing the blame. Once having transferred the guilt to the "system," he eventually developed an ideology which allowed him to sever all personal obligations for the sake of his "principles." As he assessed it, personal relationships impeded the cause, for they weakened his resolve by reminding him of others' pain and suffering. Only as he could detach himself from the lives of the real people around him, could he inflict the suffering required for the fulfillment of his higher purposes.

In Mahler's case, as for others like him, caring impulses had gone awry. His is the potential pathology of principled ideologists who eschew personal attachments. Mahler represents one extreme of the non-caring spectrum—a person whose attachment to abstractions eventually overcame his concern for real people.

At the other extreme of the non-caring spectrum is the particularist, passionately but exclusively attached to his or her own group alone.

Exclusivist attachments often begin benevolently. Enveloped in local warmth, emanating from families, political values, or churches, particularists may engage in multiple acts of generosity and care. Centered on their own groups alone, however, they may allow the larger society to become increasingly invisible or irrelevant.

Pastor Larry Beckett's evangelical church, a warm and loving group as pictured by sociologist Robert Bellah and his associates, is an example of a strongly attached local community:

There is freshly baked zucchini bread sitting out on the counter of the church's modest kitchen, and the whole community has the feeling of a family. Here members practice the virtues of their biblical ethic, learning to put the needs of others before their own . . . One must personally, as an individual, resist temptation and put the good of others ahead of one's own. Christian love applies to one-to-one relationships—I may not cheat my neighbor, or exploit him, or sell him something I know he can't afford.[5]

Enveloped by both "bread" and "love," Beckett's congregation exudes care. And who can fault an ethic that demands putting "the good of others ahead of one's own?" Yet as Bellah describes it, "the bonds of loyalty, help, and responsibility remain oriented to the exclusive sect of those who are 'real' Christians,"[6] and "real" Christians are those who subscribe to this church's views. And according to Beckett, these views are God's views; unchanging and inerrant, they include the divinity of Christ and the authority of Scripture. As Beckett says, "God doesn't change. The values don't change. Jesus Christ doesn't change. In fact, the Bible says He is the same yesterday, today, and forever."[7] As a consequence, observes Bellah, members have no sense of how the Church has coped with the world historically and no language to deal with contemporary social reality. And their "emphasis on love," he notes, so apparent in their own community, "is not shared with the world, except through missionary outreach."[8]

For Bellah, evangelicals like Beckett reflect a shared American moral malaise. By focusing on a personal, private morality rather than a social and public one, it separates members from attachment to the wider society. Yet, it can be argued that if this type of insulation and rigidity does not promote attachments to the wider society, it is reasonably harmless, particularly in democratic societies undergirded by a pluralistic ideology. Even fundamentalists, who more aggressively seek power over others by creating external enemies, are contained within democratic societies.[9] But under conditions of political uncertainty and instability, groups marked by exclusivist attachments and loyalties—religious, ethnic, or racial—can fuel unbridled violence.

The "ethnic cleansing" campaigns which have accompanied the breakup of Yugoslavia are but one recent reminder of the savagery that can surface under periods of political transition. Religiosity, ethnicity, or race underlay as many as twenty-five of the thirty-two wars fought around the globe in 1988: Protestants and Catholics in Ireland, Muslims and Jews in the Middle East, Sunnites and Shiites in the Persian Gulf, Buddhists and Hindus in Ceylon, Hindus and Sikhs in India, Christians and Muslims in Armenia and Azerbaijan, Buddhists and Communists in Tibet.[10] When an entire society is dominated by competing exclusivist groups, such as Lebanon, the results can be a tragic, unending cycle of violence.

More than 120,000 lives were lost in Lebanon between the beginning of the civil war in 1975 and 1989, and most observers see no resolution in sight. The problem, says Sandra Mackey, does not lie in Lebanon's multiple religious sects, seventeen of which are officially recognized, but rather in their exclusivist sectarian commitments. As a result, writes Mackey, "Lebanon never functioned as an integrated society, only as a collection of individuals united in close-knit communal groups jealously guarding their own interests." Hence, long before the onset of war, two-thirds of the population paid no taxes and politicians routinely used bribery and intimidation to con-

duct public life. Legalities have no meaning outside the group to which a
Lebanese owes his or her allegiance, says Mackey, for the ties which bind
him and supersede all others are "kinship, fealty, and confessional loyalties."[11]

If in Horst Mahler's case, abstractions had replaced all sense of kinship
and personal loyalties, in the case of Lebanon's sects, kinship and personal
loyalties are all that matters. Both models of care are deeply and perniciously
flawed; the ensuing suffering their adherents cause appears to us not accidental but inevitable given their posture. Real caring needs to be rooted in
both personal attachments to one's groups and inclusion of others outside
them.

The salience of this dual rootedness was brought home to us in a study
we completed in 1988 and to which we refer often. The people we studied
were non-Jews who, without benefit of any external rewards, had risked their
lives, and sometimes those of their families, to help some Jews survive the
Nazi Holocaust. Rescuers, as they are commonly called, constituted less than
one-half of one percent of the total population under German occupation.
Hence they were extraordinary by virtue of their altruistic behavior as well
as their numbers. What influenced them to take on these risks, we wondered,
and how did they differ from nonrescuers, the vast majority of their countrymen? By the time we concluded our study, we felt we understood some
of the personality and situational factors that distinguished them so markedly.

To better explain their behaviors, we compared a sample of rescuers with
a sample of nonrescuers; that is, persons who had lived in the same geo-
graphical areas during that period but had not rescued Jews. Two of the
significant differences between these groups were the degree to which rescuers felt attached to those around them and the degree to which they felt
obligated toward diverse other groups. More typically than nonrescuers, rescuers described their family relationships as very close and their parents as
caring models. More typically than nonrescuers, too, they made Jewish
friends even when both groups had similar opportunities for doing so in
their schools, neighborhoods, and places of work. And more typically than
nonrescuers, rescuers expressed a sense of commitment to the broader society and rejected ethnocentric attitudes while emphasizing their psychological similarity to diverse groups: rich and poor, Jews and Gypsies.[12]

The scope of the schematic framework we propose, and which underlies
this book, is directly related to the above considerations. It consists of eight
social processes, four of which focus on means to promote attachments with
those in our immediate settings, and four of which focus of promoting
caring relationships with those outside our immediate settings and groups,
extending to the globe.

We call the first four attaching processes. They include opportunities for
(1) *bonding*: forming positive connections and a sense of communion with

others; (2) *empathizing*: understanding others' feelings and emotions, sometimes even feeling what they feel; (3) *learning caring norms*: acquiring caring rules and values; and (4) *practicing care and assuming personal responsibility*: participating in caring activities and developing a sense of personal obligation for doing so.

We call the last four including processes. They include opportunities for (5) *diversifying*: interacting in a collegial way with different types of people for the purpose of getting to know and understand them; (6) *networking*: working together with multiple diverse others for the purpose of developing and implementing shared objectives; (7) *resolving conflicts*: learning the strategies for using and resolving conflicts for mutually beneficial purposes; and (8) *establishing global connections*: linking the here-and-now with people and places far-and-wide throughout the planet in the service of care.

People who participate in institutions that provide opportunities for all these processes to occur, we believe, are more likely to feel cared for and are more likely to care for others. They are also more likely, we believe, to resist the excesses of ideological dogma and exclusivity.

The eight processes identified above, the core of our scheme, serve as the organizing concepts for the chapters which follow. Each chapter highlights one of them and proposes strategies and conditions to encourage their implementation. So as to suggest their broad applicability, each chapter includes examples that reflect a wide diversity of social contexts. The educational and business contexts receive special attention because they illustrate best how these concepts can be manifested even in institutions that differ sharply in ideology and goals. We hope the reader will not be too disconcerted by these contextual shifts—from school to business, from community scenes to social agencies among others—but will rather understand the underlying idea; namely that each concept can be applied to a single and particular social institution.

Omitted from what follows is any lengthy discussion of theoretical and empirical complexities or a critical analysis of the personal or institutional constraints which may inhibit the implementation of the above processes. Many factors hinder expressions of care, and even highly benevolently inclined individuals can become persuaded of the futility of trying to overcome them. The rescuers in our 1988 study offer a sharp reminder of this point; unlike some kindly disposed bystanders (people of good intentions who did not extend help), they preferred to concentrate on what they needed to do rather than on what might have kept them from doing it. We offer our suggestions in that spirit.

A tone of optimism underlies the pages which follow. We presume that social institutions are modifiable, that individuals within them have both the desire and the potential for making them more responsive to caring concerns, and that conscious choice can arrest thoughtless drift. While we certainly do not presume that attending to the social processes we propose is all that is required to make society more caring, we believe it can help move us toward that goal.

NOTES

1. Irving Bernstein, *A Caring Society: The New Deal, the Worker, and the Great Depression* (Boston: Houghton Mifflin, 1985).

2. This account is based on an article by Otto Billig, "The Lawyer Terrorist and His Comrades," *Political Psychology*, 6:1 (1985): 29–46. Clinical Professor of Psychiatry in the School of Medicine at Vanderbilt University, Billig based his interpretations on publicly available sources, including interviews published in Germany.

3. A. Jeschke and W. Malanowski, "Der Minister und der Terrorist" (Hamburg: Spiegel Buch, 1980), cited in Billig, 38.

4. Jeschke and W. Malanowski in Billig, 43. The paragraph from which this quotation is taken actually reads as follows: "He (Mahler) stressed that his past upbringing had taught him that it was only 'honorable to overcome cowardice in the face of the enemy but there is also cowardice that confronts us when meeting a friend that must be overcome. It hinders us to shake taboos established by the consensus of the group that keeps us from posing questions and that prevents us from gaining new insights that would switch our actions to new tracks.' "

5. Robert N. Bellah et al., *Habits of the Heart: Individualism and Commitment in American Life* (Berkeley: University of California Press, 1985), 231.

6. Bellah et al., 232.

7. Bellah et al., 230.

8. Bellah et al., 232.

9. Martin E. Marty and R. Scott Appleby, directors of the Fundamentalism Project of the American Academy of Arts and Sciences, say that fundamentalists deliberately create this dualistic view (they use the word "scandalize" to describe the strategy) so as to ensure that followers understand clearly and unflinchingly the fundamental nature of the issue and will resist any temptation to compromise or negotiate. As they observe, however, some "Marxists, secularists, rationalists, scientists, feminists, and liberals . . . bear a family resemblance to some religious fundamentalists when it comes to intolerance" (Martin E. Marty and R. Scott Appleby, *The Glory and the Power: The Fundamentalist Challenge to the Modern World* [Boston: Beacon Press, 1992], 198).

10. This is the estimate given by The Santa Barbara Peace Resource Center, cited in the Arthur Schlesinger, Jr., review of *The Opening of the American Mind*, by Alan Bloom, *The New York Times Book Review*, July 23, 1989, 1+.

11. Sandra Mackey, *Lebanon: Death of a Nation* (New York: Congdon and Weed, 1989), 82.

12. Samuel P. Oliner and Pearl M. Oliner, *The Altruistic Personality: Rescuers of Jews in Nazi Europe* (New York: Free Press, 1988).

CHAPTER 2

Bonding

There are certain places in Europe which are particularly troublesome to history and geography teachers: Trieste, the Saar Basin, Schleswig-Holstein. Just such a sore spot is the city of Vilna. In the last half-century it belonged to various countries and saw various armies in its streets.

During my school and university years the city belonged to Poland. It lies in a land of forests, lakes, and streams, concealed in a woody dale. Travelers see it emerge unexpectedly from behind the trees. The steeples of its scores of Catholic churches, built by Italian architects in the baroque style, contrast in their gold and white with the blackness of the surrounding pines.

The life of the town unfolded in a rhythm that was slower and less subject to change than forms of government or borders of kingdoms . . . On Sundays, crowds filled the narrow street leading to the old city gate upon which, in a chapel, was housed the picture of the Virgin known for its miraculous powers . . . In the little streets of the Jewish quarter on a Friday evening, through the windows one could see families seated in the gleam of candlelight . . . Great fairs on Catholic holidays attracted peasants from neighboring villages to the city, where they would display their wooden wares and medicinal herbs on the ground . . . In the winter the steep streets were filled with boys and girls on skis, their red and green jerkins flashing against a snow that became rosy in the frosty sun.

During that time, every spring . . . the trees would turn green; and ever since, nowhere else has the green seemed so joyous to me.[1]

Czeslaw Milosz, the Nobel Prize prize poet, wrote these words in France, several years after he left Poland. They leave little doubt about the ties he continued to feel. Vilna's grand forests, lakes, and sky are an inextricable part of his youthful joys. Its history, whether reflected in the details of its architecture or the fate of its people, cannot be separated from his own. Even as its tragic past continues to haunt him—the city and its populations have been repeatedly violated by conquerors—the Vilna of his youth nourished him with majestic images and sensory delights.

"Bonds" is a shorthand way of describing such feelings. They refer to the attachments people make to places or people; those locales, individuals, or groups with which they feel intensely interconnected, related, affiliated, and identified. Bonds remain real and ever-present internally even if their sources are externally transformed or removed.

The bonds Milosz expresses in the above passage are primarily to *place*. The physical setting dominates his memories, and the people he mentions are not individuals but groups, notable because they lend color and vibrancy to the place.

For Russell Baker, an American journalist growing up in Belleville, New Jersey, during the Depression, "home" was far less grand but no less nourishing. Like Milosz, the bonds he continued to feel some fifty years later remain very strong, but their objects are quite different. The following excerpt taken from his book *Growing Up* captures some of this difference:

Often, waking deep in the night, I heard them down in the kitchen talking, talking, talking. Sitting around the table under the unshaded light bulb, they talked the night away, reheating the coffee, then making fresh coffee, then reheating the pot again, and talking, talking, talking. I would lie on my daybed half awake listening to the murmur of voices, the clatter of cups, the splash of water in the sink, the occasional burst of laughter, the warning voice saying, "Hold it down, you'll wake the children."

Now and then I could make out a distinct phrase or two. "Lucy, remember the time old Mr. Digges . . . ?" This was Uncle Charlie addressing my mother. "—reminds me of the time the cops arrested Jim over in Jersey City." This was Uncle Allen retelling a story I'd heard many times. Uncle Hal's mellow drawl would come in: "—so I didn't do a thing but tell that dirty scoundrel, 'Man, don't you ever try—' " And I would drop off to sleep again, lulled by the comforting familiarity of those kitchen sounds.[2]

Baker's kitchen, as he describes it, had little merit of its own, and its austerity highlighted its real purpose. The hub of family talk, it provided a functional setting for family intimates to act out their relationships. The nightly conversations affirmed their connections to one another. Ordinary and predictable, the talk warmed Baker, rooting him in a sense of dependable continuity and ongoing familial connections.

The bonds Baker expresses in the above are to *people*; more precisely to individuals who played an extremely important role in his life. Psychologists call this social bonding, and they know more about its consequences than they do about bonding with place. Many of them are persuaded that the ability to care about others depends on successful social bonding.

People who fail to form satisfactory social bonds, claim many psychologists, are likely to feel deprived, abandoned, and needy and to experience the world as precarious. Rather than focusing on others' positive characteristics and trusting them, they tend to reject others.[3] Their sense of deprivation, vulnerability, and distrust promotes self-centeredness and demanding expectations of others. Conversely, people who bond with others are more likely to feel competent and to have a sense of personal control over their lives. They are also more likely to be optimistic and have a more positive view of other people and trust them.[4] Their sense of competence, optimism, and trust heightens their tendency to be giving and generous.[5]

Many people associate bonding with infancy; the months immediately after birth, they believe, are the critical period for bonding to occur.[6] Along with many other psychologists, we believe this is an overly deterministic view.[7] Rather than viewing infancy as the only period for bonding to occur with parents alone responsible, we view bonding as an ongoing opportunity that social institutions other than families can provide and through which they can strengthen caring impulses.

In the following pages, we propose some conditions that can promote social bonding in varied contexts throughout life. What they share is their ability to connect individuals to the group, helping them feel that they are important and valued members of the group. We conclude the chapter with a discussion of the similarities and differences between women and men as they relate to bonding needs.

We start with a condition which might be considered so obvious that it would not merit noting except that it is so often overlooked, sometimes with dramatic consequences. Good bonding environments attend to basic biological needs. Like Baker's kitchen, they can be simple, but they need to make sure that people can relieve their hunger, thirst, and physical distress and interact with others in comfort. Migrant workers who have no adequate toilet facilities, for example, are not likely to feel welcome. Disabled people will be effectively barred from participating in any place which does not provide appropriate size doors, ramps, and lifts. And children who spend their school years in densely packed classrooms, without adequate ventilation or light, begin to understand how little others care about them and have little reason to bond with the larger society which produces such circumstances.

Educational crusader Jonathan Kozol gives us a compelling look at what happens to children whose lives are spent in decaying neighborhoods and schools. After spending the years between 1988 and 1990 looking at schools in the inner cities, poor suburbs, and rural areas—New York, San Antonio, East St. Louis, Chicago, Washington, D.C.—he concludes that public schools for non-white ghetto children are "extraordinarily unhappy places." Some sense of how hopelessness develops as early as kindergarten emerges from Kozol's description of one such school, New York Public School 261 in District 10:

The principal . . . tells me that the school's "capacity" is 900 but that there are 1,300 children here . . .

Two first grade classes share a single room without a window, divided only by a blackboard. Four kindergartens and a sixth grade class of Spanish-speaking children have been packed into a single room in which, again, there is no window . . .

I return to see the kindergarten classes on the ground floor and feel stifled once again by lack of air and the low ceiling. Nearly 120 children and adults are doing what they can to make the best of things: 80 children in four kindergarten classes, 30 children in the sixth grade class, and about eight grown-ups who are aides and teachers . . .

As I leave the school, a sixth grade teacher stops to talk. I ask her, "Is there air conditioning in warmer weather?"

Teachers, while inside the building, are reluctant to give answers to this kind of question. Outside, on the sidewalk, she is less constrained: "I had an awful room last year. In the winter it was 56 degrees. In the summer it was up to 90. It was sweltering."

I ask her, "Do the children ever comment on the building?"

"They don't say," she answers, "but they know."

I ask her if they see it as a racial message.

"All these children see TV," she says, "They know what suburban schools are like. Then they look around them at their school. This was a roller-rink, you know . . . They don't comment on it but you see it in their eyes. They understand."[8]

Not surprisingly, only fences and guards can keep youngsters from damaging such schools further, and only extraordinary teachers can persuade them of their value or the value of an education.

If basic biological needs are often overlooked, the need for play tends to be vastly undervalued. Children have a strong need to play, but so do adults. Good bonding environments provide many opportunities to play.

Consider for example this description of Ben Cohen, cofounder of the highly successful Ben & Jerry's Homemade, Inc., and Rick Brown, the company's sales director, who, encircled by a ring of employees, spontaneously decided to wrestle each other one day in this very unconventional manner:

A year ago . . . Ben stripped down and swathed himself sumo style, then marched out into the shipping-and-receiving bay at Ben & Jerry's headquarters in Waterbury, Vermont. Rick Brown, the company's director of sales, came out dressed the same way. They squared off amid the cheers and blood-lust stomp of nearly all the company's employees . . . Ben and Rick puffed out their pale and prodigious stomachs and bounced each other, a couple of human bumper cars trying to determine once and for all who had the baddest belly in the Ben & Jerry's empire."[9]

Given the cheers that went out from the spectators who watched them, Ben and Rick's performance was highly entertaining. But what could have conceivably motivated two grown men, two successful business executives, to bounce their stomachs around in this fashion? And what effects might such behavior have had?

Ben and Rick may very well have been acting out what they already knew as infants and a scenario they learned as men. Play delights both men and women, but it is a primary bonding mechanism for men in particular.

Males generally, boys and men, invest passionate energies in physical activities; the friendships they form with their "playmates" often last for years. And most adult males depend on play, especially physical play, not only to bond with other males, but also with children. Fathers, for example, not only play with their children more often than mothers[10] but also play with them differently. Mothers prefer verbal games, repetitive phrases, and "pat-a-cake"; fathers prefer horseplay, rolling their babies over, tickling them, and tossing them in the air.[11] This may cause mothers anxiety, but infants develop strong attachments to their fathers through such play, sometimes even stronger than to their nurturant mothers as they grow older. Up to six months, for example, infants generally respond more to their mothers; after that time, they frequently begin to show a preference for fathers—smiling, looking at them, and vocalizing more in their presence.[12]

But Ben and Rick did more than play in typical masculine fashion; they played "playfully." Playfulness has a prankish, unpredictable, and humorous quality; and evidence suggests that playfulness not only delights even more than play itself, but promotes group solidarity. As early as three months, for example, infants are already entranced by games such as "peekaboo," where familiar people apparently emerge out of nowhere, and facial distortions, which make known faces unknown.[13] Adults who must spend a great deal of time together in serious activities often depend on playfulness to reduce group tensions, relax conventional rules, and get to know one another. The pranks, elaborate costumes, extravagant dancing and singing which accompany parties in the workplace may appear bizarre in the eyes of uninvolved spectators, but they do help keep groups together.

The importance of play in keeping groups together was dramatically demonstrated among the rescuers we studied. Their lives and the lives of the people they were helping, depended on a combination of extraordinary deception and trust. A word to the wrong person about what they were doing could have tragic consequences. They therefore avoided sharing routine intimacies even with ostensibly trustworthy others for fear of disclosing some bit of information that might be revealed in a moment of weakness or extracted under pressure. Simultaneously, they were enormously dependent on others to provide them with basic necessities to keep their charges alive—such things as food, medical services, and transportation as well as false identity papers and ration cards.

Tensions often reached unbearable levels as rescuers tried to keep everybody at a distance while simultaneously consolidating the feelings of comradeship they so desperately needed to sustain one another. Like the working colleagues described above, one way they dealt with it was through exuberant "parties," pranks, and "black humor." A Dutch rescuer, for example, remembers the boisterous parties of that time, in which food was no more than hot water and a single tea bag, and party garb meant simply exchanging clothes, often men with women. And an Italian priest recalled laughing heartily at a "joke" he contrived to make fun of the very situation which could terrorize both him and the Jews he was hiding:

> One night Morris' mother and sister had their lights on at ten-thirty, so I stomped up to their room and shouted, "Police! Police! Open up!" We could joke about it. One night we had a party. I had a nice piano, and we all sang—loud, like crazy people, late at night. One of them said, "Do you realize that if you turned us in, you could get a bounty of twenty pounds sterling?"[14]

As many rescuers recalled in later years, events like these contributed to their feelings that "people in those times were really united," and that even though those had been the worst of times, they were also the best.

In addition to promoting group bonds, playfulness performs yet another important function, particularly relevant for schools and businesses. According to organizational theorists Karl Weick, James March, and Herbert Simon, playfulness and foolishness, rather than discipline and command, are essential for experimental creativity.[15] In other words, parents and teachers, business executives and politicians looking for innovation and achievement would be better advised to prescribe less and discourage drudgery, and to encourage others to play more with ideas and each other. Ben apparently believes this, for according to observers, his business meetings are almost as playful as his recreational spectacle with Rick, which may help explain in part his company's spectacular success.

Good bonding environments also provide a sense of emotional safety and reassurance. Physical touch is one way of assuring people they are worthy, understood, and cared for.

Angered and worried by media reports of abuse, particularly of children, Americans have become increasingly wary of physical touchers. Yet more than ever, psychologists are emphasizing the importance of physical contact. Diane Ackerman, for example, believes that touch triggers our deepest emotions and is more essential than all other senses. Without caresses, she argues, people of all ages can sicken.[16]

Parents understand this instinctively; they routinely pick up infants when they cry, holding them close to their body. Not all people like to be touched of course—for personal or cultural reasons—but those whom others prefer not to touch—the ill and very old, those who are "different" in some way— often find touch restorative for body and soul.

Lewis Thomas, a self-proclaimed "medicine watcher," not only agrees that touch is critically important, but claims that it once provided the foundation for particular attachments between doctors and patients. When doctors routinely depended on "laying on of hands," patients felt strongly bonded to them. As he describes the process, it resembled a caress:

The doctor's oldest skill in trade was to place his hands on the patient. Over the centuries, the skill became more specialized and refined, the hands learned other things to do beyond mere contact. They probed to feel the pulse at the wrist, the tip of the spleen, or the edge of the liver, thumped to elicit resonant or dull sounds over the lungs, spread ointments over the skin, nicked veins for bleeding, but at the same time touched, caressed, and at the end held on to the patient's fingers.[17]

Nurses, even more than doctors, once provided such comforts, sponging and washing, feeding and grooming their patients. Like doctors, they have largely succumbed to mechanized medicine. Preoccupied by administrative tasks and dependent on machines for diagnoses and pills for treatment, they leave much of the touching undone. While cures have increased, so have patient suits and hostility.

Paradoxically, physically abused children, for whom contact can be terrorizing, may be particularly susceptible to affectionate touching. This helps explain why they often are loathe to sever ties with sexual abusers; in the context of their generally abusive environment, such physical intimacies may provide some relief or even appear affectionate. Appropriate touch can, however, be a source of spiritual healing and strong emotional ties for the abused.

Frederick Douglass is a case in point. Born into slavery from the union of his white, cruel master and a black slave woman, he eventually became an internationally respected voice for oppressed people everywhere. Allison Davis credits this evolution to the love he received from three women: his black grandmother, his white half-sister Lucretia, and her sister-in-law, Sophia Auld. Badly hurt on several occasions, Douglass spoke of their touch many years thereafter. Of Lucretia, he wrote: "With her own soft hand she washed the blood from my head and face, fetched her own balsam bottle, and with the balsam wetted a nice piece of white linen, and bound up my head."[18] Already eighteen years of age, when Sophia was no longer the totally compassionate woman of his childhood, he nonetheless recalled:

She kindly drew a chair by me, and with friendly and consoling words, she took water and washed the blood from my face No mother's hand could have been more tender than hers. She bound up my head and covered my wounded eye with a lean piece of fresh beef. It was almost compensation for all I suffered.[19]

Amidst increasing numbers of disclosures of sexual abuse, many pre-school teachers resist holding and cuddling children. Many of these same children spend hours of the day untouched in settings away from home.[20] Such deprivation, some observers believe, accounts for the increase in youthful aggression and violence.[21] Rather than focusing on overburdened parents, who for assorted economic and psychological reasons absent themselves from homes, realists argue that child raising is legitimately a societal concern. One solution they offer is to incorporate day-care facilities at the workplace site, thus allowing parents to feed, hug, and play with their children during lunch hours and breaks. Some enlightened businesses are beginning to investigate such possibilities; a few are already experimenting with them.

If caretakers for the very young are dissuaded from providing contact comfort, this is even more the case for teachers of older students. Elementary and secondary school teachers are routinely warned not to touch children, particularly adolescents, for fear of being misunderstood or violating cultural taboos. Yet touch was a fundamental way the very popular principal of one particularly successful high school demonstrated his care for students as well as staff. The following comments by one teacher and student, exemplifies what Harvard Professor Sara Lightfoot describes as Mr. Mastruzzi's characteristic style:

"He is very physical, very demonstrative and it affects all of us. Even the kids hold hands in friendship and support . . . it's amazing" . . . "He doesn't draw back from you," says a dark-skinned Black boy who claims that his junior high school teachers were often repelled by and afraid of students of darker hue. "They'd never touch you. Sometimes I felt like I was diseased . . . But I've seen Mastruzzi reach out to all kinds of kids."[22]

Mastruzzi's touch apparently infected the entire school in a literal and emotional way according to this account. As teachers and students touched each other, they felt a sense of group support. Echoing Diane Ackerman's view about the "sickening" effects an absence of affectionate touch can cause, the formerly untouched young man found Mastruzzi's style restorative.

Just as physical touch can provide basic comfort, so can sharing losses. Loss comes in many forms: divorce, illness, and death among them. Largely unacknowledged and unrecognized are the losses which frequently accompany any form of change: school graduation, promotion, retirement. Even as each of these may promise new rewards, each also requires giving up old statuses and familiar ties. Good bonding environments allow people to express and share their grief as old bonds dissolve.

One of the most common workplace losses, largely unacknowledged, occurs when companies merge with others, even if employees retain their jobs. A telling example of the effects of mergers is given by W. Brooke Tunstall, who interviewed former American Telegraph and Telephone (AT&T) employees after its dissolution in 1982.[23]

By almost all accounts, AT&T was an exceptional company. Despite its one million employees and twenty-four thousand buildings, AT&T is almost uniformly described as having been a paradigm of a strongly bonded organization. Its forced breakup by horizontal divestiture of its local exchange companies traumatized many of its employees. Feelings ranged from numbness, anger, resentment, and powerlessness to a loss of identity itself. As one employee expressed it:

I knew the old Bell System, its mission, its operation, its people, its culture. And I knew my niche in it. In that knowledge, I had identity and confidence about my company and myself. Now I work for a new company, one fourth its former size, with only a partial history and no track record. With the loss of our mission—universal service—and the fragmentation of the very business of providing telephone service, I find myself asking, "Who are we?" "Who am I?"[24]

How should companies deal with such feelings? Terrence E. Deal, who lectures to corporations across the country about business culture, proposes they institute grieving rituals, an idea he implemented in a subsequent presentation to a Bell operating company shortly after the AT&T divestiture. Unaware at the time of the actual sentiments of the group about the divestiture, Deal began his presentation by talking generally about what he calls "corporate culture" and the potential impact of its loss. It was not too long before he realized that he had provided those present with a much needed opportunity to share their grief collectively:

Addressing an audience of 200 Bell managers, I talked about corporate culture and the potential impact of its loss. I amplified the points . . . without fully knowing the situation or the actual sentiments within the group. In the midst of the session, I realized that this was not a typical presentation to a detached crowd. Most of the people in the audience had tears in their eyes. The room was painfully hushed. At the end of the presentation, several of the participants lined up to continue the conversation; they wanted to tell me how the change was affecting them personally. Many were visibly anguished. All reported the agony of "being pulled apart inside."[25]

Deal believes that grieving experiences of this type help people bury the past, without which they may not be able to prepare for new roles and form new bonds. Hence he warns that businesses, schools, hospitals, or any other organizations that do not acknowledge and resolve the painful consequences of change may find themselves unable to "move on" and create something new.

A personal experience highlighted this for us at the high school one of our sons attended. Driving while drunk one night, Mark, a fellow student, had an accident that left him in a coma. The doctors gave little hope for recovery; at best Mark might survive, but with his mental and physical faculties severely limited. Accomplishing even this much would require extensive and prolonged physical therapy, some of which could be performed by people other than physical therapists.

Confronted with this tragedy, Mark's distraught parents sought some means to assuage their grief, one which might not only afford them some comfort but might also give this event some meaning. They contacted the high school principal and asked permission to meet with the entire school. At that assembly, the parents shared their feelings about their son and his fate, and then went on to say that the only way their loss could have any meaning was if it kept other young people from drinking and driving. They concluded by inviting students to help with Mark's physical therapy.

Students wept openly and copiously. Mark's accident had touched them deeply for it reminded them acutely of their own vulnerability, which young people generally suppress. That Mark's parents could find some meaning in this loss allowed them to do the same; rather than simply resuming their normal activities under a shroud of unnamed anxiety and fear, they had confronted their feelings directly and collectively. Being able to participate in Mark's care—many volunteered to do so—allowed students to reintegrate him into their high school community; a way of saying that the separation was not final. As our son reported it, students did drink less for some months thereafter. And ten years later, he, along with other students, was still visiting Mark, who never did recover all his faculties, whenever he returned home.

In AT&T's case, as in that of Mark's, a way of grieving was provided accidently; the product of chance, rather than an anticipated response. People need opportunities to create and innovate, but they also require predictability. Rituals, shared patterned and repeated practices, provide people with a sense of continuity, order, control, and meaning; without them, people often feel adrift and isolated. Good bonding environments not only attend to people's emotional needs spontaneously, but also through rituals.

Religious groups have long understood the bonds that rituals create. As the orthodox among them insist, to "be religious" is nothing less than "a way of life," by which they mean participation in ritualized behaviors not only to mark singular life events, such as birth and death, but also the mundane and the ordinary: rising and going to bed, eating, dressing, and making love. Non-believers may regard these as obsessive and irrational constraints;

the faithful depend on them for emotional certainty, guidance, and a sense of shared transcendant meaning.

The sense of extraordinary well-being that ritualized behaviors of this sort can confer is captured by English literature scholar Richard Rodriguez as he recalls the Catholic Church of his youth:

I remember my early Catholic schooling and recall an experience of religion very different from anything I have known since. Never since have I felt so much at home in the Church, so easy at mass . . . Catholicism shaped my whole day. It framed my experience of eating and sleeping and washing; it named the season and the hour.

The sky was full then and the coming of spring was a religious event. I would awaken to the sound of garage doors creaking open and know without thinking that it was Friday and that my father was on his way to six-thirty mass. I saw without bothering to notice, statues at home and at school of the Virgin and of Christ. I would write at the top of my arithmetic or history homework the initials *Jesus, Mary,* and *Joseph.* (All my homework was thus dedicated.) I felt the air was different, somehow still and more silent on Sundays and high feastdays. I felt lightened, transparent as sky, after confessing my sins to a priest. Schooldays were routinely divided by prayers said with classmates. I would not have forgotten to say grace before eating. And I would not have turned off the light next to my bed or fallen asleep without praying to God.[26]

Rodriguez no longer feels quite comfortable in the church of his youth, and he mourns its loss. Those who integrate such religious rituals into their adult lives often find uncommon strength in them. Some rescuers in our study understood this, even if they themselves did not necessarily share such feelings. One Dutch woman, for example, went to great lengths to find candles for the Jewish woman she was keeping, so that she could continue to light the Sabbath candles. When the brother of two Jewish children he was hiding died, their Polish protector contrived what he thought was a Jewish burial for the child. For both, it was a way of affirming some normalcy and meaning in the midst of a social world which had literally turned all values and meaning "upside down."

More than religious rituals, which some people feel less than comfortable with and others reject summarily, individuals depend on family household rituals to provide them with a sense of purpose, continuity and predictability. Such rituals can range from routine "small-talk"—exemplified by Russell Baker's family nightly kitchen exchanges—to elaborate festivities. At their best, they provide a means for relating to the past, future, and present—an arena for celebrating personal triumphs and sharing disappointments, a helping network in times of need, and an ongoing group with whom to share information, accumulated wisdom, and values. Whether families alone can be depended on to perform these vital functions in the wake of industrialization is questionable.

The family structure has changed dramatically, and evidence suggests that such changes are likely to be with us for some time to come. The "typical family"—father, mother, and children living together—accounted for only 26.3 percent in 1990 as compared with 30.5 percent of American households in 1980 and 41.4 percent in 1960. More people are living alone: their number increased to 24.6 percent in 1990 as compared with 22.7 percent in 1980 and 21.5 percent in 1960.[27] Among the working population, young adults may be most affected. In the computer world of California's Silicon Valley, for example, almost half the work-force is under thirty, living away from parents and childhood friends, and unmarried.[28]

Adding to people's sense of separation and detachment is not only the numbers of hours many spend working, but the changing nature of jobs. More of them require what Arlie Russell Hochschild calls "emotional labor," the need to suppress feelings and put on a proper "face" in order to produce an appropriate state of mind in others. Airplane stewards, for example, must learn to project tranquility and assuredness in the face of drunken passengers or electrical storms; middle-range business executives must learn to deny their angers and insecurities as they confront demanding bosses and subordinates.

Hochschild estimates that six of the twelve standard occupational groups used by the U.S. Census depend heavily on emotional labor, including professional and technical workers, managers and administrators, sales workers, clerical workers, and service workers. While emotional labor continues to be performed primarily by women, Hochschild suggests that at least one-fourth of the jobs requiring it are held by men.[29] Such physical and psychological isolation may help explain a curious finding by a recent University of Michigan study. Whereas increased freedom and affluence have contributed to lower levels of anxiety and depression than in the past among older Americans, younger Americans are "growing more fretful, anxious, off balance and goalless."[30]

In light of the above, the importance of integrative rituals in educational and business institutions is increasing. Schools and the workplace represent natural local communities in which people meet routinely and frequently. Whether in fact they become communities depends on the degree of integration and social solidarity they achieve.

Management consultants Trice and Beyer propose five types of integrative rituals which can help promote group solidarity in any organization. *Rites of enhancement* are public recognitions of individual and organizational accomplishments. *Rites of conflict reduction*, such as celebrations and play events, help restore group equilibrium when tensions mount. *Rites of integration*, often occurring in weekend retreats or in-service training sessions, revive values shared by the group. *Rites of renewal*, in which organizations provide concrete services such as child-care facilities or counselors, help organizational members and their families function effectively. *Rites of passage* facilitate entry into new statuses, new jobs, and new roles.[31]

Those who have fond memories of people and places, tend to recall just these very elements, as the following excerpt written by John Witte about a former workplace demonstrates:

At SI my wife and I observed and shared the rituals of retirement ceremonies, awards, management pep talks, and massive Christmas parties. But we also celebrated the births of children and the marriages of sons and daughters; we attended parties where managers and workers drank, sang, and argued without consciousness of rank or position; we witnessed the fear of workers and the anguish of managers when layoffs were required; and we joined hundred of employees in burying an all too young manager whose entire working life had been spent with the company.[32]

Not all rituals of course, religious or otherwise, share such benevolent components. Some are deliberately designed to cultivate "in-group" bonds by degrading outsiders. Tyrants spend lavish amounts on theatrical ritual spectacles for the purpose of separating the "elect" from "enemies" in preparation for the latter's punishment. Robespierre as much as Hitler, ultra-nationalists as well as religious zealots, past and present, depend on rituals to cement "in-group" bonds by inflaming poisonous hatred of "outsiders."

But degradation rituals are also found in more routine contexts; like others of their type, they divide the "good" from the "bad." For example, public evidence of personal failure—such as widely disseminated annual business reports ranking the performance of all departments or publicly posted grades—may seem nothing more than the presentation of "objective data" to those who use them, but their consequence—even if not their intent—is to discredit others. Good bonding environments avoid degradation rituals.

But even among the benevolently inclined, rituals can exclude rather than include, separate rather than bond. Exclusion often takes the form of omission, a failure to note some individual or group need. This was the case in a well-intentioned annual circular distributed to students and parents in a city high school. Designed to help the senior class plan for graduation and the year thereafter, it duly noted the dates and sites for college entrance exams and college recruitment presenters. What it omitted was any reference to prospective planning for the non-college bound, the overwhelming majority of the student body.

Perhaps the most subtle way to exclude is to attend to others' needs in a way that stigmatizes them, that is, marks them as distinctly different. Affirmative action is one such example. Designed to integrate "special populations"—ethnic minorities and women—it often winds up stigmatizing the very groups it is intended to serve. Recipients not only face others' doubts about their qualifications, but their own. Even should they not have such doubts, recipients frequently feel guilty for having succeeded when other equally talented minority members may not have similar opportunities and often feel burdened because their failures may reflect on their group as a whole. Affirmative action may be the best short-run solution for overcoming institutional racism and sexism, but in the long run cannot integrate minorities until their "exceptional status" is overcome.

"At risk" youngsters, that is, students who appear to be headed for school failure, are another example of a group subject to such stigmatization even as their schools may want above all to integrate them. One way schools have attempted to meet their needs is to create programs designed specifically for them, such as special classes, special counselors, and special initiation procedures. It does not take too long before children in such programs recognize that "special" means "not quite normal."

One sensitive school district overcame this problem in the following way. The school routinely sponsored a kindergarten pre-registration procedure for "at risk" students, to which they invited parents as well as children, and at which they provided information about the school's resources and ways the school could help. As planners became more sensitive to the way this procedure distinguished these children and their families from others, they decided to alter the procedure. They began by asking themselves this question: "How can we meet the special needs of these children while simultaneously emphasizing their commonalities with others?" All entering kindergartners, they decided, shared one dominating characteristic: all were "newcomers" to the school. All newcomers and their parents could benefit from an initiation procedure like the one they had previously provided for "at risk" students only.[33]

The Newcomer Initiation Program, which has been adopted by several school districts,[34] encouraged group bonding in two ways. By introducing all entering students and parents to the school as a whole, it helped these newcomers become part of it. And by removing the stigma of "different," it helped integrate "at risk" children and their parents with so-called "normals."

Herein lies a lesson which all social institutions can profit from. Helping people bond does mean attending to their special needs, but in ways which focus on their commonalities with others rather than their exceptionalities.

The need to affiliate and belong is a strong human need, but according to many psychologists, so is the need to affirm independence. Good bonding environments provide opportunities for people to express their distinctiveness and autonomy. Bonding implies a self connected to the group, but it is different from a smothered self, engulfed and swallowed by the group.

Some sense of how group bonds can smother the self is given by journalist David Shipler in a book he wrote some years ago about the former Soviet Union. One of the things that impressed him was the care the community at large bestowed on young children. Parents lavished attention on them, indulging them with expensive gifts they could ill afford. Strangers, as well as parents and grandparents, hovered over them in public, protecting them from getting hurt or dirty, making sure their coats were buttoned, and cautioning them to walk straight. Older children, even adolescent boys, would pick them up and hug them. And public parks, preschools, and kindergartens were carefully designed and furnished to meet their needs. Here's how he describes one such kindergarten, representative of many he saw:

Every class of twenty-five children, grouped by age, had a complex of rooms: a large, airy playroom with huge windows that allowed a flood of daylight to wash over them; a big changing room for shedding sopping boots and snowsuits, with benches arranged so that each child could sit in front of his own cubbyhole; a spacious bathroom with a rack of cream-colored potties (in the section for two-year-olds), each painted with black numerals designating a particular child; and finally, for those still in the nap-taking stage, a fourth room full of beds.[35]

The setting was so fine, says Shipler, that even "the most privileged and creative American or European educator would have been seized with envy." Yet despite the luxurious surroundings, the curriculum was monotonously and uniformly the same from "Moscow to Central Asia." Almost nothing expressing an individualistic impulse appeared on the walls wherever he went; there were no opportunities to browse or select a book of one's choice, or to draw or do anything different. Children who did not do it "right" were gently but firmly guided to follow the prescription. Much the same atmosphere prevailed in higher grades, where lessons were taught by rote, and memorization was the key to success. "Certainty is such a solid foundation of Soviet education," says Shipler, "that by the time many Russians reach their teens they have already developed a virulent allergy to ambiguity."

Shipler of course is a North American, clearly influenced by western psychological assumptions, as we are. The notion that children and adults need opportunities for self-expression is rejected by many cultures, including the Japanese and Chinese. Yet the rapidity with which old bonds dissolved in the former Soviet Union suggests that environments which do not allow opportunities for autonomy risk explosive surges for self-assertion. Several Russians we spoke to on our visit to that country a few years ago, including those who despised the former regime and supported democratization, shared a similar fear. What some said they now feared more than political coercion was anarchy, the only two alternatives which they believed the Russian psyche was prepared for.

What these Russians appear to be implying is what American psychologists generally believe. Pressed to subordinate their individual selves to the group, people may find themselves lacking an identity separate from it, permanently dependent on it, and unable to cope with uncertainty. Bonds can thus become chains, walls which keep people imprisoned and unfit to create something new even should they want to. Frustrated and angry should these bonds dissolve, they may well see violence as their only alternative.

Having suggested that good bonding environments provide opportunities for affiliation with the group and asserting independence from it, can we assume that both men and women share these needs equally? Men, purportedly more independent and achievement oriented, are presumably more likely to seek escape from affiliative bonds but may need them more. Women, on the other hand, purportedly more concerned with emotional attachments, are presumably less concerned with autonomy. What does the evidence suggest?

A considerable amount of evidence suggests that males more than females value and push for independence. As children, boys more than girls seek independence from adults and spend more time with their peers.[36] While they develop more friendships than girls, their relationships are less intense[37] and more competitive; more than girls, boys participate in games that produce winners and losers.[38] As adults, men rate themselves as more independent and achievement oriented than women, whom they perceive as more expressive and dependent; women's perceptions of men and themselves are largely congruent with those of males.[39] As compared with women, men are less interested in and nurturant toward infants and younger children[40] and more concerned with their careers. Such evidence suggests that men have less need for affiliative bonds than females.

Conversely, some evidence suggests that men may be more fragile than women, physically and psychologically, and more dependent on social support and enduring social bonds. Male infants, for example, are more vulnerable to problems during pregnancy and birth.[41] They are more irritable and demand more of their mothers' attention[42]; when they fail to get it, they are more likely than girls to become uncooperative and difficult.[43] Boys are more vulnerable to divorce; they are more likely to become aggressive and noncompliant as a result.[44] At all ages, males are more aggressive.[45] While women are more likely to be clinically depressed and suffer from mental health problems, men are more likely to engage in antisocial or self-destructive behaviors.[46]

One conclusion suggested in the above is that males generally have difficulties sustaining positive relationships with others. Carol Gilligan supports this view and offers an explanation to account for it. Based on her own research and that of others, Gilligan asserts that women develop differently from men, the consequence of which are different adult problems. This assertion is a major departure from the more conventional view proposed by Erik Erikson[47] which presumed identical developmental patterns. According to the conventional view, boys and girls first gain their sense of identity and self sometime during the period of adolescence. Once having passed through this stage successfully, they are then able to move on to intimacy, relationship, and care in maturity. Gilligan believes this model is flawed in two ways. Adolescent females find their identity primarily through relationships and thus do not acquire a sense of "self" during adolescence. Males, on the other hand, do develop a strong sense of themselves during adolescence, but rather than progressing to intimacy thereafter, tend to remain self-focused well into their adult years. As a consequence, they feel more isolated than women and more indifferent to others' welfare.[48]

All the above suggest that even as they push for independence, males may be particularly in need of supportive bonds to inhibit their aggression and sustain them in positive relationships. If Gilligan and others cited above are right, then the environments in which men in particular spend most of their childhood and adult years need to encourage affiliative bonding. Under increasing pressures to perform stressful emotional labor, as well as assert their independence, men may need encouraging integrative environments even more than women if they are to develop caring behaviors.

Yet to overemphasize gender differences is to obscure a more fundamental point: men and women share more needs in common than the above studies imply. Several of the above studies are based on attributions—that is what people say about themselves and others—rather than what they really are. Attributions are frequently the products of stereotypic thinking; men and women tend to see themselves in conventionally acceptable ways. Some studies are methodologically flawed or based on small samples primarily drawn from the United States, which helps explain why results are often inconsistent, particularly when samples are drawn from other countries. Meta-analyses—statistical procedures to study the aggregate effects of variables of combined independent studies—generally conclude that the differences between the sexes are much smaller than the similarities.[49] Overlapping is considerable at all ages; many men possess "feminine" characteristics, and many women are independent and achievement oriented. Moreover, "feminine" and "masculine" characteristics frequently occur in the same individual.

While some gender differences may be the consequence of biology, many more appear to be the consequence of culture and role. Both men and women modify their gender-associated behaviors and attitudes depending on the social roles they assume over the life-cycle. The differences between them sharpen when they become parents, presumably because men grow more concerned about their role as breadwinner and women become more concerned about mothering.[50] As they grow older and these roles weaken, however, men perceive themselves as becoming more expressive and nurturant, while women view themselves as becoming more autonomous.[51]

Such findings suggest that culture plays an important role in shaping masculine and feminine needs and that both sexes share independence and affiliation needs. Many psychologists agree. Humans generally, says David Bakan, are driven by two needs: the need for self-assertion and differentiation from others, which he calls "agency"; and the need for joining with and becoming part of others, which he calls "communion." Agency and communion, says Bakan, are the dualities of human existence, and they provoke lifelong tension.[52] Robert Kegan says much the same thing; people are ever engaged in progressive motion, trying to make meaning of their world by separating themselves from others and by merging with them.[53] Gilligan also acknowledges that separation and attachment anchor the life cycle for all.[54]

The critical point it seems to us is maintaining an appropriate balance. Good bonding environments, we suggest, address both needs for males and females; they encourage autonomy, divergence, and innovation, but they simultaneously promote integration and group solidarity.

NOTES

1. Czeslaw Milosz, *The Captive Mind*, trans. J. Zielonks (New York: Alfred A. Knopf, 1951), 135–136, 145.

2. Russell Baker, *Growing Up* (New York: Congdon & Weed, 1982), 115–116.

3. John Bowlby, *Attachment and Loss*, vol. 1 (New York: Basic Books, 1969); Langdon E. Longstreth, "Revisiting Skeels' Final Study: A Critique," *Developmental Psychology* 17 (1981): 620–625; Michael Rutter, "Maternal Deprivation, 1972–1978: New Findings, New Concepts, New Approaches," *Child Development* 50 (1979): 283–305.

4. Everett Waters, Judith Wippman, and L. Alan Sroufe, "Attachment, Positive Affect, and Competence in the Peer Group: Two Studies in Construct Validation," *Child Development* 50 (1979): 821–890; Alicia F. Lieberman, "Preschoolers' Competence with a Peer: Relations with Attachment and Peer Experience," *Child Development* 48 (1977): 1277–1287; Mary D. S. Ainsworth, "Infant-Mother Attachment," *American Psychologist* 34 (1979): 932–937; L. Alan Sroufe, "The Coherence of Individual Development: Early Care, Attachment, and Subsequent Developmental Issues," *American Psychologist* 34 (1979): 834–841; Mary Main and Donna R. Weston, "The Quality of the Toddler's Relationship to Mother and to Father: Related to Conflict Behavior and the Readiness to Establish New Relationships," *Child Development* 52 (1981): 932–940.

5. Data from our study of rescuers tend to support the above assertions. Rescuers, as compared with non-rescuers, were more focused on others' needs and did have a greater sense of control over their lives. They also felt significantly closer to their families (Samuel P. Oliner and Pearl M. Oliner, *The Altruistic Personality: Rescuers of Jews in Nazi Europe* (New York: Free Press, 1988).

6. Mothers, fathers, and others who assume caretaking roles during this time, they assert, can shape enduring attitudes and values depending on how they respond to their babies' needs. If babies learn to trust their caretakers, they are likely to become adults who trust and care for other people; babies who learn that caretakers cannot be trusted are likely to become adults who do not trust or care for others. The "prototype hypothesis," as this is often called, is most associated with Sigmund Freud and John Bowlby (*Maternal Care and Mental Health: A Report for the World*

Health Organization [Geneva: World Health Organization, 1952]). More recently, pediatricians Marshall H. Klaus and John H. Kennell argued that infants need to bond with their parents during the first few minutes of life for optimal future development (Marshall H. Klaus and John H. Kennell, *Maternal-infant Bonding* [St. Louis: C. V. Mosby, 1976]). Although subsequent research did not support this idea (Michael E. Lamb and Carl-Philip Hwang, "Maternal Attachment and Mother-neonate Bonding: A Critical Review," in *Advances in Developmental Psychology*, vol. 2, eds. Michael E. Lamb and Ann L. Brown [Hillsdale, N.J.: Lawrence Erlbaum, 1982], 1–40), many hospitals changed their practices as a consequence.

7. E. Bergler, *Parents Not Guilty of Their Children's Neuroses* (New York: Liveright, 1964); Bettye M. Caldwell, "The Effects of Infant Care," in *Review of Child Development Research*, vol. 1., eds. Martin L. Hoffman and Lois Wladis Hoffman (New York: Russell Sage Foundation, 1964). Further support for this view comes from our rescuers study. Not all rescuers in our sample felt close to their families of origin, and many nonrescuers who did failed to respond to others' needs.

8. Jonathan Kozol, *Savage Inequalities: Children in America's Schools* (New York: Crown, 1991), 85–88.

9. Erik Larson, "I Scream, You Scream . . . ," *Utne Reader*, January/February 1989: 64–75.

10. Jay Belsky, "Mother-Father-Infant Interaction: A Naturalistic Observational Study," *Developmental Psychology* 15 (1979): 601–607; K. Alison Clarke-Stewart, "And Daddy Makes Three: the Father's Impact on Mother and Young Child," *Child Development* 49 (1978): 466–478; Ross D. Parke, "Perspectives on Father-Infant Interaction," in *Handbook of Infancy*, ed. Joy D. Osofsky (New York: John Wiley & Sons, 1978).

11. Clarke-Stewart, "And Daddy;" M. Elissa Lamb, "Paternal Influences and the Father's Role," *American Psychologist* 34 (1979): 938–943; Parke, "Perspectives."

12. M. Elisa Lamb, "Father-Infant and Mother-Infant Interaction in the First Year of Life," *Child Development* 48 (1977): 167–181.

13. Christina M. B. Arco and Kathleen A. McCluskey, "A Change of Pace: An Investigation of the Salience of Maternal Temporal Style in Mother-Infant Play," *Child Development* 52 (1981): 941–949.

14. Oliner and Oliner, 204.

15. Karl E. Weick, *The Social Psychology of Organizing*, 2d ed. (Reading, Mass: Addison-Wesley, 1979); James G. March and Herbert A. Simon, *Organizations* (New York: John Wiley & Sons, 1958).

16. Diane Ackerman, *A Natural History of the Senses* (New York: Random House, 1990).

17. Lewis Thomas, *The Youngest Science: Notes of a Medicine-Watcher* (Toronto: Bantam Books, 1983), 56.

18. Cited in Allison Davis, *Leadership, Love and Aggression* (San Diego: Harcourt, Brace, Jovanovich, 1983), 24.

19. Cited in Davis, 44.

20. Accusers blame mothers who, they charge, work for personal gratification. Yet statistics show that economic need compels most women to enter the work force; commonly in low status jobs which pay little, many of them work reluctantly (J. L. Norwood, *The Male-Female Earnings Gap: A Review of Employment and Earnings Issues* [U.S. Department of Labor, Bureau of Labor Statistics, Report 673, Septem-

ber], 1982); N. F. Rytina, "Earnings of Men and Women: A Look at Specific Occupations," *Monthly Labor Review*, April 1982, 251–71; C. D. Foster, M. A. Siegel and N. R. Jacobs, eds., *Women's Changing Roles* (Wylie, Tex.: Information Aids, 1988).

21. Several pre-school teachers have made such observations to us in informal conversations.

22. Sara Lawrence Lightfoot, *The Good High School: Portraits of Character and Culture* (New York: Basic Books, 1983), 64, 76.

23. W. Brooke Tunstall, "Breakup of the Bell System: A Case Study in Cultural Transformation," in *Gaining Control of the Corporate Culture*, eds. Ralph H. Kilmann et al. (San Francisco: Jossey-Bass, 1985), 44–65.

24. Tunstall, 59.

25. Terrence E. Deal, "Cultural Change: Opportunity, Silent Killer, or Metamorphosis," in *Gaining Control*, eds. Kilmann et al., 292–331, 295.

26. Richard Rodriguez, *Hunger of Memory: The Education of Richard Rodriguez: An Autobiography* (Boston: David R. Godine, 1981), 80.

27. Judith Waldrop and Thomas Exter, "The Legacy of the 1980s," *American Demographics* (March 1991): 32–28; George Masnick and Mary Jo Bane, *The Nation's Families: 1960–1990* (Cambridge, Mass.: Joint Center for Urban Studies, 1980).

28. Kate Ludeman, *The Work Ethic: How to Profit from the Changing Values of the New Work Force* (New York: E. P. Dutton, 1989), xv.

29. Arlie Russell Hochschild, *The Managed Heart: Commercialization of Human Feeling* (Berkeley: University of California Press, 1983).

30. Institute for Social Research, *ISR Newsletter* 7:1 (Ann Arbor, University of Michigan): Winter 1979.

31. Harrison M. Trice and Janice M. Beyer, "Using Six Organizational Rites to Change Culture," in *Gaining Control*, eds. Kilmann et al., 370–395.

32. John F. Witte, *Democracy, Authority, and Alienation in Work: Workers' Participation in an American Corporation* (Chicago: University of Chicago Press, 1980), 168.

33. Personal interview with Marianne Pennekamp who participated in the project.

34. *Bridges: Promising Programs for the Education of Immigrant Children* (San Francisco: California Tomorrow, 1989).

35. David K. Shipler, *Russia: Broken Idols, Solemn Dreams* (New York: Penguin Books, 1986), 57.

36. Bernice Lott, "Behavioral Concordance with Sex Role Ideology Related to Play Areas, Creativity and Parental Sex Typing," *Journal of Personality and Social Psychology* 36 (1978): 1087–1100; Roy Roper and R. Hinde, "Social Behavior in a Play Group: Consistency and Complexity," *Child Development* 49 (1978): 570–579.

37. Mary F. Waldrop and Charles F. Halverson, Jr., "Intensive and Extensive Peer Behavior: Longitudinal and Cross-sectional Analyses," *Child Development* 46 (1975): 19–26.

38. Andrew Ahlgren and David W. Johnson, "Sex Differences in Cooperative and Competitive Attitudes from the 2nd Year Through the 12th Grades," *Developmental Psychology* 15 (1979): 45–49; George P. Knight and Spencer Kagan, "Apparent Sex Differences in Cooperation-Competition: A Function of Individualism," *Developmental Psychology* 17 (1981): 783–790.

39. I. K. Broverman et al., "Sex Role Stereotypes: A Current Appraisal," *Journal of Social Issues* 28:2 (1972): 59–79; Janet T. Spence, Robert L. Helmreich, and Joy Stapp, "Ratings of Self and Peers on Sex Role Attributes and their Relation to Self-esteem and Conceptions of Masculinity and Femininity," *Journal of Personality and Social Psychology* 32 (1975): 29–39; Thomas L. Ruble, "Sex Stereotypes: Issues of Change in the 1970's," *Sex Roles* 9 (1983): 397–402.

40. Phyllis M. Berman, Lori C. Monda, and Rodney P. Myerscough, "Sex Differences in Young Children's Responses to an Infant: An Observation Within a Day-care Setting," *Child Development* 48 (1977): 711–715; Shirley S. Feldman and Sharon C. Nash, "Interest in Babies During Young Adulthood," *Child Development* 49 (1978): 617–622; M. Elissa Lamb, "Twelve-month Olds and their Parents: Interaction in a Laboratory Playroom," *Developmental Psychology* 12 (1978): 237–244.

41. Eleanor E. Maccoby, *Social Development: Psychological Growth and the Parent-Child Relationship* (New York: Harcourt, Brace, Jovanovich, 1980).

42. John A. Martin, "A Longitudinal Study of the Consequences of Early Mother-Infant Interaction: A Microanalytic Approach," *Monographs of the Society for Research in Child Development* 90:46 (1981); Maccoby, *Social Development*.

43. D. Baumrind, "Sex-related Socialization Effects," paper presented at the biennial meeting of the Society for Research in Child Development, San Francisco, March 1979; J. A. Martin, "A Longitudinal Study."

44. E. Mavis Hetherington, "Divorce: A Child's Perspective," *American Psychologist* 34 (1979): 851-858; E. Mavis Hetherington, Martha Cox, and Roger Cox, "Stress and Coping in Divorce: A Focus on Women," in *Psychology and Women: In Transition*, ed. Jeanne E. Gullahorn (Washington, D.C.: V. H. Winston and Sons, 1979), 95–130; Michael Rutter, "Sex Differences in Children's Response to Family Stress," in *The Child in His Family*, eds. E. James Anthony and Cyrille Koupernik (New York: John Wiley & Sons, 1970), 165–196.

45. Eleanor E. Maccoby and Carol N. Jacklin, *The Psychology of Sex Differences* (Stanford: Stanford University Press, 1974); Irene H. Frieze et al., *Women and Sex Roles: A Social Psychological Perspective* (New York: W. W. Norton, 1978); Ronald P. Rohner, "Sex Differences in Aggression: Phylogenetic and Enculturation Perspectives," *Ethos* 4 (1976): 57–72; Eleanor E. Maccoby and Carol N. Jacklin, "Sex Differences in Aggression: A Rejoinder and Reprise," *Child Development* 51 (1980): 964–980.

46. Hilary M. Lips, *Sex and Gender: An Introduction* (Mountain View, Calif. Mayfield, 1988).

47. Erik H. Erikson, "The Human Life Cycle" in *A Way of Looking at Things: Selected Papers from 1930–1980, Erik H. Erikson*, ed. Stephen Schlein (New York: W. W. Norton, 1987), 595–610.

48. Carol Gilligan, *In a Different Voice: Psychological Theory and Women's Development* (Cambridge: Harvard University Press, 1982).

49. Alice H. Eagly and Linda L. Carli, "Sex of Researchers and Sex-typed Communications as Determinants of Sex Differences in Influenceability: A Meta-analysis of Social Influence Studies," *Psychological Bulletin* 90 (1981): 1–20; Nancy Eisenberg and Randy Lennon, "Sex Differences in Empathy and Related Capacities," *Psychological Bulletin* 94 (1983): 100–131; Janet S. Hyde, "How Large are Cognitive Gender Differences?," *American Psychologist* 36 (1981): 892–901.

50. Barbara Abrahams, Shirley S. Feldman, and Sharon C. Nash, "Sex-role Self-concept and Sex Role Attitudes: Enduring Personality Characteristics or Adaptations to Changing Life Situations?," *Developmental Psychology* 14 (1978): 393–400.

51. Shirley S. Feldman, Zeynep C. Biringen, and Sharon C. Nash, "Fluctuations of Sex-related Self-attributions as a Function of Stage of Family Life Cycle," *Developmental Psychology* 17 (1981): 24–25; Shirley S. Feldman, Sharon C. Nash, and Carolyn Cutrona, "The Influence of Age and Sex on Responsiveness to Babies," *Developmental Psychology* 13 (1977): 675–676.

52. David Bakan, *The Duality of Human Existence* (Boston: Beacon Press, 1966).

53. Robert Kegan, *The Evolving Self: Problems and Process in Human Development* (Cambridge: Harvard University Press, 1982).

54. Gilligan.

CHAPTER 3

Empathizing

I didn't want any part of them here. They belong with their own, and
we belong with our own—that's what we all said. Then those two kids
came here, and they had a tough time. They were all by themselves. The
school had to get protection for them. We didn't want them, and they
knew it. But we told them so, in case they were slow to get the message.
I didn't hold back, no more than anyone else. I said, "Go, nigger, go"
with all the others. I meant it. But after a few weeks, I began to see a
kid, not a nigger—a guy who knew how to smile when it was rough
going, and who walked straight and tall, and was polite. I told my parents, "It's a real shame that someone like him has to pay for the trouble
caused by all those federal judges."

Then it happened. I saw a few people cuss at him. "The dirty nigger,"
they kept on calling him, and soon they were pushing him in a corner,
and it looked like trouble, bad trouble. I went over and broke it up. I
said, "Hey, cut it out." They all looked at me as if I was crazy, my white
buddies and the nigger, too. But my buddies stopped, and the nigger
left. Before he left, though, I spoke to him. I didn't mean to actually!
It just came out of my mouth. I was surprised to hear the words myself:
"I'm sorry." As soon as he was gone, my friend gave it to me: "What
do you mean, 'I'm sorry!' " I didn't know what to say. I was as silent
as the nigger they stopped. After a few minutes, we went to basketball
practice. That was the strangest moment of my life.[1]

The above episode, recounted by Robert Coles, occurred in one of Atlanta's
public schools during the period of desegregation. The speaker, a fourteen
year-old, was the first white youth to speak to a black one. Coles describes
him as a "poor student" and a "tough athlete," who came from a family

conventionally labeled as "redneck." Yet, at a crucial moment, for reasons not entirely clear even to Coles himself, he apparently experienced a sharp sense of compassion for someone he had previously learned to see as a threatening alien. He was never to be quite the same again. He became the black youth's champion and eventually an advocate of desegregation.

Psychologists might attribute his behavior to an emotion called *sympathy*; more likely they would call it *empathy*.[2] While these two terms are often used interchangeably, their motivational sources, and more importantly their consequences, are generally presumed to be quite different.

Because empathy is more likely to result in effective care, we focus here on strategies to encourage empathy and conditions which are likely to result in empathic behaviors. We begin first by distinguishing between empathy and sympathy and illustrating the effects each has on responses to others' needs.

Sympathy means pity or commiseration *for* another's condition. It implies looking at the other person from one's perspective and at a distance. Sympathizers feel uncomfortable with others' apparent unhappiness, but they do not understand how others themselves feel about that condition. Sympathy thus is basically self-centered: an interpretation of another's state based on one's own feelings and thoughts.

Empathy, on the other hand, means feeling *with* the other person. It implies looking at others from their own perspective and responding to them on their own terms. Rather than self-oriented, empathy is other-oriented; requiring what Alfie Kohn calls "entering" *into* the other.[3]

Both sympathizers and empathizers help others, but they are usually not equally effective nor do they elicit similar emotional responses from those they help. Because sympathizers act on the basis of their own needs and thoughts, the help they give often misses the mark while those they help frequently perceive them as condescending, patronizing, or paternalistic. Because empathizers act on the basis of others' needs and thoughts, they are able to respond more appropriately while those they help are more likely to feel appreciative.

To illustrate the differences between a sympathetic and empathic response, consider the following two examples: one taken from the treatment of the homeless in Santa Barbara, California, the other from a rescuer response to a child.

Santa Barbara, an affluent California city, has three main shelters to house the homeless. Here's how sociologist Peter Marin describes them:

There are three main shelters in the city—all of them private. Between them they provide fewer than a hundred beds a night for the homeless. Two of the three shelters are religious in nature: the Rescue Mission and the Salvation Army. In the mission, as in most places in the country, there are elaborate and stringent rules. Beds go first to those who have not been there for two months, and you can stay for two nights in any two-month period. No shelter is given to those who are not sober. Even if you go to the mission only for a meal, you are required to listen to sermons and participate in prayer, and you are regularly proselytized—sometimes overtly, sometimes subtly. There are obligatory regimented showers. You go to bed precisely at 10 o'clock: lights out, no reading, no talking. After the lights go out you will find 15 men in a room with double-decker bunks. In the morning you are awakened precisely at 5:45. Then breakfast. At 7:30 you are back on the street.[4]

That private organizations would voluntarily provide this service betokens their willingness to tackle a problem which many others have chosen to avoid. And given the limited accommodations and presumed monetary constraints, the rules seem reasonable. The two-month lodging rotation assures that some three thousand people will have the opportunity to shower and sleep in a clean bed at least twice during that period, and the rules about lights and talking make it possible for all to rest. Even the sermons and prayers are understandable since those who insist on them are themselves likely to be persuaded of their curative powers. Yet according to Marin, who has spent many hours talking to the homeless, many, if not most, of the recipients feel humiliated by the process. The reason, he implies, is that the program fails to address their goals and wants on their terms and from their perspectives.

What would such perspectives be? There are at least three types of constituencies among the homeless. The first, by far the majority, are the formerly "respectably" employed, now without jobs or money.[5] What they want above all is to find a job, take care of their families, and rejoin mainstream society. The regimentation and the forced prayers underscore their neediness and "child-like" status and do not address their real needs. The second type are the physically and/or emotionally ill, their condition itself sometimes caused by being homeless. They need long-term help; an occasional bed and wash hardly suffice to alleviate their pains.

The above two groups are relatively new recruits to "homeless" status. The third group, transients—Marin calls them "voluntary exiles"—have been part of society's homeless for a long time. Unlike the first two, they actually choose a way of life which keeps them on the peripheries of society. Since they neither recognize the need for help nor want it, they resent efforts to reform them. Formerly accommodated by a hidden infrastructure—cheap shelters, flophouses, temporary employment agencies—they were largely invisible to mainstream society. Modernization has destroyed this infrastructure, thrusting them into the very centers of middle-class life and sensibilities. What they need, Marin implies, are structures which will accommodate their chosen life-styles more hospitably.

If Marin is right, self-centeredness and sympathy rather than empathy motivate much of the current concern for the homeless. Now forced to confront them on the streets where they live and work, middle-class people seek to relieve their own uncomfortable feelings of distress by embracing any effort which keeps this group out of sight. Rather than escape it, sympathetic and well-intentioned groups, such as the ones Marin describes, do try to deal with the problem directly, but on their own terms. An empathic response would require meeting the needs of the homeless on *their* terms; obviously more than our society is willing to do.

By way of contrast, consider this example of two rescuers, a Dutch couple, who agreed to hide a Jewish child in 1942. Here's how the husband, whom we shall call Peter, describes the little boy and what he and his wife did to help him:

The little boy, three years old, had asthma and wet the bed. My wife kept saying, "I'm so glad we got this boy and not someone else." And then the little boy kept talking about his sister. So I began to snoop around and found out where she was. She was only a year and a half old. I decided that these kids should not be apart, and I brought her home as well.

When the little boy was five years old, someone came from the church to press us to send the boy to Sunday school. We talked about it and decided we had the obligation to save those children, not convert them—we did not have that right. Besides, we would have confused them. This way, they could go back to their mother with their own beliefs and own religion.[6]

That this couple could view an asthmatic child who wet his bed as a gift rather than an overwhelming burden is remarkable in itself. That they could further understand his need for rootedness in continuing relationships—with his sister and his mother in the future—suggests that they were able to see the world through his eyes and feelings. When their mother returned some two years later to reclaim her children, the couple demonstrated that they could also see the world from *her* viewpoint. The children, who had learned to love Peter and his wife as their own parents, did not want to go back with their mother who was now almost a stranger. Yet Peter and his wife, who had also learned to love the children and would have happily adopted them, helped support both mother and children through this transition. Some two years later, when the children's mother became terminally ill, the couple again offered to adopt the children after her death. When she again rejected the offer and chose instead to send them to relatives in Israel, the couple once more "understood." As Peter explained: "She wanted them to be raised Jewish. We understood."

How did this couple acquire such developed empathic understanding? We don't really know enough about the details of their lives to answer this question. More than likely it was a combination of some innate characteristics and learned responses.

Many writers, past and present, believe that the capacity for empathy may well be part of human nature, a type of innate psychic equipment which people have simply by virtue of being human. David Hume believed this,[7] as did Rousseau[8] and Adam Smith.[9] Many contemporary psychologists agree.

Pointing to the fact that newborns who hear other infants cry often cry themselves, some psychologists believe that a rudimentary form of empathy is already present at birth.[10] Martin Hoffman does not regard this as true empathy, however, because infants do not have a sense of themselves as distinct entities, let alone others. Hence, he calls this "empathic distress," a type of "global" reaction in which infants sense that whatever is happening to the other is happening to themselves. He proposes that the capacity for true empathy develops with maturity, in progressively more complex stages.

Somewhere between one and two years of age, children develop what Hoffman calls "egocentric empathy." Still self-centered at this stage, they are nonetheless aware that others exist independently of themselves. What they cannot do is recognize that others can have feelings and thoughts different from their own: whatever comforts them, they think, will comfort someone else. They overcome this during the third stage, when "empathy for another's feelings" emerges. But they are unable to grasp how complex others' feelings and thoughts can be. The final stage is a sophisticated one; Hoffman calls it "empathy for another's life conditions." Children can now understand that others not only have multiple thoughts and feelings, but that their individual histories and life conditions can affect their thoughts and feelings. In addition to knowing this about individuals, they recognize that whole groups of people are influenced by their histories and life conditions.[11]

All would be well if progression from one stage to another was assured. Unfortunately, this is not the case. Overwhelmingly egocentric adults, interacting with others from their own perspectives alone, are hardly rarities. They may choose this posture deliberately, of course, out of the conviction that they have most to gain by assuming it. Or they may act this way because their empathic potential has not been adequately developed. Some types of experiences can transform a potential into an actuality.

What can people do to help others develop their potential for empathy? One means is to encourage them to know themselves. Merely asking others to say what they feel and think, and doing so repeatedly, provides such encouragement.

How does knowing oneself influence empathy? As a recent study by psychologist Maria Jarymowicz suggests, people who know themselves well are more likely to differentiate between their feelings and thoughts and those of others.[12] Hence, they are less likely to believe that what they need is what others need as well. And people who are not in touch with their own selves or deny their feelings and thoughts are less likely to form caring relationships with others. "One who cannot tolerate his own range of feelings, or who is essentially a stranger to himself" writes Alfie Kohn, "is unlikely to forge an affective connection to someone else."[13]

When self-knowledge is deliberately suppressed, as is the case in totalitarian systems, not only are nourishing human relationships and the capacity for empathy diminished, but also the very character of morality itself. Vaclev Havel, the new president of Czechoslovakia, echoed these thoughts in his 1990 inaugural address. Denial of feelings and thoughts, he said, was Czechoslovakia's main problem, resulting in mass moral contamination:

The worst thing is that we live in a contaminated moral environment. We felt morally ill because we became used to saying something different from what we thought. We learned not to believe in anything, to ignore each other, to care only about ourselves. Concepts such as love, friendship, compassion, humility or forgiveness lost their depth and dimensions and for many of us they represented only psychological peculiarities, or they resembled gone astray greetings from ancient times, a little ridiculous in the era of computers and spaceships . . . When I talk about a contaminated moral atmosphere . . . I am talking about all of us.[14]

As Havel implies, the road to recovery lies in reestablishing a connection with oneself.

But just as national crises such as Havel describes frequently demand a particularly sharpened authenticity—a sense of who one is and what one's beliefs and feelings are—so do personal ones. Effective help during periods of anxiety, change, and uncertainty often depends on a genuine engagement with one's innermost self. According to some, those who are able to comfort the dying, for example, must encounter them from a position of empathy which can only emerge from penetrating self-knowledge. Hospice volunteers, who work with the dying and their families, stress this capacity repeatedly. The inauthentic Hospice volunteer, say many, risks being detected. Unless they have carefully scrutinized their own feelings about death and resolved them, they are unlikely to be able to offer real comfort to the dying or their families. As one Hospice volunteer expressed it:

Being a Hospice volunteer is risky. Because you are dealing with people at one of the most intimate times in their lives, there is a responsibility in that. You have to be as sincere and as genuine as you can, and at times that is risky . . . it gets scary for the volunteer.[15]

One means to encourage people to know themselves is simply to ask them what they think and feel. Such invitations have to be genuine inquiries, intended to know and learn. If responses become fodder for attacks and assigning blame instead, people will learn not to trust the inquirer and self-exploration will quickly come to a halt.

But even if genuinely intended, invitations to disclose thoughts and feelings may have little effect if internal inhibitions are too strong. Providing the right conditions, which take into account special needs, can often make a difference. Men, for example, generally incline less toward introspection as compared with women, presumably because of their societal roles: it interferes with their ability to be successful competitors. Self-exploration may reveal doubts and confusion whereas society demands of them assuredness and certainty. They may be more willing to be self-reflective with other men similarly engaged, particularly if they perceive such men as competent males.

The size of the group and the frequency and predictability of their meetings also make a difference. People tend to be more silent in large groups, or to talk mechanistically, relying on stylized patterns acquired over time in similar situations. Small groups encourage more authentic interactions, particularly if participants know that they will continue to meet predictably for some specified amount of time. Prolonged interactions help promote a climate of trust.

Is empathic understanding then an inevitable consequence of self-exploration and authenticity? Not necessarily. Rather than empathy, self-exploration can uncover antipathy and anger. Whereas empathy requires a sense of connection with others, hostility implies separation from them.

Threats loom behind hostile expressions; most people prefer not to hear them. Yet, the opportunity to ventilate anger can sometimes defuse it; it can even result in a renewed sense of relationship. Just this very self-generated process is illustrated in a moving article written by Anthony Walton, a young, highly educated, middle-class black male.

Walton writes that only recently has he realized that he has been the victim of a cruel hoax. Assured by parents, relatives, and teachers alike that if only he stayed in school and conformed to middle-class standards, he would realize the American dream, he performed appropriately. A series of small incidents—the refusal by a temporary doorman to let him enter the building where he lived, a query by a friend's landlord about whether he lived there, a futile attempt to get a cab while others succeeded—made him aware in a very concrete way of what Walton calls his veil of double consciousness; an American and a black. In his blackness, he could at any moment be seen by white society as Willie Horton, the murderer. This belated recognition makes him feel "suckered":

I might meet Bernard Goetz on the subway; my car might break down in Howard Beach; the armed security guard might mistake me for a burglar in the lobby of my building. And they won't see a mild-mannered English major trying to get home. They will see Willie Horton.

I think we, the children of [Martin Luther King's] dream, often feel as if we are holding 30-year bonds that have matured and are suddenly worthless. There is a feeling, spoken and unspoken, of having been suckered. This distaste is festering into bitterness. I know that I disregarded jeering and opposition from young *blacks* in adolescence as I led a "square," even dreary life predicated on a coming harvest. And now I see that I am often treated the same as a thug, that no amount of conformity, willing or unwilling, will make me the fabled American individual . . . I think it has something to do with Willie Horton.[16]

Even as his hostility might lead an external listener to imagine ominous consequences, so it apparently disturbs Walton himself. For while acknowledging being angry enough to "start World War III over perceived slights," he concludes with a sense of his connectedness to humanity generally:

In light of the events of recent years, I begin to see that we are, competing or not, winners or not, irrevocably chained together, black and white, rich and poor. New York City is a glaring microcosm of this interrelatedness, which can be thought as either a web of fear ensnaring and enslaving us, or as a net of mutuality that strengthens us all.[17]

Having begun only with his own fears and anger, Walton concludes with the recognition that others—rich and poor, blacks and whites—may share similar anxieties. By acknowledging that all of the segments of the microcosm he describes may be ensnared by a common web of fear, Walton demonstrates a capacity for some perspective taking. The latter allows him to reconnect with others in recognition of a common fate and shared choice of opportunities, shared capitulation to mutual fears or shared transcendance of them.

Walton demonstrates an important point in the above. Acknowledging one's feelings, including angry ones, may be an important first step, but ultimately may do little to encourage empathy unless accompanied by the effort to relate to others' perspectives.

Perspective taking, also called role taking, refers to the ability to understand others. Primarily a cognitive skill, it requires the ability to correctly infer what others are thinking and feeling. Responding to others on their own terms—an essential component of empathy—depends on accurate understanding.

Like empathy, the capacity for perspective taking develops reasonably early in life. By age twelve, says social psychologist Robert Selman, children already have the cognitive capacity for sophisticated perspective taking. In addition to being able to recognize that others have feelings and thoughts which can differ from their own, they also have the capacity to maintain several perspectives simultaneously and to recognize that theirs is not always the correct one. Additionally, they can simultaneously consider and coordinate their own needs and intentions with those of others, and are able to compare their own perspectives with the "generalized" and multiple others who comprise society.[18]

Like empathy, perspective taking remains a potential which can be deliberately and consciously cultivated.

Merely asking people to imagine what others are thinking and feeling is one way to promote perspective taking. When this is accompanied by "role-playing," the effects on behavior can be dramatic.

"Role-playing" invites people to "act out" someone's role but without providing them with a prepared script to do so. The strategy generally requires giving some information about the character's background and position and providing a context where she or he "acts out" the role. Several characters—usually no more than five—with differing points of view are then cast into a pre-determined scene, and each is instructed to improvise a dialogue consistent with the assigned character. No character, however, is to represent his or her real self. The characters in a scene involving an automobile manufacturing decision might be an automobile purchaser, an assembly line worker, the chief executive officer, an energy conservationist, and a successful foreign competitor. The characters in a scene designed to increase family understanding might reverse roles among parents and siblings, while characters in a scene designed to increase ethnic and racial understanding would similarly reverse roles. A critical part of the role taking experience is that the actors receive feedback on the accuracy of their portrayal from those who view it.

Using a combination of methods—clarifying their own feelings, recognizing and discriminating among others' feelings as well as role-playing—Norma Feshbach demonstrated how behavior can change even with children as young as eight and nine years of age. Although children participated in this experience for only a short period—three hours a week over a ten-week period—the results were impressive. As compared with children who had not received the training, their understanding of others as well as cooperative and helping behaviors increased while their aggressive behaviors decreased.[19]

That role-playing can be effective even with delinquents was dramatically demonstrated by Michael Chandler. The children, between eleven and thirteen years of age, were serious offenders who would have been charged with felonies had they been adults. After comparing them with nondelinquent children, Chandler concluded that they had great difficulty describing any situation that required taking any perspective other than their own. In addition to asking the youngsters to play the roles of different types of young people their own age in short skits, Chandler videotaped the skits and then gave them feedback on the accuracy and quality of their depiction. At the end of ten weeks, the delinquents who had the role-playing experience scored significantly higher on a perspective taking test than other delinquents who did not have the training. More importantly, the role-playing group had half the number of arrests during the subsequent eighteen months as compared with the eighteen months prior to the experiment.[20]

Simulations, a more dramatic type of role-playing, can have even more powerful effects than conventional role-playing. They are as close as one can get to walking in another's shoes without really being there.

Simulations require that actors actually "become" someone else in the context of a situation where others treat them as if they were in fact the other. Unlike role-playing, which offers but a partial view of another's condition, simulations plunge people into another's more complete reality.

Short simulations, lasting from an hour to several days, might have engineers become construction laborers, students become victims of arbitrary discrimination, or doctors become patients in the hospitals they service. All these types of simulations have in fact been tried with impressive learning results. To learn more about patients in a psychiatric institution, Stanford professor David Rosenhan and seven other people engaged in a lengthy simulation which received wide attention. They had themselves admitted into several different psychiatric institutions by pretending they heard voices. While the patients quickly realized that these people were sane, it took the staff some nineteen days to realize they were despite the fact that these pseudopatients stopped reporting any symptoms immediately after entry. In the process, the simulators began to understand the sense of powerlessness, unworthiness, and general invisibility which patients routinely endured.[21]

In hopes of finding some solution to the deeply troubling political situation in Israel some few years ago, Yoram Binur, a Jewish journalist for a Jerusalem local weekly newspaper *Kol Ha'ir*, undertook a highly dangerous simulation. He became a Palestinian Arab for six months. The bitterness he encountered frightened him, and he became infuriated when one of his hosts, a Palestinian intellectual, remarked: "Those Zionists . . . they're always talking about what Hitler did to them in Europe. I don't believe that Hitler killed the Jews, they just killed each other." Despite this, he came to appreciate their sense of humiliation and anger in a new way and became even more committed to ending the bloodshed on both sides.[22]

Role-playing and simulations are so powerful in promoting empathy that participants in armed conflict resist it for fear it will weaken their resolve to fight. (War simulation exercises do encourage understanding the enemy, but for the purpose of defeating them.) For the very reason that it reduces the ability to inflict pain, role taking abilities are deliberately repressed among soldiers. "If the soldier were to imagine the suffering he is ready to bring about, he would be less eager to wage war," says Nobel Prize winner Elie Wiesel. "If he were to consider the enemy a potential victim—and therefore capable of weeping, of despairing, of dying—the relationship between them would be changed. Every effort is made, therefore, to limit, even stifle, his humane impulses, his imagination and his capacity to experience a feeling of brotherhood toward his fellow man."[23] For that very reason, role-playing and simulations are highly valued among peace promoters.

While the above strategies can help promote perspective taking, they are unlikely to yield accurate understanding of others without a climate of trust. To illustrate the effects of distrust on accurate perceptions, consider the case of the Cuban missile crisis of 1962 when the United States and the Soviet Union stood poised for a war which neither side wanted.

Before the summer of 1962, when Soviet missiles were introduced into Cuba, the Soviets and the Cubans believed that the United States intended to invade the island to overthrow Castro and his government. They believed that the missiles could be introduced secretly into Cuba without detection, and if detected, they believed the United States would not respond. The United States, however, had no intention of invading Cuba, but having once learned of the missiles' presence, was determined to take military action. The United States also believed that the Soviets would not retaliate. In fact, the Soviets were quite determined to retaliate somewhere in the world, most likely against U.S. Jupiter missiles in Turkey or NATO forces in Berlin.

These gross miscalculations, reported by Robert McNamara, did not become known until January 1989, when representatives from both sides met for an unusually candid meeting in Moscow. They occurred despite a highly sophisticated information collection system on both sides because of what McNamara calls deep-seated mistrust.[24]

As Sissela Bok points out, everyone may need a certain measure of distrust to discern dangers,[25] but if we are determined to see others as adversaries or enemies, we are unlikely to interpret their behaviors correctly, empathize with them, or respond appropriately. Whether the context is international or interpersonal, the same principle applies.

The object of empathy is to be an effective helper and that usually requires at least two types of understanding: understanding others' total life conditions as well as their distinctiveness and uniqueness. It is this dual capacity, sometimes called "mature empathy," which makes it possible to develop realistic and achievable goals.

Consider for example this comment given by Vera Brooke, a high school teacher whom sociologist Bob Blauner interviewed. Vera was trying to explain how she managed to succeed with a student whom others had given up on:

The caring factor . . . That's how I got the kid that walked in my classroom in 1970 reading at third-grade level [to] graduate at grade level three years later. And I didn't have any special books and I didn't just work with him. But I was interested in his progress, interested in his difficulties, and when he bullshitted me, I told him, and when I was bullshitting him, he told me. That kind of dealing is real important . . . [26]

What Vera calls "caring" is a persistent interest, which included not only the progress this youngster was making but also "his difficulties." Vera does not specify what those "difficulties" were, but she implies that they included more than just his academic difficulties. Vera probably spent a lot of time just talking with this youngster, learning about his interests, family, and friends as well as his academic shortcomings and strengths. Based on this more complete understanding, she developed some realistic expectations about what could and could not be done. As a consequence, she refused to coparticipate in perpetuating his failure and developed some appropriate tasks that he could achieve.

Because they have high but realistic expectations for themselves and others, many highly empathic people often look "tough" rather than "soft." Chris Zajac, the fifth grade teacher who was the subject of Tracy Kidder's best selling book, *Among Schoolchildren*, shares many of Vera's qualities.

Like Vera, Chris insists on knowing much more about her students than just their academic progress. Pedro, for example, never misbehaved, always tried to do his homework and please her. Yet he hardly ever talked, cried frequently, and was often absent from class. Not content with the fact that he caused her no trouble and suspecting that he might have some learning disability, Chris tried to get him evaluated by available school experts, which required a note from his mother. When Chris tried to get his mother to come to school, she received a note in Spanish telling her: "I am sick with high blood pressure. I can't walk much. I want to die." Chris told the principal, who reluctantly dispatched the guidance counselor (there was only one at the school for the approximately six hundred students) to Pedro's house only after the suicide prevention center told him they couldn't become involved unless the victim asked for help. The conditions at home were very depressed, but the counselor did manage to get Pedro's uncle and grandmother to school while Chris continued to work with him on an individual basis as much as possible and to encourage him with praise.[27] A year's observation persuaded Kidder that Chris acted much the same way with all her students.

Based on his initial impressions, Kidder would never have predicted the type of teacher Chris is:

"I was kind of shocked by her at first," Kidder says of Zajac. "She was so tough. She took a little bit of getting used to. It took me a while to figure out what she was trying to do." Zajac, he realized, was tough but not mean, and her toughness was part of what made her such a good teacher.

"I guess I am strict," Zajac says. "The teachers who affected me the most were the ones who expected a lot out of me."[28]

For Vera Brooke and Chris Zajac, high expectations for themselves and their students were inextricably linked. Implementing them did not mean requiring standardized and uniform expectations, but rather the ability to recognize unique differences and adjust their goals and methods accordingly.

Yet, even as it is based on a recognition of differences, mature empathy also requires an appreciation of a shared humanity. While Vera Brooke and Chris Zajac paid attention to the unique qualities of their individual charges, they also understood that, like themselves, students wanted to achieve and succeed. Alfie Kohn proposes that advanced empathy consists of "a twofold attitude toward the other. On the one hand, we appreciate, as it were, the other's otherness; on the other hand, we appreciate the humanness that we have in common."[29]

That high level empathy need not be confined to other humans alone, is suggested by Nobel Prize winner Barbara McClintock, who has made some major discoveries in the field of cytogenetics. Like other empathizers, she focuses on singular differences as well as comprehensive understanding. Describing how she approaches plants, she says:

No two plants are exactly alike. They're all different, and as a consequence, you have to know that difference . . . I start with the seedling, and I don't want to leave. I don't feel I really know the story if I don't watch the plant all the way along. So I know every plant in the field. I know them intimately, and I find it a great pleasure to know them.[30]

As Evelyn Keller, her biographer, describes it, what she acquires in the process is something she calls a "feeling for the organism" and what we would call advanced empathic understanding—a sense that she knows the "autobiography of each plant" intimately, understanding it not only cognitively but also feeling into it in a way she cannot articulate. And the small details she observes provide the key for understanding not only the single organism but its underlying principles, and the connection between such principles to yet other organisms and other principles.[31]

Bill Devall and G. Sessions, advocates of what is called "deep ecology," argue that we need to extend this view not only to plants and trees, but also to all natural phenomena, including rocks, streams, rivers, and lakes. Among all "others," we tend to conceptualize these as the most distant from ourselves, hence using them as objects for our immediate convenience. Ecologists like Devall and Sessions believe that we will continue to use them in this way unless we develop empathic respect for all the elements of our natural surroundings. Without such feelings, they contend, we cannot even begin to address the global issues that threaten us.[32]

Does empathy then lead to action on others' behalf? Not necessarily. According to psychologist C. Daniel Batson, empathic emotion evokes altruism, a genuine desire to enhance another person's welfare. Having conducted some twenty-five systematic experimental studies designed to assess alternative explanations for helping others, Batson speaks with particular authority on this matter.[33] But as he and other psychologists note, acting on the basis of these emotions depends on certain conditions.

One of the primary conditions is what psychologists call perceiving a need, and the greater the magnitude of the perceived need, the more likely it is that people will act on it. Merely reading about others is sufficient for some people to perceive a need. But one of the most effective ways to help people perceive a need is to provide them with a direct visible encounter with someone in distress. Actually seeing others' misery often prompts empathically disposed people to respond, a matter that has significantly elevated television's influence on foreign policy, for example. Our involvement in Somalia and our contemplated action in Bosnia can in large measure be attributed to television's ability to bring the horrors vividly into our visual consciousness.

But too many visible encounters with distress risks desensitization. The homeless are a case in point; overwhelmed by their numbers, we have resigned ourselves to their presence, evading our eyes as we pass them on the street. The cost of helping, even when we perceive a need, is sometimes too high. When the price of empathy is too dear, we devise many strategies to repress our feelings. We suppress the knowledge or deny the need, as did the German nonrescuer who said: "I must admit that I knew the Jews were transported, but I didn't have the foggiest idea that they were all being massacred. The rumors were there, but I could not believe they could be such beasts."[34] And sometimes we blame the victims themselves, accusing them of deserving their fate.

People are more likely to overcome such avoidance techniques if the information is salient to them. The more isolated people are, the more likely they are to dismiss information about others' needs as relevant to them. The less people interact with others, the more they become focused on themselves alone;[35] hence, the importance to society of avoiding isolation in the workplace or school, and encouraging sustained interpersonal face-to-face interactions with others generally.

But it is the people we interact with routinely and on a daily basis who are likely to be the most salient to us. It is easier to identify with them and to respond to them because they have a heightened reality for us. This helps explain why non-Jews who had Jewish friends, worked with Jews, and lived among Jews were more likely to become rescuers than those who did not.[36] It also helps explain why helpful behaviors are more common in rural environments than in larger cities[37] and why executives who have a sustained interpersonal relationship with employees over time are more likely to respond empathically to their needs.

Such was the case, for example, with Steven Simpson who was appointed to preside over the demise of Sun Ship, a Sun Company shipyard subsidiary located in Chester, Pennsylvania. Faced with continuing heavy financial losses at Sun Ship, the parent company, Sun Company, decided to sell. At stake were some thirty-one hundred jobs, many of them held by thirty-year veterans. The city itself, an economically blighted area, faced equally impressive losses. Local businesses that depended on Sun Ship's employees were threatened, as were the city's tax base and community projects to which the company as well as its employees customarily contributed. To prepare themselves and the community for the impending sale scheduled for 1982, Sun Ship decided they needed advice. They hired Steve Simpson, a local man, as chief counsel in 1978.

Simpson had a difficult role. As an attorney with what he describes as a realistic understanding of the economic necessities, his job was to administer the company's dissolution. But, because of his relationships with Sun Company employees over many years, he had strong personal feelings which became apparent when David Freudberg interviewed him for a radio talk show:

Freudberg: I'm going to ask you to take off your lawyer's hat and your Sun Company management hat. Did the phasedown decision bother you a lot?

Simpson: Sure. Sure. I had social friends who had worked at the shipyard during the Second World War. My father had friends who had worked at the shipyard before that. My father's first job was in Chester as a pharmacist. His first pay was a gold coin, and the guys from the shipyard used to go buy pharmaceuticals.

Freudberg: How do you sort that out?

Simpson: That's the essence of being a businessman. It's the essence of being a lawyer . . . Decisions are made on the basis of facts. Lawyers give legal advice on the basis of the law and the facts as they're presented to them . . . It was probably the most painful period of time that any of the decision makers experienced in their business lives, because as I said, we all knew people who had worked there for three generations. It was not callous. It was, we have a problem with respect to the marketplace.[38]

The company eventually resolved it in a way which was regarded by a University of Delaware study as unusually generous. Threatened workers were offered early retirements, severance benefits, job counseling, and medical benefits. The company contributed $800,000 to the city as compensation for the tax income that would be lost; $210,000 to the United Way to make up for pledges by workers, and a grant of $360,000 for the establishment of a nonprofit agency, the Riverfront Development Corporation, for the purpose of stimulating an economic revival in the community. The total sum is estimated in the millions.

While Sun Company apparently wanted to dissolve its Chester shipyard humanely, they probably would have been unable to do so without Simpson's help. Simpson, who bore most of the responsibility for negotiating this complex settlement, had sophisticated perspective-taking skills which enabled him to balance the interests of employees and the community with

Sun's interests. But Simpson brought more than skills to the task. He also brought a high level of empathic concern, born primarily of his ongoing and direct interactions with many people and strata in the community over years.

But perhaps the most compelling condition motivating people to develop empathy and act on it will be a change in the nature of societal values. Some promising indicators in this direction already exist, and feminists deserve much of the credit for the change.

Not too long ago, when classical psychoanalytical theory dominated much of our thinking, heightened empathy was presumed to be associated with personality pathologies. Not surprisingly, these pathologies were purportedly most evident among women.

More than forty years ago, psychoanalyst Helene Deutsch argued that the willingness to embrace suffering was an essential characteristic of the adult woman's personality. Women presumably developed this masochistic orientation because their own lives were marked by suffering experienced in menstruation, pregnancy, childbirth, and menopause. While women learned to be self-sacrificing as a result, they also developed specific pathologies, including heightened emotionality and dependency needs, merging and fusing with others as well as manipulating them.[39] By way of contrast, the healthy personality was presumed to be independent, autonomous, and rational; characteristics more commonly the province of men.

Feminists—Jean Baker Miller,[40] Carol Gilligan,[41] Nel Noddings,[42] Elizabeth Janeway,[43] Adrienne Rich[44] among others—not only challenged this view, but repudiated it. They agree that women's lives are different from those of men. They also agree that women develop different attributes as a consequence, but they reconceptualized and relabeled those differences. Women, they said, seek more integrated lives; hence they emphasize relationships, connection, and caring. Whereas men learned to emphasize their distinction and separation from others, women learned to empathize with them.

Few feminists believe that women possess a heightened empathic sense because of some innate predisposition. Rather, they argue, women learn it because of their assigned cultural roles. As society's primary caretakers, they not only nurture the young, but also bear most of the care for the old.[45] They also dominate in caregiving occupations such as child care, nursing, and nursery school and kindergarten teaching.[46] Nancy Chodorow argues that it begins in early childhood, long before women assume these roles.

During their most formative years, girls and boys interact primarily with women: with mothers at home and with women teachers in school. Girls identify with these women and see themselves as continuous with them. Boys, on the other hand, know they are different. Since adult males are remote figures during this period—fathers are rarely present and elementary teachers are dominantly female—boys lack a sense of what "masculinity" is. Hence, their sense of identity revolves around being something other than female. Given too that women are powerful persons in these early experiences, boys feel compelled to eject the feminine while constructing an imagined masculinity.[47]

Some evidence supports the idea that women are more empathic than men. Women, for example, consistently score significantly higher than men on self-reported measures of empathy; that is, in response to questionnaire items such as "Seeing people cry upsets me."[48] At all ages, women appear to be better at interpreting the meaning of others' auditory cues, such as tone of voice and pitch. Adult women are also better at interpreting the meaning of visual cues, such as facial expressions and gestures.[49] While as youngsters, both boys and girls are just as likely to express emotions, boys are more likely to mask negative emotions, such as fear or anxiety.[50] As adults, women are more inclined to respond emotionally[51] and try to respond to others on their terms.[52]

Other studies, however, suggest that males are as empathic as females and in certain circumstances, equally good at perspective taking. When physiological responses (such as heartbeat) or facial and gestural expressions (in response to a laboratory induced emotional situation or videotape) rather than self-reports were used to measure empathy, gender differences disappeared in studies done by Eisenberg and Lennon.[53] After reviewing fourteen studies with twenty-two samples, twenty of whom were children, Martin Hoffman found no significant gender differences on empathy in eighteen of them, while the remaining four favored boys.[54] And a study of men preparing for or working in occupations requiring sensitivity and nurturance indicated that they were just as good as women in interpreting nonverbally expressed emotions.[55]

Parental socialization practices, both in the United States and in western Europe, appear to contribute heavily to gender differences. Consistent with western cultural norms, boys and men are expected to assume an instrumental role—performing functional tasks for family and society—while women are expected to assume an expressive role—facilitating interpersonal harmony.[56] In Denmark, England, Finland, Norway, Sweden, and the United States, parental expectations for boys emphasize achievement, competition, conformity, and control of feelings, while parental expectations for girls emphasize interpersonal relationships.[57] Parents express such expectations verbally as well as physically. They are more likely to hug and kiss girls and use affectionate language with them.[58] Mother-daughter relationships in particular encourage empathy whereas father-son relationships inhibit it; the former tend toward tolerance and affection whereas the latter emphasize competition.[59]

A recent longitudinal study demonstrates that men and women are just as likely to become empathic adults if their parents relate to them in particular ways. Based on a sample of seventy-five men and women, Richard Koestner concluded that four variables contributed to an empathic concern with others: fathers' involvement with children (the degree to which fathers spent time with them), mothers' tolerance of dependent behavior (the degree to which mothers responded to childrens' dependent behaviors), mothers' inhibition of childrens' aggressive behaviors, and mothers' satisfaction. These parental dimensions, measured when these adults were five years old, significantly predicted their levels of concern at age thirty-one. Of them, the single most important influence was paternal involvement with their children.[60] Our study of rescuers suggests that such relationships may be particularly important for men. While both men and women rescuers reported being closer to their families as compared with nonrescuers, men rescuers reported such close relationships significantly more frequently than any other group, including women rescuers.[61]

One of the important points the evidence suggests is the danger of over-generalizations. Not all women are empathic; neither are all men devoid of empathy. Pointing to what she calls a "curious coincidence" of attributions to women and minorities, Sandra Harding issues the same caution with respect to the latter. Both feminists and Africanist theorists distinguish themselves from white European males by virtue of their presumed greater tendency to view others as subjects rather than objects. As she says, not all subordinated peoples are empathic; neither are all their superordinates devoid of it.[62]

The other point relates to the importance of learning experiences. Rather than innate, gender differences appear to be largely the result of social values, social roles, and socialization practices. If women above all are assigned the responsibility for caring for others and maintaining interpersonal harmony, then they, rather than men, will develop empathic skills. If schools and the workplace, as well as other social institutions, eschew such responsibilities, empathy will continue to be primarily women's work to the detriment of men and social life generally.

NOTES

1. Robert Coles, *The Moral Life of Children* (Boston: The Atlantic Monthly Press, 1986), 27–28.

2. Definitions of sympathy and empathy differ. Nancy Eisenberg and Paul Mussen (*The Roots of Prosocial Behavior in Children* [New York: Cambridge University Press, 1989]) and Norma Feshbach ("Sex Differences in Empathy and Social Behavior in Children," in *The Development of Prosocial Behavior*, ed. Nancy Eisenberg [New York: Academic Press, 1982]) agree that empathy requires both cognitive understanding of another as well as feeling what others feel. Janusz Reykowski and M. Zuzanna Smolenska (see Samuel P. Oliner and Pearl M. Oliner, *The Altruistic Personality: Rescuers of Jews in Nazi Europe* [New York: Free Press, 1988]: chap. 8, fn

2) distinguish between what they call primary empathy and secondary empathy; the former is based on an emotional response to a direct emotional cue whereas the latter implies cognitive understanding. While C. Daniel Batson agrees that empathy is centered on the other's needs rather than the self, he says it does not require understanding others from their viewpoint or sharing their feelings. Rather, "it is a more other-oriented emotional response elicited by and congruent with the perceived welfare of someone else" (C. Daniel Batson, "Prosocial Motivation: Is it Ever Truly Altruistic?" in *Advances in Experimental Social Psychology*, ed. Leonard Berkowitz [New York: Academic Press, 1987], 65–122, 93). This conception appears to be largely similar to what Lauren Wispé calls sympathy: "a heightened awareness of the suffering of another person as something to be alleviated" (Lauren Wispé, "The Distinction Between Sympathy and Empathy: To Call Forth a Concept, a Word is Needed," *Journal of Personality and Social Psychology* 50:2 [1986]: 314–321, 318). While Wispé agrees that empathy means to cognitively understand (or to attempt to understand) another's experiences, he says its intent is accuracy rather than alleviation of another's discomfort and does not require sharing another's feelings. For a comprehensive review of the concept and its development, see Nancy Eisenberg and Janet Strayer, eds., *Empathy and its Development* (New York: Cambridge University Press, 1987).

3. Alfie Kohn, *The Brighter Side of Human Nature* (New York: Basic Books, 1990), 115.

4. Peter Marin, "Helping and Hating the Homeless," *Harper's Magazine*, January, 1987, 47.

5. Joel Blau (*The Visible Poor: Homelessness in the United States* [New York: Oxford University Press, 1992]) writes that the fastest growing group of homeless consists of families. In 1978, families constituted 21 percent of all the homeless in shelters; by 1988, their percentage had increased to 40 percent.

6. Samuel P. Oliner and Pearl M. Oliner, *The Altruistic Personality: Rescuers of Jews in Nazi Europe* (New York: Free Press, 1988), 192.

7. David Hume, "Morality, Self-Love, and Benevolence," in *Egoism and Altruism*, ed. Ronald D. Milo (Belmont, Calif.: Wadsworth, 1973, originally published in 1751).

8. Jean Jacques Rousseau, "A Discourse on the Origin of Inequality," in *The Social Contract and Discourses*, trans. G.D.H. Cole (New York: E. P. Dutton, 1950), "Preface," paragraph 11 (originally published in 1755).

9. Adam Smith, *The Theory of Moral Sentiments* (Richmond, Va.: Ibis Publications, 1986, originally published in 1759).

10. Martin L. Simner, "Newborn's Response to the Cry of Another Infant," *Developmental Psychology* 5 (1971): 136–150; Abraham Sagi and Martin L. Hoffman, "Empathic Distress in the Newborn," *Developmental Psychology* 12 (1976): 175–176.

11. Martin L. Hoffman, "The Contribution of Empathy to Justice and Moral Judgment," in *Empathy*, eds. Eisenberg and Strayer.

12. Maria Jarymowicz, "Self, We, and Other(s): Schemata, Distinctiveness, and Altruism," in *Embracing the Other: Philosophical, Psychological and Historical Perspectives on Altruism*, eds. Pearl M. Oliner et al. (New York: New York University Press, 1992), 194–212.

13. A. Kohn, 152. Several studies suggest that children who express their feelings freely are more likely to help others (Nancy Eisenberg et al., "Socialization of Pro-

social Behavior in the Preschool Classroom," *Developmental Psychology* 17 [1981]: 773–782; Susanne A. Denham, "Social Cognition, Prosocial Behavior, and Emotion in Preschoolers: Contextual Validation," *Child Development* 57 [1986]: 94–201.)

14. Vaclev Havel, "The Art of the Impossible," full text reproduced in *The Spectator*, January 27, 1990, 11+, 11.

15. Bob Jarvis, interviewed by the Altruistic and Prosocial Behavior Institute, Humboldt State University, November 13, 1985.

16. Anthony Walton, "Willie Horton and Me," *The New York Times Magazine*, August 30, 1989, 52+, 77.

17. Walton, 77.

18. Robert L. Selman, "Social-Cognitive Understanding: A Guide to Educational and Clinical Practice," in *Moral Development and Behavior*, ed. Thomas Lickona (New York: Holt, Rinehart and Winston, 1976), 299–316; Robert L. Selman, *The Growth of Interpersonal Understanding: Developmental and Clinical Analyses* (New York: Academic Press, 1980), 299–316.

19. Norma D. Feshbach, "Empathy Training: A Field Study in Affective Education," in *Aggression and Behavior Change: Biological and Social Processes*, eds. Seymour Feshbach and Adam Fraczek (New York: Praeger, 1979), 234–249; Norma D. Feshbach and Seymour Feshbach, "Empathy Training and the Regulation of Aggression: Potentialities and Limitations," *Academic Psychological Bulletin* 4 (1982): 399–413. For a description of the activities, see Norma D. Feshbach et al., *Learning to Care: Classroom Activities for Social and Affective Development* (Glenview, Ill.: Scott, Foresman, 1983).

20. Michael Chandler, "Egocentrism and Antisocial Behavior: The Assessment and Training of Social Perspective-taking Skills," *Developmental Psychology* 9 (1973): 326–332.

21. David L. Rosenhan, "On Being Sane in Insane Places," *Science* 173 (1973): 250–258.

22. Yoram Binur, *My Enemy, My Self* (New York: Doubleday, 1989), 214–215.

23. Elie Wiesel, "Are We Afraid of Peace?," *Parade*, March 19, 1989, 8.

24. Robert S. McNamara, *Out of the Cold: New Thinking for American Foreign and Defense Policy in the 21st Century* (New York: Simon & Schuster, 1989).

25. Sissela Bok, *A Strategy for Peace* (New York: Pantheon Books, 1989).

26. Robert Blauner, *Black Lives, White Lives: Three Decades of Race Relations in America* (Berkeley: University of California Press, 1989), 295.

27. Tracy Kidder, *Among Schoolchildren* (New York: Houghton Mifflin, 1989).

28. David Hill, interviewer, "Tracy Kidder," *Teacher Magazine*, September/October 1989, 74–80, 78.

29. A. Kohn, 99.

30. Cited in Evelyn Fox Keller, *A Feeling for the Organism: The Life and Work of Barbara McClintock* (San Francisco: W. H. Freeman, 1983), 198.

31. E. F. Keller, *Feeling*.

32. Bill Devall and George Sessions, *Deep Ecology: Living as if Nature Mattered* (Salt Lake City: Peregrine Smith, 1985).

33. C. Daniel Batson, *The Altruism Question: Toward a Social-Psychological Answer* (Hillsdale, N.J.: Lawrence Erlbaum, 1991).

34. Oliner and Oliner, 122.

35. William R. Looft, "Egocentrism and Social Interaction Across the Life Span," *Psychological Bulletin* 78 (1972): 73–92.

36. Oliner and Oliner.

37. Harold Takooshian, Sandra Haber, and David J. Lucido, "Who Wouldn't Help a Lost Child?," *Psychology Today*, February 1977, 67–68.

38. David Freudberg, *The Corporate Conscience: Money, Power, and Responsible Business* (New York: AMACOM [American Management Association], 1986), 95, 96. In preparation for five half-hour documentaries titled "The Corporate Conscience" (which aired on National Public Radio in 1984), Freudberg assembled a research team whose task was to identify "individual executives and entire companies which had a reputation for fairness, integrity, and a thoughtful approach to resolving business conflicts" (p. 3). The team conducted some eighty interviews, of which twenty-five were subsequently published.

39. Helene Deutsch, *The Psychology of Women: A Psychoanalytic Interpretation*, 2 vols. (New York: Grune and Stratton, 1944, 1945).

40. Jean Baker Miller, *Toward a New Psychology of Women* (Boston: Beacon Press, 1976).

41. Carol Gilligan, *In a Different Voice: Psychological Theory and Women's Development* (Cambridge: Harvard University Press, 1982).

42. Nel Noddings, *Caring: A Feminine Approach to Ethics and Moral Education* (Berkeley: University of California Press, 1984).

43. Elizabeth Janeway, *Man's World, Woman's Place* (New York: William Morrow, 1971).

44. Adrienne Rich, *Of Woman Born: Motherhood as Experience and Institution* (New York: W. W. Norton, 1977).

45. Wives and adult daughters represent more than 70 percent of caregivers to the elderly (Robin Stone, Gail Lee Cafferata, and Judith Sangl, "Caregivers of the Frail Elderly: A National Profile," *The Gerontologist* 27:5 [1987]: 616–626).

46. Among child care providers, more than 97 percent are women; among registered nurses they number more than 96 percent, and among nursery and kindergarten teachers, more than 98 percent (Andrew Hacker, *US: A Statistical Portrait of the American People* [New York: Viking Press, 1993]).

47. Nancy Chodorow, *The Reproduction of Mothering: Psychoanalysis and the Sociology of Gender* (Berkeley: University of California Press, 1978).

48. Julie Larrieu and Paul Mussen, "Some Personality and Motivational Correlates of Children's Prosocial Behavior," *Journal of Genetic Psychology* 147 (1986): 529–542; Martin L. Hoffman, "Sex Differences in Empathy and Related Behaviors," *Psychological Bulletin* 64 (1977): 712–722; Nancy Eisenberg and Randy Lennon, "Sex Differences in Empathy and Related Capacities," *Psychological Bulletin* 94:1, (1983): 100–131.

49. Peter D. Blanck et al., "Sex Differences in Eavesdropping on Nonverbal Clues: Developmental Changes," *Journal of Personality and Social Psychology* 41 (1981): 391–396; Judith A. Hall, "Gender Effects in Decoding Nonverbal Clues," *Psychological Bulletin* 41:1 (1978): 845–875; Eisenberg and Lennon.

50. Leslie R. Brody, "Children's Emotional Attributions to Themselves and Others: A Measure of Children's Defensiveness," paper presented at the annual convention of the American Psychological Association, Anaheim, California, August 1983.

51. Jon G. Allen and Dorothy M. Haccoun, "Sex Differences in Emotionality: A

Multi-Dimensional Approach," *Human Relations* 29 (1976): 711–720; Leslie R. Brody, "Gender Differences in Emotional Development: A Review of Theories and Research," *Journal of Personality* 53 (1985): 102–149; Eleanor Maccoby and Carol Jacklin, *The Psychology of Sex Differences* (Stanford: Stanford University Press, 1974).

52. Nona Plessner Lyons, "Two Perspectives: On Self, Relationships, and Morality," *Harvard Educational Review* 53 (1983): 125–145.

53. Eisenberg and Lennon; Nancy Eisenberg, *Altruistic Emotion, Cognition and Behavior* (Hillsdale, N.J.: Lawrence Erlbaum, 1986), chap. 3. Although such responses only indicate arousal rather than necessarily reflecting empathy, the validity of self-reports is also questionable.

54. Hoffman, "Sex Differences."

55. Robert Rosenthal, D. Archer, M. R. DiMatteo, J. H. Kowumaki, and P. O. Rogers, "Body Talk and Tone of Voice: The Language Without Words," *Psychology Today* 8 (1974): 64–68.

56. Talcott Parsons and Robert F. Bales, *Family Socialization, and Interaction Processes* (New York: Academic Press, 1955).

57. Jeanne H. Block, "Conceptions of Sex Role: Some Cross-cultural and Longitudinal Perspectives," *American Psychologist* 28 (1973): 512–526.

58. Howard A. Moss, "Early Sex Differences and Mother-Infant Interaction," in *Sex Differences in Behavior*, eds. Richard C. Friedman, Ralph M. Richart, and Raymond L. Vande Wiele (New York: John Wiley & Sons, 1974), 149–164.

59. Norma D. Feshbach, "The Relationships of Child-Rearing Factors to Children's Aggression, Empathy, and Related Positive and Negative Social Behaviors," in *Determinants and Origins of Aggressive Behavior*, eds. Jan Dewit and Willard W. Hartup (The Hague, Netherlands: Mouton, 1975); Norma D. Feshbach, "Sex Differences in Empathy and Social Behavior in Children," in *The Development of Prosocial Behavior*, ed. Nancy Eisenberg (New York: Academic Press, 1982): 315–358.

60. Richard Koestner, Carol Franz, and Joel Weinberger, "The Family Origins of Empathic Concern: A 26-year Longitudinal Study," *Journal of Personality and Social Psychology* 58 (1990): 709–717.

61. Pearl M. Oliner, Samuel P. Oliner, and Mary B. Gruber, "Altruism and Peace: Some Propositions Based on Gender and Cross-Cultural Comparisons," *International Journal on World Peace* VIII:1 (March 1991): 35–44.

62. Sandra Harding, "The Curious Coincidence of Feminine and African Moralities: Challenges for Feminist Theory," in *Women and Moral Theory*, eds. Eva Feder Kittay and Diana T. Mayers (Totowa, N.J.: Rowman and Littlefield, 1987), 296–315.

CHAPTER 4

Learning Caring Norms

"Come here, Rose. Look down into this bush."

"O Willie! a bird's nest! What cunning, little eggs! May we take it, and show it to mother?"

"What would the old bird do, Rose, if she should come back and not find her nest?"

"Oh, we would bring it right back, Willie!"

"Yes; but we could not fasten it in its place again. If the wind should blow it over, the eggs would get broken."

"How does the bird make the nest so strong, Willie?"

"The mother bird has her bill and her claws to work with, but she would not know how to make the nest if God did not teach her. Do you see what it is made of?"

"Yes, Willie, I see some horsehairs and some dry grass. The old bird must have worked hard to find all the hairs and make them into such a pretty, round nest."

"Shall we take the nest, Rose?"

"Oh, no, Willie! We must not take it; but we will come and look at it again, some time."[1]

No contemporary school textbook series equals the popularity of The Mc-Guffey Readers, from which the above dialogue is taken. With sales of approximately 122 million between 1836 and 1922,[2] the Readers dominated American schools for almost a century. At present they are little more than historical curiosities, largely confined to archival collections. The story of the Readers' success and subsequent demise suggests some important changing views about moral norms and how children as well as adults, learn them. As we shall see, not only schools, but also some businesses are beginning to take these new ideas seriously.

Our purpose here is to propose principles which help people learn caring norms. But we begin first by describing the McGuffey approach and the historical context in which it came to be challenged and subsequently revived, albeit with important modifications.

The McGuffey Readers had two primary objectives, one of which was to teach students how to read. The second one, more relevant for our purposes, sought to teach children morality, and in the view of many of their admirers, this objective was even more important than the first. It was critically important to their author, Scotch Presbyterian clergyman and college president William Holmes McGuffey.

A man of his times, McGuffey had clear ideas about morality and how it was to be taught. Children needed to be molded into moral beings, and adults had the responsibility and duty to shape them appropriately. Moral instruction largely meant teaching children to respect nature, to be industrious, honest, and kind, and to avoid drink, sloth, overeating, and arrogance. The way to teach these moral lessons was straightforward: tell children the rules clearly, repeat the rules often and in a variety ways as the children grow.

The Readers reflected these views. Reading selections emphasized moral lessons and the lessons themselves were repeated throughout the grades in five successive Readers, their language adjusted to suit the maturity levels of students. Stories, fables, poetry, drama, and the like provided the variety. Admire birds' nests but don't touch them is the lesson from The First Reader excerpted above; subsequent lessons in more advanced readers reiterated the idea that children needed to respect nature but not interfere with it unnecessarily.

Common sense suggests that these principles are eminently reasonable, yet for the better part of the twentieth century they were challenged at their core by philosophers, educators, and psychologists.

One critical challenge came from a prestigious Columbia University research team, headed by Hugh Hartshorne and Mark May. According to their ten-year study, published in 1930 and called the Character Education Inquiry study, these principles simply did not work. That is, knowing the rules had little effect on behavior. Students could not be counted on to practice the virtues they had been taught in any consistent way, even if they perceived themselves as possessing them. Students who described themselves as honest, for example, would cheat on examinations as often as those who did not perceive themselves as particularly honest.[3] Findings from this study persuaded many people that changing behaviors required something more than simply telling and repeating moral rules.

But the more fundamental challenge was a philosophical one: it struck at the heart of the nature of morality itself with radical implications for the way it was to be taught. The moral virtues advocated by McGuffey among others, critics observed, seemed to derive more from the needs of a harshly exploitative economic system than to reflect the inherent nature of morality. Industry and humility, for example, seemed better suited to adapt compliant employees to the needs of capitalist enterprise than to promote democratic values.[4] Whereas good employees needed but to obey their superiors, good democratic citizens needed to *think* about values as they went about creating a democratic community. Democracy, argued John Dewey, the foremost philosophical architect of the period, depended on the development of moral social intelligence. As Dewey saw it, school, like life itself, should be a place where children could test and reason about moral and social judgments rather than simply obey them.[5]

That virtue was complex and required thoughtful consideration was not a new idea, of course; philosophers had so argued for centuries. What *was* new was the idea that the "common man" could think in this way; if that were not the case, then democracy itself seemed doomed to failure. As many prominent thinkers interpreted it, authorities had the responsibility to provide a social climate where reasoning and reflecting about democratic community life could occur, and the place to begin was in the schools.[6]

While a few schools experimented with Dewey's ideas in the thirties and forties, it was not until the 1960s that they became reasonably widespread, albeit not quite the way Dewey had envisioned them. One of the most popular teaching strategies of that period was the "values clarification" approach, developed by Louis Raths, Merrill Harmin, and Sidney Simon.[7] It penetrated the school system with uncharacteristic speed. By the early seventies thousands of teachers throughout the country had participated in workshops where they learned how to use it.

Raths, Harmin, and Simon, like Dewey, argued that moral indoctrination through top-down prescriptions had not worked. Their strategy, a seven-step approach, invited students to think about their values. Based on a list of suggested questions, it asked students to explore their values as they examined their choices, reflect on those values they prized, and to consider their past and future actions with respect to them. The following is one example of how it worked:

First, the teacher asks, "If you could not be yourself but could be someone else, what is the name of the character you would most like to be?" The students are to write down on a piece of paper the name of a person chosen from real life, fiction, the news, movies, literature, cartoons, history, etc. Then the teacher asks them to write down the name of a character "You would least like to be like," and third, "the name of a character who is most like you."

When they have listed their three characters, the students are to break up into small groups of from three to five members. They take turns sharing their lists with their group and explaining their selections.

After the students have discussed their characters, the teacher might ask values clarifying questions like: Were your characters males or females? Can you think of anyone whose list of characters *you* would be on? Would your list have been different three years ago? Would your best friend be able to guess the names on your list?[8]

At its heydey, few educators envisioned the public outcry that would result as a consequence of this apparently innocuous procedure. By the early eighties, "values clarification" became a "dirty word," and schools rushed to disassociate themselves from it as rapidly as they had first embraced it.

To some degree, it was the very success of the strategy that made it controversial. Students would often reveal very personal matters—family and personal feelings about race, religion, and sex among others—which left many feeling vulnerable and embarrassed subsequently. But the real problem, as critics saw it, was that it left values open-ended. Teachers were explicitly asked to refrain from saying what was good or bad; their role was confined to raising exploratory questions. While the ultimate aim was to arrive at good values—research had persuaded Raths, Harmin, and Simon that such things as academic motivation, consideration and, self-discipline would be enhanced by the process—observers were often aghast when students used the procedure to verbally justify behaviors such as stealing and cheating without teachers saying "that's wrong."

A far more sophisticated approach to teaching values, one with a more elaborate theory and stronger research base, was Harvard psychologist Lawrence Kohlberg's "moral reasoning model." Kohlberg received greater acclaim and international recognition than the value clarifiers, but his direct influence on the classroom was considerably less than theirs, primarily because his strategy was more complex and required more training to implement.

In Kohlberg's view, morality meant being able to reason at high moral levels. High moral reasoners based their choices on principles of universal justice, equality of human rights, and the dignity of individuals. These principles, Kohlberg argued, constituted the essence of a democratic society. The objective of the moral reasoning model was to help students progress from lower levels of moral reasoning—what Kohlberg called preconventional and conventional moral reasoning—to high moral reasoning levels. The medium through which this was to be accomplished was the "moral dilemma": teachers confronted students with a problem in which two moral principles were in conflict and asked students to decide what they would do and why. Students might be asked to decide whether they would tell the police the truth if their best friend had stolen something, for example, or if they would steal a drug if it could save their mother's life and they had no money to buy it. More important than their decisions, were the *reasons* they gave for their choices. As in the values clarification strategy, the teacher was to refrain from making judgments while helping students see the inconsistencies and limitations of their reasoning by asking appropriate questions.[9]

Were these new strategies more effective than former ones in changing behavior? The answer is not entirely clear. The few studies done to assess the values clarification strategy, primarily conducted by Louis Raths himself, failed to persuade people that their purported successes outweighed their negative effects. And while research by Kohlberg and his associates demonstrated that people could progress in their moral reasoning through use of the moral dilemmas, and that children and adults who reasoned at higher levels were less likely to hurt others and more likely to behave kindly toward them,[10] the overall correlation between moral reasoning and moral behavior was low.[11] At best one could say that people who demonstrated high levels of moral reasoning were more likely to act caringly, but not consistently.

With no conclusive evidence to support the reasoning position as the best means for teaching moral behavior, psychologists began to reexamine ideas they had formerly rejected, and to experiment with new ones. The ideas which follow represent some of their current thinking.

Norms set expectations for behavior, and people need to know what they are if they are to behave appropriately is one widely adopted view regarding learning norms. Caring norms are no exception. One way to make sure people know that they are expected to behave caringly is to communicate caring norms explicitly and unambiguously.

Note that the above says "norms," not "rules." The terms are critically different in meaning with important learning implications. Norms are general and abstract; rules derive from norms and are very specific. "Help your neighbor" is a caring norm; "lend your neighbor money if s/he needs it" or "help your neighbor carry grocery packages" are rules the norm might imply. Similarly, "respect others' dignity" is a caring norm; "don't reveal others' weaknesses publicly" or "make sure everyone has a chance to participate" are rules this norm might imply.

If norms are general enough and well learned, people can potentially use them to derive many rules for behavior in specific circumstances. This observation leads to another principle: concentrate on communicating a few important norms only, and choose those which are general enough to apply to many varied situations.

Another good principle is: state norms positively rather than negatively. "Help your neighbor," is an example of a positively stated norm; "don't hurt your neighbor" is stated negatively. Similarly, "respect everyone's dignity" is stated positively; "don't offend others' dignity" is stated negatively. Positive statements tell people what to do; negative statements only tell them what not to do. "Don't hurt your neighbor," for example, could mean not hitting or insulting others; it does not necessarily imply helping them.

Bystanders and rescuers offer a dramatic example of this difference: bystanders avoided hurting Jews directly, but only rescuers helped them.

Another principle to keep in mind is that people need opportunities to discuss norms and to consider derivative appropriate rules. Rules generally become relevant in specific contexts, and they are not always clear even to those who may subscribe to the norm in a general way. Our rescuer study again offers a case in point.

The majority of rescuers and nonrescuers had been reared as Christians and most considered themselves very or at least moderately religious.[12] Many had heard the norm "love your neighbor" in their churches. Yet in the context of the Holocaust, it was not clear who "your neighbor" was and what "love" meant. Did "neighbor" include Jews? Since many churches themselves did not spell this out specifically, even those who subscribed to the norm felt Jews were not properly "neighbors." And if they did not exclude Jews, many were not clear that "loving" required actually helping them.

In those social institutions where caring norms have been most effectively taught, the above principles are often applied. To illustrate, we offer the example of two quite different contexts: one an elementary school program in San Ramon, California; the other, two large business corporations.

The central purpose of the San Ramon elementary school program, called The Child Development Project, is to promote prosocial behaviors (i.e., positive social behaviors) among children. As the staff describes it, their emphasis is on "encouraging children to be responsive to the needs of others, without at the same time inappropriately sacrificing their own legitimate needs and interests."[13] Now in existence for more than a decade—implementation in three schools began in 1982—the program evidences considerable success.[14] Outside observers find students more helpful, cooperative, and considerate than comparison classrooms, and students themselves report that their classmates are more helpful and responsible as compared with students in comparison classrooms.[15]

Many factors contribute to the program's success, but the one which interests us here pertains to what the staff calls "positive discipline." It is this component which includes teaching norms. Here's how the staff describes the way they go about it:

Key elements of positive discipline are the clear expression and communication of prosocial norms, values, and expectations; induction; fair, firm, and consistent guidance; and an amount of child participation in rule-setting that is consistent with the child's developmental level.

One aspect of the component involves the clear and emphatic communication of prosocial norms, values, and expectations. Children in this culture receive many inconsistent, mixed, or weak messages, and often appear to be uncertain and confused about cultural values and guides for behavior. Before children can act in ways consistent with prosocial norms, values, and expectations, they must know what the norms are and under what circumstances they apply. This will be provided in the program in several ways—through verbal statements by adults and other children, through implicit and explicit themes in reading materials and other curricular materials, through dramatic presentations, through school and family rules, and through comments, discussions . . . [16]

Several points make this extract of interest. One, some of the techniques advocated bear a striking similarity to the principles McGuffey employed to teach values: tell students what they are, repeat them often and through varied means. Two, the idea that even children need opportunities to derive rules through discussion is emphasized. Finally, rather than condemning society for failing to teach care, the passage points to something more subtle: its inconsistencies. The same children and adults who learn that "helping your neighbor" is a good idea, for example, also learn to mind their own business and look out for themselves. Social institutions intent on encouraging care thus need to make clear where they stand rather than depending on individuals to resolve the conflict.

Our second illustration, the world of big business, is not commonly associated with the teaching of moral norms. Yet as we shall see, a number of them do evidence at least a minimal concern with ethics, and a few of them, the most progressive ones, indicate an increasing concern with moral issues, particularly as they relate to "social responsibility." As we shall also see, the latter use some of the same principles noted above in addressing them.

One indicator of business standards are written codes of conduct, and according to researcher M. Cash Mathews, more than half of the 485 manufacturing corporations in the United States with annual sales over $100 million claim to have written codes. After much effort, Mathews was able to obtain 212 of them. What she wanted to know was whether they did indeed address ethical concerns, and if so, what kinds.[17]

What did Mathews find? After analyzing them carefully, she concluded that many business codes did indeed address ethical concerns, but of a limited type. They focused primarily on two types of unethical behavior: (a) illegal and unethical practices against the corporation, such as the misuse of funds by mid- and lower-level employees; and (b) specific illegal activities on behalf of the firm, such as bribery. What concerns corporations most then are transgressions which affect them directly. Notions of social responsibility to employees (such as considerations of safety or related work conditions) or to the broader society (such as product quality or environmental responsibilities) have yet to become a concern for most of the corporate world.

Johnson and Johnson, however, is an exception, and its exceptional history began in 1940, when the chairman and CEO Robert W. Johnson II developed a written Credo for the Company. Unlike the codes described by Mathews, it included statements regarding responsibilities to consumers, workers, and local communities as well as to management and stockholders. Persuaded that it had become a meaningless document by the mid 1970s, one which had little effect on actual practice, president James Burke decided to challenge it.

Burke invited all employees of the company to attend a series of meetings, the object of which was to reconsider the Credo. The result was not only a reaffirmation of the Credo, but also some significant revisions. For example, whereas the earlier document had emphasized job security and fair working conditions for employees, the new Credo included an "equal opportunity" clause as well as a commitment to individuality and dignity. The earlier document spoke about managers needing to be "qualified and fair minded"; the new Credo added that they must be "just and ethical." The earlier document talked about responsibility to the community in which employees lived; the new Credo talked about responsibilities to the world community, including the protection of "the environment and natural resources."[18]

Burke apparently understood two important principles. Written statements alone, however nobly expressed, are not likely to become meaningful unless people are encouraged to talk about them. And equally important, norms themselves often need modification in the light of deeper and new understandings. What might have sufficed as a normative framework in an age of short-sighted nationalism and limited notions of discrimination and environmental protection could not be adequate in a global society increasingly sensitized to injustice, minority issues, and ecological degradation.

The Norton Company of Massachusetts takes some of these same principles further. Like Johnson and Johnson, it has a very progressive written policy. But to ensure that the policy actually affects behavior, Norton has taken several pioneering steps.

One of these important steps was to establish an in-house Corporate Ethics Committee with ongoing responsibilities. The Committee serves as the final authority on policy and is also responsible for the policy's implementation. To make sure that company employees actually know the company's policies, they require all corporate officers to send a signed letter to the Committee every year stating that they understand the company code and that they have reviewed it with their subordinates. To make sure that officers assume responsibilities for implementing policies, they also require them to state in that same signed letter that they have investigated all cases of suspicious conduct and have reported significant violations to the Committee. But perhaps their most innovative procedure is the ongoing mechanism they provide for translating norms into behavioral rules.

Like Johnson and Johnson's Credo, Norton's code contains many norms referring to fairness, equity, and social responsibility. As is common with norms, rules for behavior in specific contexts are not necessarily clear. In such "gray areas," employees are instructed to seek counsel from their supervisors, and supervisors are required to make themselves easily available for such counsel.[19] This provides an ongoing consultative process, one which does not seek to attribute blame for ethical failures after the fact, but rather to clarify derivative rules through shared discussion before taking action.

Dewey would likely have been pleased with San Ramon, Johnson and Johnson, and the Norton Company, for they appear to be strongly encouraging of the moral intelligence that he advocated. All apparently recognize that moral norms and behaviors are as much the product of reflection and evolution as they are the considered inheritance of the best of past traditions. But McGuffey might have been pleased with them also for their attempts to clarify expectations and their efforts to teach them through varied means.

The above examples also illustrate the essential role that authorities generally play in promoting caring behaviors.

Authority figures—whether school principals or corporation executives,[20] clerics or parents—play a critical role in communicating values, and the more prestigious they are, the greater their influence is. Psychologist Stanley Milgram demonstrated this in a series of highly controversial experiments.

Milgram recruited a variety of volunteer subjects to participate in experiments he described as designed to study learning and memory. The volunteers were informed that they would be required to administer electric shocks of increasing intensity to "learners" when the latter gave the wrong answers. The "learners" were in fact confederates, coached to give incorrect responses and to indicate increasingly intense expressions of pain as the shocks—also faked—increased. Milgram was dismayed to discover that many subjects administered the highest voltage possible despite the pleas of the learners to release them from the experiment. They were much more likely to administer the shocks when they received instructions to do so from authorities they perceived as prestigious or associated with prestigious institutions.[21]

Prestige, however, depends on the audience. For the university students in Milgram's experiments, the most prestigious authorities were university professors. Among the religiously committed, clerics are likely to have this status. In both these cases, prestige is a consequence of official position. But this is not always the case. Among adolescents, for example, peers often have more prestige than teachers or principals, and for many employees, immediate associates may be more influential than chief executives. What this points to is that official authorities—people who hold exalted positions by virtue of official appointments—are not necessarily sufficient figures to communicate norms and that getting the most prestigious figures may mean recruiting unofficial "authorities."

But even if they have limited prestige, official authorities do have the power to punish and reward. The power-hungry official may capture more of our attention, but the overly timid authority may be more common than is popularly believed. Failure to exercise power can have dire consequences, as dramatic for civility as the despotic abuse of power. Such was the case at Hamilton High School described by sociologist Gerald Grant. It is a micro-cosm of what may happen in other social contexts when authorities fail to exercise their power in the service of the good.

Hamilton High's problems began with desegregation in the early 1970s. At this formerly high achieving public high school, learning effectively ceased as confrontations between blacks and whites erupted into violence. Personal relationships broke down as did conventional behaviors. An expe-rienced teacher recruited during this period describes his first day as follows:

The kids were off the walls. . . . When I walked into the room one of the girls said, "Who's this turkey?" She really gave me a lot of lip and when I went to see one of the assistant principals he sort of tried to talk me out of it saying she was really a good kid and didn't mean it. So many came in late. You kept getting interrupted. They would come in fifteen minutes after the bell and you'd look out in the hallway and there would still be a hundred and fifty people out there . . . just milling around. Teachers would just stick to their rooms, lock their doors because it wouldn't be unusual for students roaming the halls to open your door five times during a period, look in, glance around, then shut the door and walk on with no explanation of why . . . It was a constant struggle. During this period I gave a lot of thought to quitting.[22]

Unwilling to challenge students, administrators and teachers favored two strategies: withdrawing from the situation and attempting to please students in hopes of wooing them toward appropriate behavior. Conditions began to change only when a new principal, Joseph Kielicki, arrived on the scene.

Kielicki used several strategies to restore order, at least one of which was not entirely conventional. Rather than abandoning the hallways, he would stand in them and shout. As he describes it: "I was known as a voice. I'd stand outside the office on the first floor and I could yell and they'd hear me all throughout the building . . . The kids knew when I was upset."[23]

But Kielicki understood that shouting in the hallways had its limits and that restoring order depended on faculty as much as himself. He decided to invite some twenty teachers to his home during the summer to ask them what he should do. They recommended three things: restore a uniform code of discipline, back teachers up in classrooms and hallways, and get rid of quarter courses which wound up wasting valuable instructional time because of four sign-up and start-up periods each year. When the students came back to school that fall:

[they] found that quarter-courses had been eliminated, no cuts were allowed, and no hats could be worn in classes. They met the "shouter," who stood in the hall, confiscating radios and skateboards . . . In Kielicki's first year on the job, he handed out 351 suspensions . . . The showdown came the following June when thirty seniors

who had overcut and had failed courses were not allowed to participate in the graduation ceremonies . . . Students protested, and the local television station recorded their threats to disrupt commencement ceremonies. But Kielecki held his ground.[24]

As the above suggests, Kielicki paid a price for these new policies. Some students, as well as some teachers and parents, resented him deeply. Had his tactics been punitive alone, he might not have had any success; he augmented them by enhancing programs, particularly in the arts. By 1978 the arts and theater programs caused Hamilton to be declared a magnet school, open to all students in the city; and by the 1980s, dances and plays, which had been suspended for years, were revived. One of its consequences was the beginning of "real racial integration" among the students who formed a theater company. But most important, teachers as well as parents began to feel that Hamilton High was settling down, the consequence in large part of a renewed sense on the teachers' part that change was possible and that they themselves could make it happen.

Hamilton High thus began to recover only when administrators and teachers reclaimed their authority. The strategies they used reflect several principles about using authority in the service of care.

Kielicki and his staff initially depended heavily on punishments: shouting, suspensions, and general revocation of privileges which the students had come to expect, such as "cuts" and wearing hats in classes. Psychologists call these negative power assertion techniques. In some cases, punishments—excluding physical brutality or aggressive techniques—can be quite effective in changing behavior, sometimes even more so than rewards alone.[25] This suggests another principle for encouraging care: it is better to use punishment to ensure compliance with basic norms than to permit their continuing violation.

But as students' reactions to Kielicki demonstrate, punishments have the potential to cause long-term resentments—in some cases, even increasing aggression.[26] He overcame some of these negative effects by enhancing programs—a reward. Rewards—psychologists call them "positive power assertion" techniques—are usually more effective than punishments.

One reason rewards are more effective than punishments is that they provide more information. Punishments tell people what is wrong; rewards tell people what is right. Ridiculing an employee for getting a procedure wrong, for example, tells him he's made a mistake; praising him for getting a procedure right tells him how to do things correctly.

Rewards are more effective for yet a simpler reason: they appeal to self-interest. As psychologist Bandura explains, people are more likely to behave as others want them to if they anticipate being rewarded (anticipated consequences), are in fact rewarded, or see the outcomes that others receive for their actions (vicarious consequences).[27]

Paul F. Oreffice, president and chief executive officer of the Dow Chem-

ical Company in 1981, expressed similar ideas about punishments and rewards in an article he wrote on corporate social responsibility. Experience,
he said, had taught him the value of what former board chairman Carl
Gerstacker said at a lecture he delivered at Columbia University. As he describes it, rewards come in many forms, and some are more effective than
others:

> If you want to establish your company as socially responsible you won't get very far
> by announcing that every employee who shows signs of being socially irresponsible
> will be horsewhipped or given early retirement at his option. Coercion is not the
> route to anywhere anymore. Does that mean I believe you ought to pay bonuses to
> socially responsible employees? Perhaps, in isolated cases, and Dow does. But I have
> a different type of carrot in mind, and that carrot is the self-interest of the employee
> and the identification of his self-interest with that of the company.[28]

As Oreffice suggests, rewards can be material—money, gifts, and special
privileges. They can also be social—public attention, certificates, awards, and
praise. Both forms can be effective. But as he also implies, externally administered rewards need to be supplemented by some form of *internal reward system*. Many psychologists agree.

Rewards are not sufficient to change behavior because once they stop,
people often revert to their previous habits.[29] Should they begin to feel
manipulated, people may even reject the very norms and behaviors rewards
were meant to encourage.[30] This leads to another principle. Punishments
and rewards may serve care very well in the short-run; they are unlikely to
work in the long run unless norms became "internalized."

Internalization means incorporating norms into oneself to such a degree
that they serve as standards for behavior through a process of self-regulation.
Fear of punishment and the promise of rewards, or dependence on external
authorities generally, are no longer necessary. Research suggests that heavy
dependence on punishments and rewards inhibits internalization,[31] particularly in relation to caring norms.[32]

How does internalization occur? A subtle process, it is more the consequence of "catching" than formal teaching.

One of the ways values and norms are caught is through the language
groups use. To illustrate, we offer the example of some caring words recently
introduced into new contexts: the words "love" and "community" in universities and "social responsibility" in business.

Universities generally pride themselves on their academic rigor and high
standards, the latter most often meaning that only the most academically
competent will survive. But the response by some one thousand university
faculty to a recent address by sociologist Parker J. Palmer suggests that some
radically new values are beginning to penetrate the halls of academe.

Speaking at a conference sponsored by the National Association for Higher Education, Palmer began his talk with a critique of higher education. What students are learning, he said, is a "trained schizophrenia": they are taught to discard their subjectivity and look at the world "out there" through an "objective" prism alone. They learn to collect information and analyze it, but they are not asked to relate to it in a personal way. As a consequence, what is "out there" seems independent of them and divorced from their personal lives. The way to deepen their education and make it more personally meaningful is to develop their sense of community, he said: the means for doing so, he proposed, is to inject "love" into the curriculum:

If you ask what holds community together, what makes this relatedness possible, the only honest answer I can give brings me to that dangerous realm called the spiritual. The only answer I can give is that what makes community possible is love . . . The kind of community I am calling for is a community that exists at the heart of knowing, of epistemology, of teaching and learning, of pedagogy; that kind of community depends centrally on two ancient and honorable kinds of love.

The first is love of learning itself . . . And the second kind of love on which this community depends is love of learners, of those we see every day, who stumble and crumble, who wax hot and cold, who sometimes want truth and sometimes evade it at all costs, but who are in our care, and who—for their sake, ours, and the world's— deserve all the love that the community of teaching and learning has to offer.[33]

What made the address remarkable was not only Palmer's words, but also their reception. As described by an observer, the hushed audience in an entirely uncharacteristic fashion spontaneously arose to give him a standing ovation in the midst of thunderous applause.[34]

What does this receptivity signify? It might mean that professors themselves yearn to be loved and feel a sense of community—an idea which our experience supports. But it also may signal their readiness to accept new obligatory norms: norms which do not necessarily reject entrenched notions but go much beyond them. Study and teaching cannot be entirely the same if words like "love" and "community" become as well accepted as "academic excellence," "merit," and "competence."

Analogously, the word social responsibility, which expresses many similar ideas, has introduced new normative expectations in the workplace.

For many people, business and social responsibility is an oxymoron. Businesses, says Lynn Peters, are organized around three core values: materialism, economic individualism, and rationality.[35] The social responsibility of business, argues prominent economist Milton Friedman, is to increase its profits.[36] If an executive acted otherwise—such as spending more money on reducing pollution than the law and the best interests of the corporation require, or hiring the hardcore unemployed rather than those best fitted for the job—he would actually be spending the money of his stockholders or his customers since it would result in higher prices and lower wages. The manager should spend his own money to do that, not the money of others. Many executives agree.

Nonetheless, the language of social responsibility is beginning to penetrate the business world. *Fortune* magazine, for example, now includes "community and environmental responsibility" among the eight categories it uses to rank America's "Most Admired Corporations." Ethics courses are becoming increasingly common in business schools, and some management leaders not only talk about "participatory management" and "collegiality," but "caring."[37]

That this message is having behavioral effects is supported by some evidence. One example is the success of an entirely new type of journal, devoted entirely to helping businesses promote ventures that respect environmental and social concerns. Founded by editor and publisher Jerome Goldstein[38] and titled *In Business: Managing by Environment (M.B.E.)*, the journal is now in its tenth year. Almost every issue includes some examples of businesses that have experimented with such new ideas and often succeeded.

Business projects which call themselves "socially responsible" offer another example. The Vermont National Bank, for example, launched what it called "The Socially Responsible Banking Fund" in 1989. Depositors with savings and checking accounts, money market accounts, and certificates of deposit can specify that their funds be specifically allocated to accomplish social purposes in Vermont. Designated purposes include environmental/conservation projects, affordable housing, education, small business development, and farming. Jim Valliere, creator of the Social Banking Program, says that many banks throughout the nation are interested in developing similar programs.[39]

Some companies are also beginning to accept the view that they bear some responsibility for the welfare of families. For example, the O'Melveny and Myers law firm and the NCNB Corporation (a bank holding company based in Charlotte, North Carolina) are allowing employees to work part time, without having to abandon their roads to corporate advancement.[40] And a handful of companies are beginning to include the old and the infirm among their concerns. According to a survey by Wyatt Company, some 2 percent of companies around the country have some form of elder-care benefits, ranging from insurance options for long-term care dependents, to actual on-site adult care facilities, from company sponsored seminars on how to cope with elderly relatives to actual help in finding local services to provide for their care.[41]

And if business ethics professors Kenneth E. Goodpaster and John B. Matthews, Jr., are correct, several corporations do incorporate socially responsibility principles in making decisions. As examples, they point to the fact that some monitor their employment practices as well as the products they produce with respect to their impact on health and the environment, and that when faced with profit goals which conflict with community welfare, they frequently consult with boards of directors and managers, listen to community representatives, and then choose action geared to the needs of the community.[42]

Of course, the above does not imply that businesses have abandoned the profit motive any more than schools can be expected to abandon academic goals if they embrace "love." And the mere presence of caring language does not ensure its practice. History offers a roster of sadistic acts undertaken in the name of "love," even as some people today justify the most heinous offenses in its name. At its best, however, caring language can structure thinking along positive lines, and promote desirable aspirations and expectations. One principle then to help people catch caring values is to use caring language.

Catching someone doing some caring deed and then telling them they possess this attribute is another way to promote internalization. Research shows that people who are labeled "caring" or "concerned" by others are more likely to behave accordingly.[43] Social scientists explain it this way. People largely develop a sense of themselves—their self-image—through others' eyes. Charles Horton Cooley—a sociologist who developed this idea—called it the "looking glass self."[44] First, they imagine how they look to others and then they consider how others evaluate that characteristic. That evaluation in turn gives them a certain feeling, such as pride, shame, or guilt. Values which promote people's self-esteem in the eyes of others are more likely to be internalized than those which suggest their weaknesses. If other people value kindness and think we're kind, we're likely to feel good; as a consequence, we're more likely to do something kind because it enhances our self-esteem. But if others value kindness but tell us we're selfish, we're more likely to reject kindness as a value because endorsing it means rejecting ourselves.

What Martin Hoffman calls "other-oriented induction" reasoning is yet another technique which encourages internalization.[45] Other-oriented induction reasoning means that rules and behaviors are explained in terms of their consequences for others. Telling people they should pay taxes so as to avoid punishment may be effective, but the underlying reason appeals to self-interest. Asking people to donate money because generosity is a noble ideal may also be effective, but the underlying reason appeals to their self-esteem. By way of contrast, explaining that their taxes will provide health care for neglected children or that their donated money will clean up the pollution for the people living in Smith Valley appeals to transcendent interests. Not surprisingly, people who hear self-enhancement reasons often are more likely to internalize self-enhancement norms; people who hear inductive reasons often are more likely to internalize caring norms.

Norms and values are also "caught" through myth, history, and the stories we tell; in fact, myth and history are stories.

Myths—the exaggerated stories we tell about people and events—have many functions; one of them is to teach norms and values. The Horatio Alger myth, so popular during the nineteenth century, conveys the message that hard work will be rewarded while the King Midas myth teaches the dire consequences of greed. Some national figures acquire mythological characteristics: George Washington's purported devotion to truth was captured in the "cherry tree" myth, and Florence Nightingale, the "angel of mercy," came to symbolize healing and reprieve from suffering.

One common mythical motif shared around the world focuses on the "hero." The hero figure has been the role model for generations of males in the past and continues to shape masculine normative expectations currently. The question we need to answer is whether this figure is the best model we can offer men.

What is this hero figure? According to Joseph Campbell, whose studies of myths have become very popular, heroes characteristically engage in what he calls a "mythological journey" and the journey itself, Campbell claims, has this universal formula:

A hero ventures forth from the world of common day into a region of supernatural wonder: fabulous forces are there encountered and a decisive victory is won: the hero comes back from this mysterious adventure with the power to bestow boons on his fellow men.[46]

The journey thus begins in separation from the ordinary, including separation from family and community. It involves a struggle of titanic proportions, which the hero wins. As a consequence, the hero gains new powers, which he then may choose to share with others or withhold. In sum, the journey is an eminently individualistic quest, which cannot be pursued except by leaving others behind. It must involve a power struggle, and the desired goal is to gain the power the other holds. And while the hero ultimately returns to family and community, the relationships are permanently altered because of his new power. The myth thus not only tells us what males are supposed to do, but also the relationships they are supposed to achieve as a consequence.

As Campbell sees it, the journey is uniquely human and extraordinarily exciting. For unlike animals, whose destinies are fixed, a man can become "an astronaut, a troglodyte, mariner, tiller of the soil, or sculptor." And neither common sense nor reason dictates his choice, but "infusions of excitement" and "visions that fool him out of his limits."[47]

Histories often reflect similar themes. Like myths, they frequently concentrate on warriors; heroic men who have overcome great obstacles to achieve their aspirations as they struggle for power with other men, try to wrest new knowledge from nature so as to better control it, or achieve glory through creative enterprise. Singularly missing, or sometimes added as an afterthought, are the achievements of the nurturers—those who care for young and old, collect the garbage and maintain the trees, seek to resolve conflicts peacefully and save lives.

Society needs heroes of the type Campbell describes, but unless they are augmented by alternative hero figures that bind them to people with equal power, we should not be too surprised if citizens wind up doing scientific experiments on unwitting subjects or on concentration camp victims. As myth and history would have it, it is women who must do the caretaking and support men in their quest, whatever it might be. If women have felt oppressed by this vision, so also do many men. The heroes we need to celebrate should be men and women, but particularly men, who root themselves in connection rather than separation, and who measure their achievement by standards of care as much as individual accomplishment.

But even as we wait for such new myths and revised histories, we can make it a point to tell stories of ordinary people who demonstrate the above qualities. In fact, stories about people we live and work with are often more powerful messengers. Fathers, husbands, and sons—as well as mothers, wives, and daughters—who nurture their families even when they have to endure dangerous or monotonous jobs—are the types of heroes we need to tell stories about. So are community volunteers and working people who try to perform their jobs with concern for others.

Robert Mastruzzi, the high school principal we have met before (see Chapter 2), seems like a good subject; so does Jim Treybig, chief executive officer of Tandem, a successful computer company in Silicon Valley. Each, in his own way, we propose, offers an alternative type of male cultural model.

Our sense of Mastruzzi's character comes from Harvard professor Sara Lightfoot; he is one of five principals featured in her book *The Good High School: Portraits of Character and Culture*. Not everyone loves him, of course, but he emerges as a person who cares about students and expects students to care about others. Lightfoot captures this quality best in the following description:

Time and time again, I heard Mastruzzi refer to his belief that "all our students are winners" and that "winning" has more to do with being a good, caring, and generous person than with visible and lofty achievement. It is an inclusive, rather than an exclusive, educational vision—one that does not focus superior or prideful attention on the narrow band of top achievers, or create a school image based on their great successes . . . Each year the principal offers the message of charity to the graduating seniors. He rehearses the words to me with great feeling, "I tell them, you need to leave this school with a sense of appreciation for other human beings. That is the primary lesson we teach at this school. I don't care if you are going to Columbia University pre-med, or if you have been tops in our Honors program. If you don't give a bit of yourself to someone else, you are a failure."[48]

As Mastruzzi may model the attributes of an educational leader, Jim Treybig may serve as a business model—or what business likes to call a "human management" model. Treybig we know through Deal and Kennedy's books. As described by one of his employees, he is a symbol of Tandem's philosophy, "a sign that every person here is a human being."[49]

This sentiment appears to be largely the result of deliberate policies that Treybig and his company have adopted. For example, the company has an open door managerial policy, which means that all employees have access to anyone in the company, including the president. The company has also extended privileges once reserved for management only—such as flexible hours—to non-managers. And some part of this sense of status equivalency is the consequence of what the company has failed to do. Managers, for example, have no reserved parking spaces, and the company as a whole has few formal rules, meetings or memos, and no formal organizational chart. The consequence, as another employee expressed it, is that "everyone here, managers, vice-presidents, and even janitors, communicate on the same level. No one feels better than anyone else."[50]

The more stories we tell of such persons—ordinary but caring individuals of diverse occupations, ethnicities, and religions—the more likely it is that others will "catch" the values they represent.

But perhaps the most compelling way people internalize caring values is by associating them with joy. Many people do kind things for others, and their motives vary. People who do something generous but subsequently express disappointment because the recipients fail to reciprocate or violate other expectations, communicate the futility of care. Those who regard caring activities as obligations or duty communicate their burdensome qualities. Conversely, those who convey a sense of gratification, pleasure, even exuberance, impart self-satisfaction.[51] Whether expressed verbally or nonverbally, statements of self-satisfaction inform observers that caring bestows joy. What observers may also learn is that the pleasure of generous living is not given by someone else but rather a gift bestowed by oneself.

Frances Lappé, whose life's work has focused on the problem of world hunger, appears to have grown up in just such an environment. Here's how she describes her childhood memories:

When I was four years old, they (my parents) and their closest friends founded the First Unitarian Church of Fort Worth. My most vivid childhood memories are of being toted to endless committee meetings, playing on the scaffolding as they repainted the church sanctuary, and packing up for family church camp.

The church fellowship provided a forum for my parents and their friends, not only to express their spirituality, but to discuss and participate in the burning social issues of the day. Since my parents' goals included a racially integrated congregation, not surprisingly they faced many obstacles.

Despite the inevitable conflict, my fondest memory of these years is this: I am lying in my bedroom half asleep, down the hallway from the kitchen. It is a Saturday, close to midnight. I can hear my mother's and father's voices, animated, intense, amid a jungle of other familiar voices. Occasionally there is laughter. I can't make out the meaning of much of it, but I love the intensity of this hum from the kitchen. Every once in a while, the percolator goes back on the stove and the familiar smell of coffee drifts in. I love that, too. But mostly I love knowing that the grown-ups are doing what grown-ups do—talking about the big, important things.

They didn't always agree. Not at all. But they were talking about things they cared about deeply—about how to make our world better.

So you see, I grew up in a family that took for granted that one of life's greatest joys is engagement. We assumed that developing one's thinking in lively interchange in order to act responsibly is part of what it means to be fully alive.[52]

As Lappé implies, caring norms are most likely to be internalized in an atmosphere of laughter, collegiality, and creative enterprise rather than onus and exaction.

NOTES

1. William H. McGuffey, "The Bird's Nest," *McGuffey's Revised Eclectic First Reader, 1879,* in *The Annotated McGuffey: Selections from the McGuffey Eclectic Readers: 1836–1920,* ed. Stanley W. Lindberg (New York: Van Nostrand Reinhold Company, 1976), 19–21.

2. Harvey C. Minnich, *William Holmes McGuffey and His Readers* (New York: American Book Company, 1936), 30–89; Harvey C. Minnich, "William Holmes McGuffey and the Peerless Readers," *Miami University Bulletin* (1928).

3. Hugh Hartshorne and Mark May, *Studies in the Nature of Character,* 3 vols. (New York: Macmillan, 1928–1930). For a summary, see Hugh Hartshorne and Mark May, "A Summary of the Work of the Character Education Inquiry," *Religious Education* 25 (September 1930): 607–619, (October 1930): 754–762.

4. Analysts Richard Mosier and Joel Spring argue that theirs was largely a conservative message; one which justified discrepancies between the rich and poor which were widening in the context of the Industrial Revolution (Richard Mosier, *Making the American Mind: Social and Moral Ideas in the McGuffey Readers* [New York: Russell & Russell, 1965], 167–170; Joel Spring, *The American School: 1642–1985 Varieties of Historical Interpretation of the Foundations and Development of American Education* [New York: Longman, 1986]).

5. John Dewey, "Ethical Principles Underlying Education," *The Third Yearbook of the National Herbart Society* (Chicago: National Herbart Society, 1897); John Dewey, *Democracy and Education* (New York: Macmillan, 1916).

6. Exemplifying this trend was the influential Tenth Yearbook of the Department of Superintendence titled *Character Education* (Washington, D.C.: National Education Association of the United States, 1932). The objective of character education, said the prestigious educational committee that authored it, is the creation in each situation of the best moral solution; one which "promises the most for the satisfaction of himself and everyone else concerned" (55).

7. Louis E. Raths, Merrill Harmin, and Sidney B. Simon, *Values and Teaching* 2d ed. (Columbus, Ohio: Merrill, 1978).

8. Sidney B. Simon, Leland W. Howe, and Howard Kirschenbaum, *Values Clarification: A Handbook of Practical Strategies for Teachers and Students* (New York: Hart, 1972), 219–220.

9. Lawrence Kohlberg, *Collected Papers on Moral Development and Moral Education* (Cambridge: Laboratory of Human Development, Harvard University, 1973).

10. Kenneth H. Rubin and Frank W. Schneider, "The Relationship Between Moral Judgment, Egocentrism and Altruistic Behavior," *Child Development* 44 (1973): 661–665; Dennis Krebs and Alli Rosenwald, "Moral Reasoning and Moral Behavior in Conventional Adults," *Merrill Palmer Quarterly* 23 (1977): 77–87; Sumriu Erkut, Daniel S. Jaquette, and Ervin Staub, "Moral Judgment-situation Interaction as a Basis for Predicting Prosocial Behavior," *Journal of Personality* 49 (1981): 1–14; Nancy Eisenberg-Berg, "Relationship of Prosocial Moral Reasoning to Altruism, Political Liberalism, and Intelligence," *Developmental Psychology* 15 (1979): 354–355.

11. Delmont Morrison, Michael Siegal, and Robin Francis, "Control, Autonomy, and the Development of Moral Behavior: A Social-Cognitive Perspective," *Imagination, Cognition, and Personality* 3 (1984): 337–351.

12. Samuel P. Oliner and Pearl M. Oliner, *The Altruistic Personality: Rescuers of Jews in Nazi Europe* (New York: Free Press, 1988).

13. Staff of the Child Development Project, *A Program to Promote Interpersonal Consideration and Cooperation in Children* (San Ramon, Calif.: The Child Development Project, October 1982), 1.

14. The project staff incorporated a rigorous research component into the program from the start and has published more than a dozen research reports to date. Now in its thirteenth year, it reports findings indicating that children's prosocial development and behavior in this program as compared with other schools has been significantly enhanced (Victor Battistich et al., "Effects of an Elementary School Program to Enhance Prosocial Behavior on Children's Cognitive-Social Problem Solving Skills and Strategies," *Journal of Applied Development Psychology* 10 [1989]: 147–169; Daniel Solomon et al., "Enhancing Children's Prosocial Behavior in the Classroom," *American Educational Research Journal* 25 [1988]: 527–554).

15. *Evaluation of the Child Development Project: Summary of Findings to Date* (San Ramon, Calif.: Child Development Project, April 1990).

16. Staff of the Child Development Project, *A Program*, 19.

17. M. Cash Mathews, *Strategic Intervention in Organizations: Resolving Ethical Dilemmas*, Sage Library of Social Research, vol. 169 (Newbury Park, Calif.: Sage Publications, 1988).

18. Wendy K. Smith under the supervision of Richard S. Tedlow, "James Burke: A Career in American Business," in *Managerial Decision Making and Ethical Values: Instructor's Manual*, eds. Mary C. Gentile, Kenneth E. Goodpaster, and Thomas R. Piper (Boston: Harvard Business School, 1989): Section 8.

19. Case prepared by James A. Weber, "Case: Corporate Codes of Conduct, in *Business and Society*, ed. Donna J. Wood (Glenview, Ill.: Scott, Foresman/Little, Brown Higher Education, 1990), 284–287.

20. Several studies point to the critical role played by chief executive officers in modeling behaviors (Robert K. Mueller, "Criteria for the Appraisal of Directors," *Harvard Business Review* (May/June 1979): 48+; Victor H. Palmieri, "Corporate

Responsibility and the Competent Board," *Harvard Business Review* (May/June 1979): 46–48; M. Davis Ermann, "How Managers Unintentionally Encourage Corporate Crime," *Business and Society Review* 59 (Fall 1986): 30.

21. Stanley Milgram, "Some Conditions of Obedience and Disobedience to Authority," *Human Relations* 18 (1965): 57–76; Stanley Milgram, *Obedience to Authority* (New York: Harper & Row, 1974). Subjects acted more compassionately when the authority giving the instructions was perceived as someone of low status (someone in a clerical role) and when the institution in which the instructions were being given had low prestige.

22. Gerald Grant, *The World We Created at Hamilton High* (Cambridge: Harvard University Press, 1988), 63.

23. Grant, 75.

24. Grant, 75–76.

25. Robert B. Cairns, "Meaning and Attention as Determinants of Social Reinforcer Effectiveness," *Child Development* 41 (1970): 1067–1082; Scott G. Paris and Robert B. Cairns, "An Experimental and Ethological Analysis of Social Reinforcement with Retarded Children," *Child Development* 43 (1972): 717–729; Janet T. Spence, "Verbal Reinforcement Combinations and Concept-Identification Learning: The Role of Nonreinforcement," *Journal of Experimental Psychology* 85 (1970): 321–329.

26. G. R. Patterson and J. A. Cobb, "A Dyadic Analysis of 'Aggressive' Behaviors," in *Minnesota Symposium on Child Psychology*, vol 5., ed. J. P. Hill (Minneapolis: University of Minnesota Press, 1971).

27. Albert Bandura, *Principles of Behavior Modification* (New York: Holt, Rinehart and Winston, 1969); Albert Bandura, "Social Learning Theory of Identificatory Processes," in *Handbook of Socialization Theory and Research*, ed. David A. Goslin (Chicago: Rand McNally, 1969); Albert Bandura, *Social Learning Theory* (Englewood Cliffs, N.J.: Prentice-Hall, 1977).

28. Carl Gerstacker, cited in Paul. F. Oreffice, "Social Responsibility at Dow Chemical," in *Corporations and Their Critical Issues and Answers to the Problems of Corporate Social Responsibility*, eds. Thornton Bradshaw and David Vogel (New York: McGraw-Hill, 1981), 199–207, 201.

29. Joan E. Grusec and R. Mills, "The Acquisition of Self-control," in *Psychological Development in the Elementary Years*, ed. Judith Worell (San Francisco: Academic Press, 1982).

30. Wendy S. Grolnick and Richard M. Ryan, "Autonomy in Children's Learning: An Experimental and Individual Difference Investigation," *Journal of Personality and Social Psychology* 51 (1987): 890–898; James P. Connell and Richard M. Ryan, "A Developmental Theory of Motivation in the Classroom," *Teacher Education Quarterly* 11 (1984): 64–77; Mark R. Lepper and David Greene, *The Hidden Costs of Reward* (New York: John Wiley & Sons, 1978).

31. Mark R. Lepper, "Intrinsic and Extrinsic Motivation in Children: Detrimental Effects of Superfluous Social Controls," in *Minnesota Symposia on Child Psychology*, vol. 14, ed. W. A. Collins (Minneapolis: University of Minnesota Press, 1981); Darl J. Bem, "Self-perception Theory," in *Advances in Experimental Social Psychology*, vol. 6, ed. Leonard Berkowitz (New York: Academic Press, 1972), 1–62.

32. Martin L. Hoffman, "Moral Internalization: Current Theory and Research," *Advances in Experimental Social Psychology*, vol. 10, ed. Leonard Berkowitz (New

York: Academic Press, 1977); Barclay Martin, "Parent-child Relations," in *Review of Child Development Research*, vol. 4, ed. Frances D. Horowitz (Chicago: University of Chicago Press, 1975).

33. Parker J. Palmer, "Community, Conflict, and Ways of Knowing: Ways to Deepen Our Educational Agenda," *Change* 19:5 (September/October 1987): 20–25, 25.

34. Russell Edgerton, "Editorial: Filling the Void," *Change* 19:5 (September/October 1987): 6.

35. Lynn H. Peters, "The Essential Values of Business," in *Management and Society*, compiler Lynn H. Peters (Belmont, Calif.: Dickenson Publishing, 1968), 53–59.

36. Milton Friedman, "The Social Responsibility of Business is to Increase its Profits," *The New York Times Magazine*, September 13, 1970, 32+.

37. "Management for the 1990's," *Business Week*, April, 1989.

38. Jerome Goldstein is the author of *The Least is the Best Pesticide Strategy* (Emmaus, Pa.: J. G. Press, 1978).

39. Jerome Goldstein, "The Bank with the Welcoming Environment," *In Business*, September/October 1989, 18–19, 19.

40. Lorraine Dusky, "Mommy Tracks that Lead Somewhere Good," *Working Woman* 14:11, November 1989, 132–134.

41. David Tuller, "The Latest Job Benefit—Care for Elderly Relatives," *San Francisco Chronicle*, August 7, 1989, 136+.

42. Kenneth E. Goodpaster and John B. Matthews, Jr. "Can a Corporation Have a Conscience?," *Harvard Business Review* (January–February 1982): 132+.

43. Joan E. Grusec and Erica Redler, "Attribution, Reinforcement, and Altruism: A Developmental Analysis," *Developmental Psychology* 16 (1980): 525–534; Roger E. Jensen and Shirley G. Moore, "The Effect of Attribute Statements on Cooperativeness and Competitiveness in School-age Boys," *Child Development* 48 (1977): 305–307.

44. Charles H. Cooley, *Human Nature and the Social Order* (New York: Schocken, 1964, originally published in 1902).

45. Martin L. Hoffman, "Moral Internalization: Current Theory and Research," in *Advances in Experimental Social Psychology*, vol. 10, ed. Leonard Berkowitz (New York: Academic Press, 1977); David G. Perry, Kay Bussey, and Kathryn Freiberg, "Impact of Adults: Appeals for Sharing on the Development of Altruistic Dispositions in Children," *Journal of Experimental Child Psychology* 32 (1981): 127–138; Justin M. Aronfreed, *Conduct and Conscience: The Socialization of Internalized Control Over Behavior* (New York: Academic Press, 1968).

46. Joseph Campbell, *The Hero with a Thousand Faces* (New York: Pantheon Books, 1949), 30.

47. Joseph Campbell, *Myths to Live By* (New York: Viking Press, 1972), 242.

48. Sara L. Lightfoot, *The Good High School: Portraits of Character and Culture* (New York: Basic Books, Inc., 1983), 117–118.

49. Terrence E. Deal and Allan A. Kennedy, *Corporate Cultures: The Rites and Rituals of Corporate Life* (Reading, Mass.: Addison-Wesley, 1982), 11,

50. Deal and Kennedy, 11.

51. James H. Bryan, "Model Affect and Children's Imitative Behavior," *Child Development* 42 (1971): 2061–2065.

52. Frances Moore Lappé, *Rediscovering America's Values* (New York: Ballantine Books, 1989), xiii–xiv.

CHAPTER 5

Practicing Care and Assuming Personal Responsibility

Leonard is a medicine man as well as a civil rights leader. This means that we have ten times more guests than the usual Sioux household. The whole place is like a free hotel for anyone who cares to come through. The red OEO house in which I and Leonard live simply began to come apart from all the wear and tear. When I moved in, the place was a mess. Nobody tried to clean up or help out. They all came to eat, eat, eat, expecting a clean bed and maybe to have their shirts and socks washed. I spent a good many years feeding people and cleaning up after them. It is mostly men who stop by at the house, and only very few women, and you cannot tell men to do anything, especially Sioux men . . .

Most other medicine men do not go all out as Leonard does. They keep their homes tight, a little more to themselves . . . Leonard pities people. Whenever we go to town we pick up somebody who is walking, and then usually we have him for dinner, and then breakfast. Some come and stay for days, weeks, or even months. Many Indians have no place to go, no one to feed them, so they come to Crow Dog's Paradise. If we see somebody who is out of gas, Leonard stops and syphons some off into his tank, and then we ourselves get stuck five miles from home. If Leonard notices someone having car trouble, he stops, takes out his tools, and fixes the car—an automobile medicine man on top of everything else. Money I am supposed to use for food or household things he gives away to anybody who asks.[1]

The above excerpt, taken from her recently published autobiography, is a representative example of what constitutes most of Mary Crow Dog's current activities. But unlike Leonard, who had been trained for his role as medicine man from birth, Mary's beginnings hardly prepared her for the life she describes as his wife. Reared in impoverished conditions on the Rosebud Reservation in South Dakota, Mary could hold down a pint of whiskey by age ten. Sent away to Catholic missionary school where the sisters beat her for "disobedience," she was raped at age fifteen and left the school. She became a drifter and a petty thief, addicted to alcohol and pot—a life-style she shared with a group of similar adolescents who traveled from one town to another in loosely formed transient groups, their behavior marked by frequent bursts of violence.

Mary attributes the beginning of her recovery to two events: the birth of her child, the product of an ill-fated earlier marriage, and her chance encounter with AIM (American Indian Movement) in the early 1970s. From the first, she learned the joys and burdens attending the care of a helpless infant. From the second, she began to experience the exhilaration of participating in a community. While hostility toward whites was the initial impetus, increasingly it has become a spiritual bond based on the revival of suppressed Sioux religious traditions. What apparently sustains Mary in her exhausting and often unappreciated duties is her relationship to the Indian community and appreciation for the critical role her medicine man husband performs in maintaining it, as well as the personal relationship she is developing with Leonard. What is striking about Mary Crow Dog's autobiography is its sense of ongoing change and unfinished reflection. It is a life in process, in which experience begets new thinking and thinking begets new experiences.

But Mary's story raises some unresolved issues, the answers to which have important implications for teaching care. One of them relates to the relationship between values and behaviors. Did Mary change her values first and then her behaviors, or was it the other way around? She implies that her early years taught her little about caring norms and the Native American community. Some people, most particularly her grandparents, may have helped her become receptive to the possibilities of her new experiences. But actually participating in those experiences themselves appears to have modified her values considerably. If values and norms influence behavior, behavior may have an equal influence on values and norms—perhaps even a more powerful one.[2]

That beliefs and values may follow behavior rather than precede it is supported by several studies. Those who harm innocent victims, for example, are more likely to subsequently disparage them even if they have previously had no such views.[3] Those who assume new occupational roles, such as becoming a manager after having been a laborer, are likely to adjust their attitudes to fit their newly required behaviors rather than maintain their previously held beliefs.[4] And attitudes and beliefs about minority groups frequently change as a consequence of integration, rather than preceding it.[5]

Psychologists explain this as a striving for consistency; people prefer to think of themselves as behaving congruently with their values and self-image. When they act inconsistently, they experience what psychologists call cognitive dissonance. Since they no longer have control over their past behaviors but can still control their current values, they are more likely to change their values to accord with their behavior.

This points to the importance of providing opportunities for people to participate in caring activities. Actually caring for others not only helps reinforce and intensify caring values, but may even convert non-carers as they begin to appreciate its benefits for themselves as well as others.

The second question Mary's story raises relates to the objectives of care. Mary has apparently become very skilled in fulfilling her husband's and her community's needs. Yet Mary also experiences emotional exhaustion, what some have called "burnout." Overwhelmed by her burdens, she has fled on at least two occasions (only to return when Leonard found her) and she is not entirely admiring of those she serves—in fact, she appears somewhat resentful of them. Although apparently able-bodied, they remain permanently dependent on her services.

What then is the objective of care? Is it merely to help others, risking the costs of burnout and learning to overcome it? Or is it to empower others to care for themselves and also to care for others? If it is the former, then caring may well become the task of a class of professionals, paid and nonpaid, whereas those they serve will become professional dependents. Even if carers were invulnerable to resentment, the number of dependents might well exceed their capacities to respond. Moreover, dependency itself breeds its own forms of discontent, frequently accompanied by escalating demands. While care sometimes requires taking care of others, whenever possible its objective should be empowering them. In fact, it could well be argued that this is the best way to express care *for* others. The twelfth century Jewish philosopher Maimonedes apparently had something similar in mind when he proposed that giving a poor man money was an important charitable behavior, but the highest form of charity was to help him earn his own living.

Whether intended to take care of others or to empower them, effective caring requires competence: a matter often overlooked by those who believe that good intentions are all that matters. In Mary's and Leonard's case it means knowing how to cook, launder clothes, and repair cars. These represent specialized skills often required for taking care of others' needs. Our focus here is on general caring skills, particularly those which empower others. They include social skills, by which we mean general communication skills which help people feel cared for and encourage them to solve problems rather than depend on others. They also include general techniques whereby people learn to assume personal responsibility for others' welfare and some motivational strategies for encouraging this attitude. As we shall suggest, such skills are applicable in ordinary contexts as well as extraordinary ones.

Practicing care often requires social competence. Research suggests that people who are more social (that is, like being with people) and socially skilled are more likely to help others than those who are not.[6] Additionally, people tend to perceive socially skilled people as more caring than others and like them more. Most important, socially skilled people tend to bring out the best in others: in their presence, people are likely to be more helpful, cooperative, and generous themselves.[7] Social skills can be taught.

What does "socially skilled" mean? Among other things, it includes the ability to communicate effectively. Effective communicators do several things particularly well: they observe carefully, listen actively, and make comments which support others.

Careful observers spend a lot of time just watching others. They not only hear what others say, but also observe non-verbal behaviors. Concentrated attention can suggest caring remedies even in the absence of verbal cues. Such was the case in the daughter described below; it helped her to know how to comfort her dying father as well as herself.

She had not seen him for awhile and was not prepared for his dramatically changed appearance. Rather than the man she knew, he was now a stranger: thin, pale, hairless, and very, very old. When she arrived from the airport to visit him in the hospital, he was asleep.

Thank God he was asleep. All I could do was sit near to him and try to get past this image before he woke up and saw my shock. I had to look through him and find something beside this astonishing appearance of a father I could barely recognize physically.

By the time he awoke, I'd gotten part of the way. But we were still quite uncomfortable with one another.

Several days later, I came into his room and found him asleep again. Again such a hard sight. So I sat and looked some more. Suddenly this thought came to me, words of Mother Teresa, describing lepers she cared for as "Christ in all his distressing disguises."

I never had any real relation to Christ at all, and I can't say that I did at that moment. But what came through to me was a feeling for my father's identity as . . . like a child of God. That was who he really was, behind the "distressing disguise." And it was my real identity too, I felt. I felt a great bond with him.

For the remaining months of his life we were totally at peace and comfortable together. I usually seemed to know just what was needed. I could feed him, shave him, bathe him, hold him up to fix the pillows—all these very intimate things that had been so hard for me earlier.

In a way, this was my father's final gift to me: the chance to see him as something more than my father; the chance to see the common identity of spirit we both shared; the chance to see just how much that makes possible in the way of love and comfort. And I feel I can call on it now with anyone else.[8]

Quiet focused attention allowed this daughter to reconstruct a severed relationship; no longer merely father and daughter, they had become two equals sharing similar human identities. Once having reconnected to him in this new way, she understood what he needed and was able to do things for him she had previously thought impossible. In the process, she acquired a new sense of power, a feeling that she could share love and comfort with anyone. She calls this a gift from her father, but without her own gift for receiving it, she might well have emerged with a sense of hopelessness and despair. The potential beneficiaries of helping others effectively are as much the helpers as the helped.

In addition to observing carefully, socially competent people listen actively. Good listeners hear what others say; active listeners seek information beyond what they hear. They ask appropriate questions and seek clarification when messages are ambiguous.

Business consultant Tom Peters claims that good business managers are obsessed with listening, but the typical business conversation Peters reports hearing shows little understanding of what it means. Its characteristic form is something like the following:

"We've really got to get in closer touch with our customers, communicate with them better."
"Yes, we have a big problem there."
"They don't understand the new features. It's all there. We just need to spend time with them."
"Yes, you're right, we've got to educate them."[9]

As Peters observes, the conversation began with the stated desire to "get in closer touch *with* our customers" and "communicate *with* them" but quickly deteriorated to "*they*" don't understand and educating "*them*." Rather than listening, these managers were all too ready to tell and preach under the assumption that they already knew their customers' problems and the solutions.

For Peters and others who see such interactions as problems, listening in the business context has little to do with "care." As they see it, good listening serves business interests by enabling listeners to act more effectively and by motivating speakers to solve problems on their own. The strategy described above does neither.

One problem with the above approach is that it deprives superiors of some potentially good information. Others' ideas may suggest new approaches, perhaps even overcoming management's own sense of incompetence and impotence. For another, it encourages dependence on authorities for solutions rather than promoting initiative. Those who are treated in this way learn that their ideas are not valued, and their sense of competence and self-esteem becomes diminished. All of this discourages them from trusting themselves, and also persuades them that their superiors don't care for them.

Active listening means both hearing what others say and asking questions such as "What did you mean when you said that . . . ?" "How would that work?" "Can you elaborate?" "What would help?" and "How can we do that with the resources we have?" Note that all these questions are open-ended; that is, they invite lengthy responses rather than single phrases or "yes" and "no" answers. Questions like these convey the sense of the value of others, and because active listeners concentrate on others' ideas, rather than their own, they heighten the speaker's sense of competence and self-esteem. As a consequence, those who are listened to are encouraged to believe they can solve problems themselves and to see listeners as "caring."

Good listeners use such techniques when others seek them out and create opportunities for such interchanges to occur. As Peters suggests, good listeners invite others to talk (informally and formally), consistently and frequently (on a regularly scheduled time as well as less routine occasions), listen "naively" (without intention to preach), give quick feedback (verbally or in writing), listen intently, have the "guts to ask dumb questions" and act on what they have heard. Additionally, rather than waiting for others to seek them out, they create opportunities for listening by circulating wherever others are and asking them questions.

Active listening is being promoted in many contexts, including teaching, counseling, and interpersonal relationships. Teaching textbooks routinely devote considerable space to the art of active listening for both learning and humanitarian purposes.[10] Family counselors who try to help couples and their children overcome tensions often concentrate on similar techniques. As sociolinguists have proposed, men more often than women use language to direct others rather than empower them and tend to perceive expressions of discontent as criticism rather than opportunities for clarification.[11] Not uncommonly, wives who complain that their husbands don't care, frequently do not mean that their husbands neglect to sit quietly while they express some frustration but rather fail to respond by asking for more information or by rushing to suggest solutions, thereby unconsciously invalidating their sense of competence. Men, on the other hand, tend to perceive the very expression of frustration as blaming and disapproving. Part of the therapy process often involves changing these communication patterns.

Effective communicators also know how to interact supportively. A supportive interaction does not mean agreeing with ideas we don't like, or telling others they are wonderful when we don't believe they are. Some people may be fooled by such stratagems, at least in the short run; in the longer run, they are more likely to be perceived as manipulative and insincere. The recipients of such facile affirmations are more likely to see them as dismissals than as evidence of care, ways of dealing which do not really require much attention. Supportive interactions often do affirm others in a positive way, but they are authentic as well as positive. More often than not, they are simply neutral.

Consider for example the case of Mr. Appleby, a popular white teacher of English in a rural low socioenomic and predominantly black high school classroom. Observer and educational researcher Deborah Dillon describes a typical day as follows:

As the students filed into the classroom they were greeted informally by Appleby, who stood in the hallway outside the room on hall duty . . . The students chatted informally, walking around the room, until the bell rang. Approximately two minutes before the bell rang Appleby walked into the room. He joined in on the student conversations, answering questions, giving advice when it was asked for, joking or joaning—playing the dozens—with students, and encouraging or supporting individuals when they needed it . . . This same informal interaction time was evident in the closing minutes of the class period.

The students are pretty talkative today about the Prom (this past Saturday). At the beginning of class Appleby, a Prom chaperone, commented on how great his students looked, dressed up in their special clothes. He asked them what their evening was like and commented on their dancing.[12]

What exactly did Mr. Appleby do here which might explain his popularity? He greeted the students at the door, joined them in their conversations both in the beginning and end of class, and made some flattering comments about their appearance and dancing at the Prom which he had chaperoned. Apparently no more than common courtesies, there is more here than meets the eye. Prominent sociologist Erving Goffman, who spent a lifetime studying just such common interactions, provides a useful way for analyzing them.[13]

Appleby began the day by greeting students at the door. We don't know exactly what he said but more than likely they were conventional greetings: "good morning," "hello," and the like. Goffman might call them "ritual offerings," that is, routine salutations by which individuals acknowledge others' presence. Often considered trivial, they assume greater significance in their absence, portending even ominous consequences in certain situations. When neighbors stopped greeting them in the days preceding the extermination camps, Jews suspected they had already been excluded from conventional obligatory norms. But even in more ordinary situations, failure to receive the customary "good morning" from a friend or a superior can provoke considerable anxiety—"Is she angry with me?" or "Will I get fired?" Rarely, or never, to receive such acknowledgments can persuade non-recipients they are inconsequential, even invisible. Many high school students share both feelings, and such routines can at least suggest they are noticed in some positive way.

The next move Appleby makes is to enter the classroom, two minutes before the bell. Rather than taking charge of the talkative students, a be-havior authorities commonly assume, he joins them, joking with them at their level and responding to questions they initiate. Goffman might call these "reciprocal courtesy exchanges," entering into others' conversations and prolonging them rather than terminating them abruptly. Entering into others' conversations suggests that the ideas are worth pursuing; it's also a way of equalizing status. Ending others' conversations suggests their insig-nificance; it's also a way of reminding them that the terminator controls matters.

Appleby does yet one other thing. He comments about their attractive appearance and dancing at the Prom and also asks what the evening was like for them. Goffman would probably call this "grooming talk"; asking people about their health, a trip they may have taken, or the consequences of what they have done belong in this category. Such comments go beyond mere notice or momentary exchange. They suggest an interest which ex-tends to the whole person, investing all her/his activities with importance.

Other ways to express supportive interchanges include addressing others by name, waiting patiently for responses, crediting their ideas, providing hospitality—sharing food and other possessions—and placing oneself in physical proximity—voluntarily standing or sitting next to them. The im-portant point to remember is that they need to include everyone, even those whom one might prefer to avoid.

Well-intentioned people often exclude others unconsciously rather than deliberately. Most teachers, for example, do care about students, yet research demonstrates that they interact with boys more than with girls, with whites more than minorities, and with high achievers more than low achievers.[14] Of course, such patterns might be reversed in other contexts: women or minorities might receive more attention in other situations; religion and social class might be what counts in yet others. Only conscious attention can reveal prevailing habits, and consciousness often needs to precede action. More aware of their patterns as a consequence of the above research, many schools, for example, are now trying to eliminate inequitable behaviors through cooperative learning and programs such as TESA (Teacher Expec-tations and Student Achievement) and GESA (Gender Equity and Student Achievement). Appleby, apparently, already understood the importance of equity; as one student commented, "Some teachers only likes the smart people—and Coach Appleby don't do that." The empowering aspect of his small courtesies is suggested by this same student who went on to say: "He makes me want to work, he makes me want to give and do something."[15]

Social competence can be learned, as can other caring behaviors. Moti-vating people to learn or to use what they know on behalf of others, or even themselves, is another matter. This often requires overcoming their sense of impotence and fear of looking foolish and persuading them they have a personal responsibility for doing so.

What inhibits many people from learning or using what they know is less a lack of concern than a sense of impotence. What distinguished some bystanders from rescuers in our study was not the absence of sympathy, but their feeling that nothing could be done. A sense of power frequently emerges from participating in care; yet getting people to participate means overcoming their sense of impotence. Mary Gonzales, associate director of the United Neighborhood Organization, feels her major task is to persuade people that they can change things. "If I can get people to believe that they can in fact make the difference," she says, then the problems will be solved.[16]

Sometimes, simply requiring that they solve problems can help overcome others' sense of impotence. Earl Babbie, chair of the department of sociology at Chapman College, did this with his university students.

One summer, Babbie found himself teaching a course in social problems at the University of Hawaii. Unhappy with the grades they received on their mid-term exam, several students asked if they could do something to raise them. During a subsequent class discussion, all agreed that the only justifiable purpose for the course was to actually solve social problems rather than merely learning about them. This became the basis of an extra-credit course project Babbie subsequently offered to hundreds of students.

The course project obliged students to "find a social problem and fix it." The problem had to be "social," that is, something that bothered others as well as themselves, and it could not be a problem they themselves created. No credit would be given for simply describing a problem or who was to blame for it, or for complaining about how bad things were and telling what authorities said about the problem. Nor would it be acceptable for the students to simply *try* to solve the problem; they needed to *actually solve it.* Hence, Babbie warned them, it would be inadvisable to take on problems like "world hunger, racism in America, or the threat of thermonuclear war."

What students did take on were problems such as litter, traffic issues, grubby bus seats, dirty public toilets, and unfriendly dorms. They not only "solved" them, but often found that their actions galvanized others to participate as well. One student, for example, decided to solve the problem of potholes on his street; they were both messy and dangerous. Although he had no experience, he decided to repair them himself and recruited his brother to help. They went to the hardware store at the intersection to buy sand and cement. Upon learning what they were planning to do, the storeowner lent them some additional tools—a shovel and a concrete mixer. He also lent them the services of his son. By the time they finished the project, about twenty neighbors had participated—neighborhood children and adults as well as some passing motorists who directed traffic around them.

From an embarrassing experience of his own, Babbie recognized that one of the impediments to such "do good" activities is the risk of looking foolish. Far from being praised, those who undertake voluntary tasks which no one expects them to are frequently mocked for being "suckers" or suspected of base motives. Overcoming such fears requires courage, he says, for the acts themselves, small as they may appear, are really "revolutionary":

The more I have read reports of others joining in, the clearer it has become that most people would be willing to clear up the litter they find in public places—except for what they fear others would think of them. The social agreements that constrain us are often just too strong! Yet, when one person breaks through the agreements and takes responsibility anyway, that revolutionary act suddenly makes it safer for others to do what they really want to do.

It takes courage to break with convention and assume a personal responsibility for having the world work the way you want it to work. You just never know how it's going to turn out. You may find yourself becoming a leader of a social movement, a hero of social reform; or you may find yourself simply looking silly. That's the risk, and it's not as trivial as it sounds when you are simply reading about it.[17]

To help students prepare for this revolutionary act, Babbie added one more requirement to the project: students were to describe the reactions of those who saw them solving the social problem. As he expected, students met with diverse reactions—appreciation and smiles, smirks and suspicion. Students who picked up litter, for example, felt sure that some passersby thought that they themselves had caused it. But by acknowledging the problem, he helped students prepare for it. Once recognizing that such feelings were shared, the students could reinforce each other's resolve to surmount them.

Babbie clearly convinced these young people of their powers and helped prepare them for the task. But perhaps his most persuasive technique was simply to threaten them with a failing grade. In the absence of such power, persuasion requires much more.

Persuasive powers depend on many skills, among them an astute recognition of others' needs and the capacity to enlist them. Curtis Sliwa, the founder of the controversial Guardian Angels, was keenly aware of the needs of the young people he sought to recruit. As we shall see, he also had other characteristics associated with masterful persuaders.

Increasingly angered by the muggings and beatings he observed as he rode the New York subway, acts the police were doing nothing to prevent, Sliwa conceived the idea of organizing a "train watch": an interracial group of people who would ride the subways as visual deterrents to crime and make citizen arrests if necessary. The recruits he approached were predominantly black and Hispanic and under the age of twenty-one. They expressed little enthusiasm about his proposal. As he describes it, here's the essence of what he would say to persuade them:

I would literally have to make our members feel guilty, by explaining to them, "Hey, you go back to your community, you complain about the mugging, the raping, the looting—now you have a chance to really do something about it. Finally a young Hispanic can look at you and see another young Hispanic doing something positive to replace Julio the junkie on the corner or the Savage Nomads or the Young Lords or half a dozen other organizations that had defamed their own unique individuality."[18]

Sliwa understood these young people very well—their need to feel powerful, to sense they could make a difference, to be respected, and to be models that others could look up to. He also was extremely persistent.

Resistance to Sliwa's idea came not only from the young people themselves, but also from their parents and the community. The young men could be shot, their parents warned; the police, predominantly white, would harass them. Sliwa spent hours with these parents, hoping to overcome their fears. Community organizations he approached smelled a vigilante group, and they rejected it. Undeterred, he persevered. Motivating others to do caring things requires commitment; occasional flurries are unlikely to be productive.

Sliwa demonstrated yet one other skill associated with effective persuaders: he was a *good teacher*. Like Babbie, he had to prepare his recruits for the potential risks. Unlike Babbie's students, the dangers these "do-gooders" faced were far more serious than looking foolish. He had to teach them specific skills.

Effective teaching includes understanding and delivering needed information, adjusting messages to exclude peripheral matters, and editing out ambiguities. These become particularly important when preparation time is short. Sliwa understood that constraining and apprehending muggers would require psychological and physical preparation. Role-playing and simulations were among his favored teaching strategies:

We're involved in physical training, a lot of mental preparation, how you would patrol the trains. So in civilian garb, just going through the motions of what a patrol would look like, a three-person patrol. What your position should be, what the signals might be in case you had a problem. How you would signal your partner that everything was all right, how you would move from car to car, station to station, platform to platform, how to do a patrol log, how to write down incidents, how to get help— all the variables that would exist in an environment that at times was chaotic.[19]

Sliwa's techniques were obviously successful. Now established as a non-profit, tax-exempt organization, the Alliance of Guardian Angels has groups in more than fifty cities and has expanded its activities to include drug prevention and escort services among others. While their actual effectiveness in deterring crime is unlikely ever to be known, Sliwa did succeed in persuading a significant number of young people, predominantly minority males, that they had the power to ameliorate the violence in their communities through non-violent means.

Babbie and Sliwa had at least one major obstacle in common: they had to make the people they were working with feel personally responsible for solving a problem which they themselves had not created. Personal responsibility means a sense of obligation to make a response, a feeling that one is personally accountable for the consequences regardless of cause. Without a willing assumption of personal obligation for others' welfare, people are unlikely to act on their behalf regardless of their intelligence or competence.

How do people acquire a sense of personal responsibility? Evidence suggests that certain conditions promote it. The younger they start, the more likely it is that people will act responsibly even in the absence of external persuasion.

Early childhood is not too soon to begin to teach responsibility; one way to help children become responsible is to require them to do tasks. Several studies demonstrate that children who are assigned responsibilities—such as household chores or taking care of younger siblings—tend to be more generous and nurturant as compared with those who are not assigned responsibilities.[20] In one experimental study, for example, psychologist Ervin Staub found that students assigned to teach younger children how to make puzzles were more willing afterward to make puzzles themselves for hospitalized children or donate gift certificates to them as compared with those who were not assigned teaching responsibilities.[21] Anthropologists Whiting and Whiting noted this some twenty years ago when they compared children's behaviors in various countries. Observations of 134 boys and girls between three and eleven years of age showed that children in Kenya, Mexico, and the Phillippines were more altruistic than children in Okinawa, India, and a New England community in the United States. The Whitings attributed these differences to the fact that children in the first three cultures were expected to help more with domestic and economic tasks and spent more time caring for their younger siblings and cousins.[22]

Psychologists label such expectations "maturity demands"; requirements which help children mature. As they point out, maturity demands need to be age appropriate if they are to encourage a sense of responsibility. They should begin with simple tasks, gradually becoming more complex as children's capabilities develop.

The more routine such behaviors become, the more likely it is that they will occur even when not required. In one study, for example, most of the sample of eighteen- to thirty-month-old children who assisted their parents with tasks such as sweeping or setting the table, also rose to help strangers in these same tasks although they were not asked to do so.[23] In hopes of making civic participation routine, many schools are now offering "participatory citizenship programs." Rather than simply studying about civic responsibility, students in these programs are required to actually perform civic service. At John F. Kennedy High School in New York, for example, students enrolled in The Community Service Corps course have to give fifteen to twenty hours of service to community organizations such as hospitals, nursing homes, public libraries, or student government.[24] Several schools throughout the nation have adopted similar programs.[25] Educators hope that such experiences will accustom young people to integrate volunteering and giving into the fabric of their lives.

Caring routines not only promote spontaneous helping in varied situations, but often become more encompassing over time. Even if the initial behavior is little more than a small gesture, successive acts of the same genre tend to escalate into larger ones. More than a little truth characterizes the maxim that if you want people to do a big favor for you, ask them to do a small favor first.

The "foot-in-the-door" phenomenon, as the above is often called, has been demonstrated in various experiments. In one such, California homemakers were asked to sign a safe-driving petition, put a safe-driving sign in their window, or some other small related activity. Those who complied were three times more likely to agree to place an ugly "Drive Carefully" sign in their front yard than a comparative group who had not been asked to do the small favor first.[26] In another study, people who agreed to wear a lapel pin publicizing the Cancer Society Drive were almost twice as likely to donate money to it subsequently than those who were not asked to first wear the lapel pin.[27]

The above require minor commitments, but major ones also frequently begin in deeds of increasing escalation. John Gropp, the pastor of Christ Lutheran Church in Duquesne, Pennsylvania, and Colleen Gropp, his wife, started with small acts of compassion. Their story suggests how conventional kindnesses may sometimes evolve to courageous protest.

As part of the Denominational Ministry Strategy (DMS), a Protestant interdenominational team ministry formed by the Lutheran synod and other Protestant churches, Gropp was sent to the Monongahela Valley in Pennsylvania to revive the urban church. The trouble began in the early 1980s when the United States Steel Corporation announced it was closing fourteen of its steel plants. As a consequence, a quarter of a million jobs were lost. Deeply touched by the skyrocketing suicide and divorce rate which ensued, several of the the DMS ministers petitioned the state's governor, politicians, and corporate heads to provide help for the unemployed. After being uniformly rejected, they embarked on a campaign pledging people to take their money out of the Mellon bank, which was foreclosing the mills, and put it into another bank willing to reinvest in local steel. They anticipated that the move would be unpopular with the Pittsburgh elite, but they did not anticipate the hostile reactions from their own church.

The Lutheran synod withdrew its support from the ministry and the DMS budget was cut; they also fired Charles Honeywell, originally hired to train the ministers, because he supported the resisters. The local DMS ministers re-hired Honeywell, paying him out of their own budgets, and joined forces with a local group of activist labor leaders called The Network. Disruptive activities at the bank escalated; former employees put dead fish and skunks on the floors, and dropped coins on the floor. Gropp barely managed to hold on to his post; the congregation, which included many of the affected employees, voted to retain him by a narrow margin. When Douglas Roth, another activist minister, was ousted from his congregation and subsequently arrested, fined and imprisoned, John and Colleen Gropp, along with other clergy families, decided to protest by attending services at Roth's church. Confronted by the police at the door, they refused to leave and were arrested.

Little in John or Colleen's past had prepared them for such events. As John described it, if "we had this crystal ball that would look into the future and if we had looked into it and saw four years down the road, we would never have imagined we would be doing it."[28] For Colleen, the disparity between her self-image and her behavior was dramatic:

I have always been very image conscious the way I dress, the way my hair is, the way I appear to people. When I was teaching, it was always every day look good because somebody's liable to see you. Or make sure you are doing your best because somebody's going to be watching . . . The hardest part for me was willing to go up there and be arrested. That was extremely difficult because bad people get arrested and I thought of myself as the all American kid. How could I get arrested? I never thought I would be the one who got arrested. Do I look like the arrestible type?[29]

Neither of the Gropps began as crusaders. For both, defiant acts of protest began in small caring behaviors, which ultimately affected their values, their self-image, and their sense of personal responsibility. Small, everyday behaviors, rather than conversion born in a moment of dramatic shift, determine many fateful decisions. Just as crimes often begin in small steps of aggression, and perpetrators of genocide frequently start as small scale opportunists, so caring begins in small steps. As wrongdoing tends to drift toward more of the same, doing good once increases the probability of doing it again.[30]

Assigning tasks and routinizing small caring behaviors enhances a sense of personal responsibility. So does inviting people to help shape those tasks.

Adults, as well as children, are more inclined to accept responsibilities which they themselves help fashion. This helps explain why some programs intended to promote corporate responsibility, for example, are more effective than others. Norwest, a bank in Minnesota, illustrates this point well.

Norwest, Minnesota's second largest banking insitution with some two thousand employees and $6 billion in assets, initiated a successful program to enhance corporate responsibility in 1978. As then bank chairman and chief executive officer John Morrison explained, he wanted the bank to "become more focused in terms of dealing with issues of corporate responsibility" and to develop means for responding better to the claims of different constituencies. Persuaded that management could not accomplish this alone, he insisted on a "bottom-up" as well as a "top-down" approach.

To help implement his goals, Morrison recruited the Reverend Doug Wallace as vice-president for social policy and programs. A leading figure in the corporate responsibility student internship program and executive director of the YMCA, Wallace appeared to be an ideal choice. But Wallace was suspicious. Accustomed to dealing with the corporate world, where rhetoric often substitutes for action, he needed some proof that Morrison really meant what he said. The test came when a small group of employees recommended a policy change unpopular with management but which it accepted. Now reasonably persuaded that Morrison really intended employees to work as equal partners with management to develop and implement social responsibility policies, Wallace began the work in earnest.

A firm believer in people's ability to make responsible decisions when given the authority and resources to do so, Wallace recruited volunteers from all levels of the bank and organized them into small teams. Teams were assigned different issues, including protecting the confidentiality of information about bank employees, the rights of individuals in relation to the bank, and the role of loans in revitalizing older neighborhoods. Each team had to draft recommendations, which were to be presented to the bank's senior management policy committee in a face-to-face session. To facilitate their work, teams were authorized to do research on bank time and given a budget to invite external experts.

The teams took two years to complete their tasks and management did in fact adopt many of their proposals. The thoughtful recommendations they proposed reflected what had happened to the employees in the process. As Wallace describes it, participants became very enthusiastic, investing many hours beyond their assigned time in the project. They immersed themselves in studying various reports, reviewing relevant federal and state laws and listening to experts. For the first time, many began to appreciate how issues they initially regarded as relevant to themselves alone affected customers and the community at large. Because for the first time, too, they felt they had real influence in shaping policies, they felt responsible for making meaningful ones.[31]

Some businesses are learning to value autonomous decision making for reasons other than enhancing corporate responsibility. As they are beginning to understand, it also can also increase profits. Rosabeth Moss Kanter, a sociologist with special expertise in the economic sector, provides evidence on this point. Kanter compared forty-seven companies with reputations for what she calls "progressive human-resource practices" with a similar number not sharing such reputations. Progressive practice businesses provided many opportunities for autonomous decision making by defining jobs broadly rather than narrowly and assigning tasks which were ambiguous, non-routine, and change-oriented rather than explicit, habitual, and present-oriented. They also allowed employees to act on some of their decisions without waiting for higher level approval. Kanter concluded that the progressive practice companies evidenced significantly higher long-term profitability and financial growth as compared with nonprogressive businesses.[32]

Other researchers have reached similar conclusions about the value of autonomy in the workplace,[33] leading management theorists to propose a new model for organizations generally. Called "loose coupling," this new model views employees as partners rather than subordinates in a hierarchy. Theorists advocate it for all agencies seeking to promote efficacy and responsibility.[34]

Yet a word of caution is in order. Increased autonomy may promote a sense of personal responsibility, but does it *ensure* care? Business researchers and consultants Peters and Waterman hint that it may not. Even as loose coupling characterized the excellent companies they studied, these same companies, they conclude, are what they call "tight"—even fanatic—with respect to a few core values. They do not compromise on such matters as product quality or safety, service or reliability, for example. Hence, they claim top management at IBM, McDonald's, and Marriot were "pathbreakers" with respect to progressive policies, but simultaneously were "ruthless" if standards of service and quality were violated.[35]

If organizations are serious about core values, the above implies, they cannot depend on autonomous decision making alone. To ensure behaviors consistent with others' welfare, autonomy may need to be tempered by accountability to some uncompromising authority which insists on it.

A sense of personal responsibility is certainly desirable, but it is not without costs. It often causes considerable anguish to those who feel it. The larger the numbers of people and the broader the number of groups to whom one feels responsible, the greater the probability that caring for one may result in non-care for another. Those who want to better prepare people to assume responsibility need to acknowledge these costs. The following stories about teacher supervisor Nancy and personnel manager Evelyn are representative of the distress caring people often experience when they have the power to make decisions about others' professional lives. Similar thinking characterized rescuers as they made decisions about others' very survival.

Teacher training programs customarily move teacher candidates into the profession slowly. Typically, they require satisfactory completion of a large number of college courses plus a year of professional training that usually begins in their last college year. Academic success, however, does not ensure being able to meet the practice requirement, which generally occurs at the very end of the training period. During this period, called student teaching, teacher candidates are placed in real classrooms, where they gradually assume actual teaching responsibilities under the guidance of the classroom teacher and a university field supervisor. By then, teacher aspirants have invested a great deal of money and time in their potential careers—investments they cannot easily transfer to other fields of preparation—and cooperating public school teachers as well as field supervisors feel a particularly strong responsibility toward them at this juncture. Since they commonly work very closely together on a one-to-one basis, intense personal relationships often develop.

Persuaded that her student teacher, Jenine, was incapable of performing even the most routine elementary class requirements during the preliminary practice weeks, Nancy, the field supervisor, gave her an "Incomplete." This allowed Jenine the opportunity to repeat the experience without penalty. Unfortunately, repetition yielded little improvement, and Nancy decided to fail her. Jenine was devastated, and Nancy herself felt she had failed. As told by professor of education, Christopher M. Clark, two reasons contributed to Nancy's sense of failure:

First, Nancy defined her own teacher education role as helping students reach their goal to become teachers. Jenine never did let go of that goal, and Nancy felt that she had failed in her responsibility to Jenine. Second, this was a difficult decision for Nancy in that the criteria for judging success or failure in a student teacher's field experience are not clear, clean, and easy to judge. Especially troublesome was the question of when to say, "Stop, you've tried long enough."[36]

Since Nancy could never be sure that continued help for Jenine would not have changed the outcome, she was not sure that she had done enough. Had she felt responsible for Jenine alone, without regard for the students she would potentially teach, she might have made a very different decision.

Seriously disturbed by Jenine's emotional reaction, Nancy continued to counsel her long after their official relationship ceased. She also helped the teacher education program initiate a seminar to support students like Jenine in the future.

Nancy's decision to terminate Jenine was painful, but it was fair; she would have applied the same standards to any teacher candidate. In the case of personnel manager Evelyn Grant, however, fairness for one person would have potentially hurt three other employees, as well as herself. Care for their future, and for her own, led her to make an unfair decision.

Had competence been the only criteria for ranking department heads, Evelyn would have designated Fred as number one among four. Unfortunately, Fred's general reputation in the company was extremely low—as Evelyn saw it, most likely due to a personality conflict with his former boss and an accident which kept him out of work for a year. Evelyn believed that had she given Fred the ranking he deserved, her boss would have concluded that the three other department heads were entirely incompetent:

My boss would have said, "Since we 'know' Fred is the bottom of the department head universe, if you say he is your best department head, then these other three fellows have got to be pretty bad." So, do you take the risk of tearing down the other three people to get Fred moved up?

Had I rated them as I saw them, it still might not have enhanced Fred's position, but it could have hurt the other fellow. Or if the positions were reversed at a higher management level, I could have been viewed as incompetent to rank my own department heads.[37]

Evelyn decided to put Fred at the bottom of the list, but spoke both to him and her boss about what she did. She then spent the next five years trying to raise Fred's ranking, finally succeeding in getting him from "the bottom to the middle." Her care for Fred went even further; unwilling to put Fred into the position of "owing" her something, she did not tell him about her persistent efforts to upgrade him.

Carers who feel multiple responsibilities inevitably wrestle with the problems of how to care for everyone and how to balance care with fairness. In routine contexts, such as those affecting Nancy and Evelyn, the decisions are important but not life-threatening. In other circumstances, they can have tragic consequences, leaving decision makers with memories which may haunt them for years.

Such was the case with the rescuers we studied. As they confronted the multiple tragedies around them, rescuers could not help every Jew; like Evelyn they had to make choices. Sometimes, they turned people away—because they had no more room, or judged the person imprudent and dangerous to those they were already helping, or because a reasonably safe locale would become perilous as the German Army advanced or retreated. The memories of those they rejected, or failed to keep alive, continued to disturb some even forty years after the event—the time of our interviews. Like Nancy, some ask themselves: "Did I do enough?" and "Could I have done more?"

But if the costs are high, so are the benefits. No rescuer regretted his or her decision. Rescuers know they did something when others did not; as a consequence, some say they can face the current generation with a degree of self-respect. And as compared with those who did not help, significantly more rescuers have talked about that period with their children and feel their children approve of them.[38] We suspect that other kinds of helpers experience similar forms of satisfaction.

As some rescuers experienced problems similar to more usual helpers, they also shared similar competencies. In fact, without some of the very skills we have discussed here, they would have been unable to accomplish their formidable tasks.

Rescuers, for example, were careful listeners and astute observers; they also knew how and where to get vital information. Although they had access to the same newspapers and observed the same situations as nonrescuers, they claim to have known what was happening to Jews earlier and to have anticipated the horrendous consequences sooner. Significantly more of them also claimed to understand from the beginning that the Yellow Star Jews were forced to wear portended an ominous future (several of them made a point of greeting those who wore them even as others ignored or humiliated them). Acutely observant, they depended on verbal and nonverbal clues to assess others' character, a matter of critical importance since asking the wrong people for help could have cost them their lives. When they did not have the resources themselves—false documents, food, transportation, doctors—they sought people out and knew how to ask them questions to get the information or contacts they needed without betraying their real purpose. When they did not have essential skills, such as building hiding places or forging documents, they knew how to acquire the information. And like sociologist Babbie's students, some faced others—often well-meaning relatives—who regarded them as foolish for voluntarily risking their lives for friends and strangers.

Persistent and persuasive, many learned how to recruit others in the task. Some spent weeks going from door to door, or even to other cities, seeking shelters or delivering needed monies and ration cards; some tried to keep track of those they placed. Several calculate that they spent the better part of the war years in such activities, including providing shelter in their own homes. They learned how to appeal to people's values when trying to enlist their help. A Belgian rescuer, for example, explained that when she talked with committed Christians, she called upon their sense of Christian conscience, and when talking to parents, she called upon their sense of empathy for children.

They were also effective teachers. They had to teach their own families how to lie about the people they were hiding, and they often had to help the Jews they were keeping learn new identities. As Sliwa did with the Guardian Angels, they often depended on simulations where their charges would rehearse what to say and how to act confidently. The ability to lie and deceive effectively, a skill thankfully not commonly associated with care, was one they acquired on the job, and teaching their children when to lie and when to tell the truth was particularly challenging.

Like the Gropps, rescuers rarely began as crusaders. For most, helping Jews began with a small service: delivering a message to a family member, keeping a suitcase, making a needed purchase when Jews were forbidden to shop, or keeping someone for "just one or two days." Like the Gropps, few understood just exactly where it would all end. But in fact, rescue often started much earlier, in routines acquired in hospitable households, where parents and children welcomed others, including those of different economic and religious status, and practiced small kindnesses.

Of course, not all rescuers were alike, but most had several of the attributes described above. To illustrate how some of these characteristics converged, we conclude with the story of Stanislaus, a Polish Catholic, who together with his mother, sheltered some twenty Jews.

Born to a poor family in 1920, Stanislaus and his family moved to Warsaw when he was a young boy. His mother, the primary breadwinner because of his father's chronic illness, worked as a domestic and part-time midwife. Although their means were limited, she routinely offered food and board to their many relatives who came to the city in search of work. During the war, he and his family lived near the Warsaw Ghetto, where half a million Jews, crowded into a space barely sufficient to house several hundred, tried to maintain themselves without any means of sustenance. Unable to distract their attention from the misery therein, despite the high walls which eventually surrounded it, Stanislaus and his mother brought some of their meager rations to the ghetto, throwing them over the walls. When the first Jew came in search of shelter, Stanislaus constructed a hiding place within his home. It collapsed, for he knew nothing about construction; he consulted a mason and "learned to do it right." As the numbers of people needing hiding places increased, he helped them find and construct shelters elsewhere. Asked the reasons for his behaviors, he explained:

When someone comes and says "I escaped from the camp," what is the alternative? One alternative is to push him out and close the door—the other is to pull him into the house and say, "Sit down, relax, wash up. You will be as hungry as we are because we have only this bread . . ."

Can you see it? Two young girls come, one sixteen or seventeen, and they tell you a story that their parents were killed and they were pulled in and raped. What are you supposed to tell them—"Sorry, we are all full already?"[39]

Although Stanislaus could not conceive it, he did in fact have a choice. Ever mindful of the consequences should he fail to act, his sense of personal responsibility for the welfare of these many people, many of them strangers, evolved out of small habitual routines which began long before the war started. Eighty-five years old at the time we interviewed him, Stanislaus was still helping others. Describing what he did for an old and disabled Jew living by himself, he said: "I shop for him and I visit him, I take care of his problems. I help him clean his apartment, wash windows, and so on." Consistent with his way of life, no helping task was too big—or too small.

As Stanislaus's story suggests, life tends to go on in patterns acquired through habitual responses. Whether the risks are small or life itself, whether the tasks are simple or complex, caring is a practiced art and skill, primarily born out of focused willing attention, escalating levels of participation, and a sense of evolving personal responsibility.

NOTES

1. Mary Crow Dog with Richard Erdoes, *Lakota Woman* (New York: Grove Weidenfeld, 1990), 174–175.

2. According to Ervin Staub (*Positive Social Behavior and Morality: Socialization and Development*, vol. 2 [New York: Academic Press, 1979]), actually participating in care is likely to be more effective in promoting it than learning about it or observing models. Whereas the latter are indirect, he argues, the former is direct and experiential.

3. Ellen Berscheid, David Boye, and John M. Darley, "Effect of Forced Association Upon Voluntary Choice to Associate," *Journal of Personality and Social Psychology* 8 (1968): 13–19; Edward E. Jones et al., "Reactions to Unfavorable Personal Evaluations as a Function of the Evaluator's Perceived Adjustment," *Journal of Abnormal Social Psychology* 59 (November 1959): 363–370; David C. Glass, "Changes in Liking as a Means of Reducing Cognitive Discrepancies Between Self-esteem and Aggression," *Journal of Personality* 32 (1964): 531–549.

4. Seymour Lieberman, "The Effects of Changes in Roles on the Attitudes of Role Occupants," *Human Relations* 9 (1956): 385–402. For further substantiation of the idea that beliefs and attitudes follow behavior rather than preceding it, see Daryl J. Bem, "Self Perception Theory," in *Advances in Experimental Social Psychology*, vol. 6, ed. Leonard Berkowitz (New York: Academic Press, 1972), 1–62; Mark Zanna and John K. Rempel, "Attitudes: A New Look," in *The Social Psychology of Knowledge*, eds. Daniel Bar-Tal and Arie W. Kruglanski (Cambridge, England: Cambridge University Press, 1988), 315–334.

5. A study by psychologists Morton Deutsch and Mary Evans Collins supports this view. After comparing the attitudes of white tenants living in integrated units with those living in non-integrated apartments, they found that significantly more of those living in the former as compared with the latter endorsed a policy of equal and unrestricted access to future integrated public housing (Morton Deutsch and Mary Evans Collins, *Interracial Housing: A Psychological Evaluation of a Social Experiment* [Minneapolis: University of Minnesota Press, 1951]).

6. Nancy Eisenberg et al., "The Relations of Quantity and Mode of Prosocial Behavior to Moral Cognitions and Social Style," *Child Development* 55 (1984): 1479–1485; David E. Barrett and Marion R. Yarrow, "Prosocial Behavior, Social Inferential Ability, and Assertiveness in Young Children," *Child Development* 48 (1977): 475–481; Nancy Eisenberg, *The Caring Child* (Cambridge: Harvard University Press, 1992), chap. 4.

7. Steven R. Asher, John M. Gottman, and Sheri L. Oden, "Children's Friendships in School Settings," in *Contemporary Readings in Child Psychology*, eds. E. Mavis Hetherington and Ross D. Parke (New York: McGraw-Hill, 1977); Francine Deutsch, "Observational and Sociometric Measures of Peer Popularity and their Relationship to Egocentric Communication in Female Preschoolers," *Developmental Psychology* 10 (1974): 745–747; John Gottman, Jonni Gonson, and Brian Rasmussen, "Social Interaction, Social Competence, and Friendship in Children," *Child Devel-*

opment 46 (1975): 709–718; Kenneth H. Rubin, "Relationship Between Egocentric Communication and Popularity among Peers," *Developmental Psychology* 7 (1972): 364.

8. Ram Dass and Paul Gorman, *How Can I Help* (New York: Alfred A. Knopf, 1988), 18–20.

9. Thomas J. Peters, *Thriving on Chaos: Handbook for a Management Revolution* (New York: Alfred A. Knopf, 1988), 153.

10. See for example Donald C. Orlich et al., *Teaching Strategies: A Guide to Better Instruction*, 4th ed. (Lexington, Mass.: D. C. Heath, 1994); Richard Kindsvatter, William Wilen, and Margaret Ishler, *Dynamics of Effective Teaching*, 2nd ed. (White Plains, N.Y.: Longman, 1992).

11. Deborah Tannen, *You Just Don't Understand: Women and Men in Conversation* (New York: William Morrow, 1990).

12. D. R. Dillon, "Showing Them that I Want Them to Learn and that I Care About Who They Are: A Microethnography of the Social Organization of a Secondary Low-track English Reading Classroom," *American Education Research Journal* 26:2 (Summer 1989): 227–259, 239.

13. Erving Goffman, *Relations in Public: Microstudies of the Public Order* (New York: Harper & Row, 1971).

14. Myrna Sadker, David Sadker, and Susan Klein, "The Issue of Gender in Elementary and Secondary Education," in *Review of Research in Education* 17, ed. Carl Grant (Washington, D.C.: American Education Research Association, 1991); Thomas L. Good and Jere E. Brophy, *Looking in Classrooms* (New York: Harper & Row, 1987).

15. Dillon, 243.

16. "Mary Gonzales," cited in Studs Terkel, *Second Thoughts on the American Dream* (New York: Pantheon Books, 1988), 74–78, 77.

17. Earl Babbie, *You Can Make a Difference* (Anaheim Hills, Calif.: Opening Books, 1985).

18. Bill Berkowitz, *Local Heroes: The Rebirth of Heroism in America* (Lexington, Mass.: Lexington Books, 1987), 160.

19. Berkowitz, 158.

20. Diana Baumrind, "Current Patterns of Parental Authority," *Developmental Psychology Monographs* 4 (1971): 1–103.

21. Ervin Staub, *Positive Social Behavior and Morality: Socialization and Development*, vol. 2 (New York: Academic Press, 1979).

22. Beatrice B. Whiting and John W. M. Whiting, *Children of Six Cultures: A Psychocultural Analysis* (Cambridge: Harvard University Press, 1975).

23. Harriet L. Rheingold, "Little Children's Participation in the Work of Adults, a Nascent Prosocial Behavior," *Child Development* 53 (1982): 114–125.

24. Donald H. Bragaw, "New York's Experiment: Participation in Government," *Social Education* (October 1989): 364+.

25. Todd Clark, "Youth Community Service," *Social Education* (October 1989).

26. Jonathan L. Freedman and Scott C. Fraser, "Compliance Without Pressure: The Foot-in-the-door Technique," *Journal of Personality and Social Psychology* 4 (1966): 195–202.

27. Patricia Pliner et al., "Compliance Without Pressure: Some Further Data on

the Foot-in-the-door Technique," *Journal of Experimental Social Psychology* 10 (1974): 17–22.

28. Richard Wormser, *Transcript for Fighting Ministers* 31, p. 3. Shown on POV (Point of View), PBS, in Arcata, California, September 5, 1989, 10:00–11:00 P.M.

29. Wormser.

30. Arthur L. Beaman et al., "Fifteen Years of Foot-in-the-door Research," *Personality and Social Psychology* 9 (1983): 181–196; Ervin Staub, *Positive Social Behavior and Morality: Socialization and Development*, vol. 2 (New York: Academic Press, 1979).

31. David Freudberg and Janet Dudrow, "Norwest Bank: Developing an Approach," in *The Corporate Conscience: Money, Power and Responsible Business*, David Freudberg (New York: AMACOM [American Management Association], 1986), 114–122.

32. Rosabeth Moss Kanter, *The Change Masters: Innovations for Productivity in the American Corporation* (New York: Simon & Schuster, 1983), 142.

33. Thomas J. Peters and Robert H. Waterman, Jr., *In Search of Excellence: Lessons from America's Best-Run Companies* (New York: Harper & Row, 1982). Peters and Waterman reviewed sixty-two U.S. companies in high technology, consumer goods, general industrial, service, project management, and resources based companies.

34. Karl E. Weick, "Educational Organizations as Loosely Coupled Systems," *Administrative Science Quarterly* 21 (1976): 1–19. The ultimate form of autonomy in business is worker ownership, a growing phenomenon which evidence suggests is largely succeeding (for studies on this point, see Frances Moore Lappé, *Rediscovering America's Values* [New York: Ballantine Books, 1989]).

35. Peters and Waterman, 96.

36. Christopher M. Clark, "The Teacher and the Taught: Moral Transactions in the Classroom," in *The Moral Dimensions of Teaching*, eds. John I. Goodlad, Roger Soder, and Kenneth A. Sirotnik (San Francisco: Jossey-Bass, 1990), 251–265, 257.

37. Barbara Ley Toffler, *Tough Choices: Managers Talk Ethics* (New York: John Wiley & Sons, 1986), 162.

38. Samuel P. Oliner and Pearl M. Oliner, *The Altruistic Personality: Rescuers of Jews in Nazi Europe* (New York: Free Press, 1988), chap. 9.

39. Oliner and Oliner, 197.

CHAPTER 6

Diversifying

When I was enrolled in school and entitled to join the library near Fifth Avenue on 110th, I finally walked into the place one hot spring afternoon. It was so dark and cool in there, like no other place I had ever been, and the pink cheeked lady leaning over her polished mahogany counter spoke in such a funereal whisper that something supernatural seemed to be present, something sacred that must not be disturbed by ordinary tones of voice, and so I stood on tiptoe as close to her ear as possible and whispered back the answers to her questions. My name, my address, my age, school, my mother's name—Augusta. At this something began knotting up inside my belly; no one had ever called her anything but Gus or Gussie, so I was already telling a kind of untruth, donning a disguise. Now the lady asked my father's name . . . Looking up into her blue eyes, I could not bring to voice my father's so Jewish name, Isidore. I was paralyzed, could only shake my head. "What does your mother call him?" I was trapped . . . My cheeks were burning. "Izzie" being impossible, I finally managed "Iz." She looked puzzled. "Is?" she asked. I nodded. "Is what?" I rushed out into the street, and I am sure that within minutes I was back within the gang playing ring-a-levio or banging a ball against a building in the game of stoopball.[1]

What Arthur Miller so concretely captures in the above excerpt, taken from his autobiography, is what Erving Goffman might describe as the experience of a child who has acquired a "spoiled identity."[2] By age six, he had already been "programmed," as he says, "to choose something other than pride" in his origins. And without knowing how, he had acquired the group's anxiety; becoming, as it were, a "character" in some two thousand year historical epic, in which, along with other Jews, he lived in a "beleaguered zone surrounded by strangers with violent hearts." The library belonged to the beleaguerers, and having gained admittance to it under the guise of "normalcy," he panicked at the unpredictable consequences should his true identity be revealed.

How had Arthur acquired such knowledge? As he describes it, he cannot trace its source to any discernible event. Living in a predominantly Jewish neighborhood, he had never heard an anti-Semitic comment. Had he thought about it at all, he says, he would have imagined that the "whole world was Jewish." His father, fair-skinned and blue-eyed, negotiated with Jews and non-Jews alike with what he describes as "baronial" self-confidence. The only events of portent which he remembers appeared at best to have but remote bearing on his fears. Passing an automobile accident in an urban center outside his Jewish neighborhood, his father steered him carefully away with the sole admonition to "stay away from crowds." On another occasion his Uncle Louis instructed him "never to walk under a large lighted cross overhanging the sidewalk outside a Lenox Avenue church" and if he did so, to "spit" so as to "cleanse" himself. The mild anxiety which he subsequently experienced at that site was not due to any "menacing theological or historical nuances"—he can recall none such ever being given—but rather, he says, to a concern that the cross might loosen and fall on him.

The adult Arthur, however, is aware of such concepts as denial and suppression. Hence, despite his failure to recollect any explicit source for his anxiety, he concludes that he must have learned it from comments, anecdotes, and "fear-laden vocal tones." Many psychologists would agree—children learn their identity in such ways—and children with spoiled identities may become aware of them particularly early.[3]

Having a spoiled identity means to bear a stigma: others regard the group and individuals within it as having some serious blemish, some flaw which is not normal, and which merits differential treatment. To be Jewish, blind, homosexual, a three-foot adult, or a person of color in a predominantly non-Jewish, sighted, heterosexual, above five feet, and white society is to live with the threat of prejudice, discrimination, and moral exclusion. Never sure that the normative moral code which constrains the larger society will apply to them, stigmatized groups live with anxiety and fear.

No group *chooses* a spoiled identity for itself, only others can assign it. Caring individuals and institutions obviously try to avoid it, but even they rarely escape a tacit acceptance of the larger society's views. Such views, deeply embedded in the cultures in which we live and grow, become deeply embedded in our thinking and in our way of talking about and relating to others.[4] What we call diversifying can be a means to overcome cultural distortions about groups other than our own.

Diversifying, as we define it, *is a deliberate effort to connect with groups different from our own for the purpose of seeking mutual understanding.* Deliberate means intentional rather than accidental, seeking out rather than being found, and connecting implies forming some type of personal relationship. Groups different from our own may include any group which differs from us, whether in social class, occupation, religion, sexual orientation, nationality, age, ethnicity, or race.

The purpose is critical: it is neither intended to seek or bestow approval nor to form alliances, although these may be outcomes. Its major intent is to understand, implying a readiness to entertain new questions and ideas, and a preparedness to acknowledge that some of our perceptions may in fact be partial, impaired, or distorted.

The promise of diversification is not only avoidance of further harm to others, but also self-enhancement. Stimulated by what they have come to newly understand, diversifiers are likely to find new sources of creativity and their range of choices considerably increased.[5] In this context, identities can become fluid rather than static, evolving rather than predetermined, self-defined rather than externally assigned.

In the pages that follow, we concentrate on those conditions which can make diversification more likely to achieve its purpose and promises. As we shall also attempt to demonstrate, diversification is rarely painless.

Physical proximity encourages the potential for contact and mutual understanding. As Stuart Cook puts it, physical proximity encourages "acquaintance potential"[6] and helps people discover their common interests and humanity. Not surprisingly, people commonly choose close friends from among neighbors and coworkers.[7]

But contact among previously hostile groups, that is, groups who are suspicious of each other and have distorted images of one another, can also confirm old stereotypes and exacerbate tensions.[8] Yet in relatively benevolent circumstances, these very tensions can sometimes be an important part of an evolutionary process whose goal is understanding.

School desegregation, the deliberate effort to mix diverse racial and ethnic populations in schools, offers a good example of the advantages of physical proximity and its limitations. Advocates hoped that it would lead to integration, to more normal social relations in which individual character and merit rather than race or ethnicity would determine relationships. In the view of some critics, it has done little more than intensify intergroup hostilities.

Given the rising number of hate crimes across school campuses, the critics appear to have a great deal of evidence on their side. For example, some 350 schools in Los Angeles recently reported more than twenty-two hundred hate incidents (racial slurs, name calling, grafitti, and physical violence) directed at Latinos, blacks, Asians, Pacific Islanders, and homosexuals.[9] Supremacist and Ku Klux Klan graffiti have proliferated throughout college campuses across the country[10] and anti-Semitic incidents on college campuses have increased by 7 percent, according to a 1993 survey by the Anti-Defamation League of B'nai B'rith.[11] While these may be the excesses of a minority, they tend to surface in a climate of resistance often lurking under ostensible calm.

Perhaps the most telling evidence of this resistance to integration is the fact that despite almost four decades of effort, schools continue to be largely segregated. Sixty-six percent of black children and more than 75 percent of Hispanic children across the nation attend schools with mostly minority children, according to a 1993 study by the National School Boards Association.[12] And in those circumstances where schools are in fact desegregated, students still manage to keep to their own racial and ethnic groups. Such "internal segregation" characterizes classes, extracurricular activities, and social activities. Blacks and Hispanics, for example, continue to be disproportionately underrepresented in physical science and advanced mathematics classes, and disproportionately overrepresented in vocational and special education classes. They are also disproportionately underrepresented in scholastically oriented extracurricular activities such as the National Honor Society and disproportionately overrepresented in athletic activities such as basketball.[13] And in public schools, colleges, and universities, students continue to socialize primarily with ethnically and racially similar others.[14]

Measured in terms of its initial promises of integration, desegregation has apparently failed. But measured in terms of modest gains, it has been reasonably successful. These gains, we believe, are the product of an enhanced understanding which would not likely have occurred without the contacts which desegregation made possible.

One of the major gains has been the substantial decrease in blatant racism, a conclusion with which even some of desegregation's harshest critics agree.[15] Race no longer serves as a major factor for denying minorities admission to schools or in hiring policies, and stereotypic distortions of minority groups in curricular materials are no longer the norm. School textbooks now labor to include multicultural groups, and multicultural education has become a serious concern across the nation. Even as critics argue that these are simply "add-ons" to a basically Eurocentric curriculum, they simultaneously acknowledge that they represent improvements over past practices.[16]

Other changes have been more modest and subtle, although no less important. They include such things as an enhanced understanding of mutual fears and anxieties, a greater ability to adapt to different styles of behavior, and increased numbers of positive interracial interpersonal relationships. How this occurs is probably best illustrated by a close look at what happened to the sixth through eighth grade students at a single desegregated school over a three-year period as told by research psychologist Janet Ward Schofield.

Schofield spent three years studying "Wexler" Middle School (the name is a pseudonym), beginning with its inception in 1975 as a newly launched desegregated school. During that period, she observed frequently, interviewed students and faculty, and conducted surveys. Her findings, summarized below, suggest how the positive changes noted above can occur between black and white students in a reasonably benevolent environment under conditions of physical proximity.

During the first few months after the school opened, says Schofield, students from both races tended to avoid each other but watched each other carefully. Black students feared rejection, since they (as well as white students) saw whites as "smarter." White children who knew the answers did not like sharing them with low-achieving black children, and high-achieving white students preferred working with other high achievers, thus excluding black children from shared academic tasks. White students feared physical harm since they (as well as black students) saw blacks as physically tougher and inclined to use this toughness to dominate others. When white children saw blacks fighting, they pretended not to see, and when they were "hassled" by black children, they said nothing. (High-achieving black children tended to have patterns similar to those of high-achieving white children.)

By the second year, attitudes and behaviors of both groups became somewhat modified. Black children learned to fear rejection less as they began to understand white children's fears. As one black girl explained:

First when they came here they were scared and they were tight . . . They was afraid. They wouldn't talk to nobody until people started coming over and talking to them . . . Last year they didn't know you that well. This year they do.[17]

And the majority of white children learned to fear blacks less as they realized that asserting themselves when black children tested them was the appropriate response. As one white girl explained it:

I learned to stick up for myself . . . There was a couple of black girls that tried to force me to fight this other one. I didn't know what to do . . . I got in trouble . . . I think that when they first came they had a pre-set idea of white people's behavior. When they got here they learned that not all of the white kids are going to roll over and play dead when they say "boo."[18]

Black children became more admiring of white children who stood up to teasing and aggressive behavior, as this comment by Charlene, another black girl, suggests:

Some black and white kids get along, but some don't . . . If they [white kids] show black kids they ain't scared of them . . . when black kids hit them, they could get along with blacks.[19]

But perhaps the most important change occurred in what Schofield describes as the "shift from intergroup to interpersonal behavior." What this means is that more children from both races began to see individuals within the group, rather than group stereotypes. Some white children, for example, learned to understand that many black children did not like aggressive behavior any more than they did. As one white girl expressed it: "[I learned] they can be nice. About fifty percent are nice."[20] And some black children began to discriminate between friendly and unfriendly whites as this comment by a black girl suggests: "Some black kids and white kids get along just like sisters, but some fight."[21]

As Schofield points out, this did not mean that race became irrelevant or unnoticed, but rather that it became only one of several attributes which determined behavior rather than the overriding one. One example of this shift in consciousness was in the school cafeteria, where more children sat next to someone of a different race with each passing year. Another was in the increasing numbers of friendly and cooperative interactions between black and white students, such as the following:

Mr. Cousins (white) is walking around the room checking students' work . . . At Table 2, Jeff (white) and Henry (black) are still acting playfully. They occasionally whisper, do some talking, show each other their papers and all of a sudden they have given the "gimme five" handshake to each other. They lean very close together as they continue to whisper and giggle.

Today in Ms. Hopkins's (black) class, there will be a speaker . . . Two girls, a tall black child and a long-haired white one, who came up this room together from their last class . . . are talking and holding hands.[22]

Both groups thus began by watching each other so as to find out what the other was like, followed by some cautious moves, which in turn led to some new understanding of appropriate responses and some improvements in interpersonal relationships. By the end of the third year, two-thirds of the students said some improvement in black/white relations had occurred, and on the whole, children had learned to deal with each other better. But, Schofield acknowledges, white students continued to fear physical harm and black students continued to fear rejection although less so than previously. And for some students, both black and white, school experiences had buttressed traditional hostilities rather than tempered them.

On the one hand, such achievements seem modest indeed, particularly in light of the fact that the school had opened under what appeared extraordinarily favorable conditions. Parents had voluntarily chosen the newly desegregated school, and the student population was equally divided between blacks and whites. The faculty, which included some 25 percent black teachers, favored the desegregation effort, as did the administrators and board.

Added to this were the fine physical facilities and some thoughtful planning to make the experiment work.

On the other hand, the achievements seem impressive because despite the racial balance, *social class was skewed*. The majority of white students came from middle-class families, many of them with parents having high education, while the majority of black students came from lower-class families. This factor helps explain the divisions among them as much as race.

Yet another reason for rating the achievements as impressive is that the children had not been prepared to deal with racial differences and received no guidance during the time they were together for doing so. For as was common during that period, teachers saw any discussion of race as divisive, and their ideology precluded acknowledging racial differences. Children were thus left to negotiate differences on their own.

Many advocates of school desegregation argue that if desegregation has failed to achieve integration, it is not because preventing racial separation in schools is unimportant, but rather because it is only the first step.[23] To achieve integration, educators need to incorporate some of the diversifying strategies below.

Part of Wexler's failure can be attributed to cultural misunderstandings based on race and cultural misunderstandings based on social class. If groups are to understand each other, they need to accept the reality of cultural differences and be prepared to recognize them as such.

Culture—patterned forms of behavior and thought[24]—is the consequence of a group's shared experiences and shared interpretations of those experiences. Racial, ethnic, national, and religious groups generate their own distinct cultures, but so do white and blue collar employees, rich and poor, and men and women. Contrary to popular conceptions, cultural misunderstandings between groups are more the rule than the exception; they permeate all types of human relationships, from the impersonal to the most intimate.

For example, cultural misunderstandings often arise between business organizations and their customers. What customers want more than efficiency, says management consultant Roger Harrison, is warmth, respect, caring, and kindness. They fail to get it not only because such tender feelings are hard to cultivate in the business sector, but also because even the most service oriented businesses don't understand what customers are saying:

When organizations become concerned about improving service, they tend to see it through their own cultural biases. Customers talk about wanting better service, and organizations think in terms of better systems. It isn't that customers don't want efficient systems or excellent, innovative approaches to meeting their needs. They want these, and more.

Organizations that don't learn how to listen to customers . . . don't understand what they are hearing . . . put effort into improving service in ways which customers are happy enough to have but which don't meet their deeper priorities.[25]

The personless voice messages which customers routinely encounter on their telephones are a prime example of such a systems service orientation. While they may in fact speed up service, they simultaneously communicate impersonality and lack of caring. Customers want more than increasingly efficient service, they want some recognition as individuals, some supportive confirmation of their expressed needs. But embedded in a commercial culture, business organizations interpret service to mean greater efficiency, while customers mean both efficiency and their validation as people. Although using the same word, "service," each in fact is speaking a different "language," the consequences of which are as real as though each spoke a language foreign to the other. (Engineers, accountants, and product divisions even within the same organizations also develop their own culture and speak a different language.)

Families—parents and children, husbands and wives—are equally vulnerable to cultural misunderstandings. In fact, says Raymonde Carroll:

It is indeed within the realm of interpersonal relationships where one feels the most secure, the least guarded—among friends, among lovers, among colleagues, among those closest to us—that cultural misunderstanding has the greatest chance of arising. This is so because we erroneously think that in this domain we are all basically the same.[26]

Because intimates do not understand such cultural differences, they wind up causing deep and painful wounds, creating a climate of accusation and victimization. Deborah Tannen, a sociolinguist, describes how this occurs routinely between husbands and wives, a representative example of which is the story of Josh and Linda.

When Josh's old school chum called him at work, Josh invited him to stay for the weekend without consulting Linda. When he informed her of his invitation and his plan to go out with him alone the first night, Linda became very upset. What upset her most was the fact that Josh had made his plans without consulting her. When she protested, Josh said, "I can't say to my friend, 'I have to ask my wife for permission'!"

As Tannen explains it, Linda and Josh were speaking a different "genderflect":

To Josh, checking with his wife means seeking permission, which implies that he is not independent, not free to act on his own. It would make him feel like a child or an underling. To Linda, checking with her husband has nothing to do with permission. She assumes that spouses discuss their plans with each other because their lives are intertwined, so the actions of one have consequences for the other. Not only does Linda not mind telling someone, "I have to check with Josh"; quite the contrary—she likes it. It makes her feel good to know and show that she is involved with someone, that her life is bound up with someone else's.[27]

Like many men, says Tannen, Josh spoke the language of hierarchy, status, and independence; like many women, Linda spoke the language of connection, equality, and intimacy. Echoing Harrison, Tannen says that what both wanted from each other is what most people want above all: "to be heard—but not merely to be heard. We want to be understood—heard for what we think we are saying, for what we know we meant."[28]

Once we acknowledge the reality of cultural differences and learn to appreciate their importance, we may be less inclined to explain some behavior we do not understand as perverse or malevolent. In that case, we might indeed be better prepared to understand others in the way Tannen suggests: that is, not in terms of what *we* think they are doing or saying but in terms of what *they* really mean.

Understanding groups whose culture differs from our own also requires that we recognize our own cultural biases and that we give others the opportunity to define themselves.

The first bias we need to abandon is the desire to homogenize cultures, that is, the wish to make others like ourselves. But we also need to become aware of other cultural prejudices we harbor, often the consequence of our natural tendency toward "us/them" thinking.

All living organisms evidence "us/them" group formations, leading some sociobiologists to argue that it has a genetic basis. Living beings appear to share some mechanism that allows them to recognize and join with genetically similar others while excluding differing others, say advocates of the genetic similarity hypothesis.[29] Proponents of this view attribute this capacity to an evolutionary process whereby groups with strong in-group/out-group sentiments were more successful at replicating their genes.

In a somewhat similar vein, psychoanalyst Vamik Volkan proposes that a self-versus-other mind-set derives from people's innate need for enemies and allies. Rather than accepting responsibility for their misdeeds and misfortunes, people share a need to externalize blame, project unacceptable thoughts onto others, and displace unacceptable feelings about intimate others onto strangers as a way of defending the self. This process, says Volkan, begins early, and while maturity may temper it, adults never quite outgrow their "us/them" mentality.[30]

Volkan here alerts us to an important possibility. "Us/them" thinking may not be confined to bigots alone, as many would like to believe, but may also include liberals who similarly may focus on "out-group" shortcomings as a way of avoiding their own. As recounted by psychologist Robert Coles about himself, a Louisiana member of the subsequently disbanded

White Citizens Council understood this when he shrewdly advised Coles to stop spending so much time studying racists and "go home":

Don't linger here too long, you'll just be feeding off us! You'll be so happy that you can see how bad and mean we are, that you'll never want to go home and take a look at your own backyard! No one wants to see himself in the mirror, warts and all. Everyone wants to pretty himself up, and also get a boost by looking at someone else's warts. You Yankees come down here, and oh, you're in heaven: You've got all us bad people to spot and write home about! When you do go back yourselves, you can make the rounds, giving pleasure to all who hear you—talking about us, those awful Southern folks who hate the nigras and lynch people are so bad, just as bad as can be. That's a good deal for people, to have someone else to blame for the world being bad.[31]

But more than self-protection lies behind "us/them" thinking. The genesis of this dichotomous thinking may well lie less in the need to find "enemies," as Volkan proposes, and more in the innate human trait to categorize and to conserve mental energy. Very early in life, children learn systems for classifying people and objects; the systems they learn depend on the cultures in which they live. Once having formed these systems, they tend to hold on to them because of what psychologist Gordon Allport calls "the principle of least effort." In other words, people tend to maintain established preconceptions for as long as they appear to be useful, even if they are inaccurate, because of what could be called "cognitive economy."[32]

The principle of least effort helps explain how even reasonably well-intentioned people may nonetheless offend other groups. When fellow employees continued to call Chinese-American lawyer Karen Kwong by the name of the one other Asian person in the firm, they were more likely manifesting a disinclination to expend the effort required to discern differences than a willful desire to humiliate her.[33] Similarly, Arab-Americans from allied countries—such as Kuwait, Saudi Arabia, and Egypt—harrassed subsequent to the Iraqi invasion of Kuwait in July 1990 may have been as much the victims of this inclination to conserve cognitive energies as general bigotry. Discriminating among the twenty-two countries comprising the Arab world was taxing; it was much easier to yield to general impressions than to distinguish friends from foes.[34]

Once acknowledged, however, cultural biases and stereotypic thinking can be controlled. As a series of recent studies demonstrates, what distinguishes those low in prejudice from the highly prejudiced is not their failure to have stereotypes—in fact, they know them and activate them as automatically as the latter—but their ability to consciously monitor them and replace them with thoughts of equality and negations of stereotypes.[35] Such internal monitoring helps explain in part the disappearance of blatantly offensive derogatory labels from the speech of the less prejudiced.

Rather than suppressing them or pretending they don't exist, say several educators, people need to talk about their cultural prejudices and stereotypes in a climate of acknowledgement rather than accusation. An Anti-Defamation League program, "World of Difference," hopes to combat racism in just this way. In one of its videotapes, the teacher solicits from students commonly held stereotypes—Asians play the violin and are smart, Hispanic and black women have many live-in lovers, the Irish are alcoholics—and duly records them on the blackboard as items for discussion.[36] But such discussion needs to begin much earlier, says Louise Derman-Sparks, and, moreover, needs to be done with the right attitude. What is the proper attitude? For Derman-Sparks and the preschool teachers who developed the ABC Curriculum (The Anti-Bias Curriculum) for preschoolers, it means teachers and parents talking about such differences objectively and comfortably, and coming to terms with their own differences.[37]

Talking about such differences comfortably, however, is difficult to achieve. For many people, terms like "black" or "white," "Christian," "Jew," or "Muslim" are not descriptions but judgments. The intense discomfort of this white principal, for example, is probably more the rule than the exception:

He was young, bright, and articulate; but when forced to talk about race, he stumbled, finding complicated circumlocutions to avoid the words "white" and "black." Partly he had been taught, in college, that race was not the issue—that blacks were really the same as white people (except perhaps that they were culturally deprived). He had also been taught that race was not to be talked about in polite society. And he was scared.[38]

Lest we think such discomfort is confined to elementary and secondary teachers, historian Patricia Limerick alerts us to the same discomfort among university professors. Describing a race-relations seminar she and a friend had organized, Limerick says, "The white people attending were on such rigorously good behavior, instantly sympathizing with and declaring that they understood whatever minority people said, that the discussion risked being dull and certainly stood little chance of educating the participants." Ironically, it was her conservative sister who wound up saving the occasion when she pointedly asked: "Just what do you people want?" The whites in the group immediately tried to distance themselves from this foolish comment, but the net consequence was a more productive and frank exchange as they began to acknowledge that there might be some things they did not fully understand either. Understanding, concludes Limerick, requires "risk, danger, and willingness to put our feet down confidently on land mines."[39]

Although apparently less threatening, even social class differences are difficult to talk about. While doing a radio interview on class issues, journalist Barbara Ehrenreich (author of *Fear of Falling: The Inner Life of the Middle*

Class) reports a woman who called in to ask, "Do we have to talk about class? Why can't we just treat everyone as an individual?" "For this woman," says Ehrenreich, "class . . . is not a category that helps to explain the individual condition," but a pernicious concept that threatens the myth that Americans are overwhelmingly middle class, with some suspect exceptions.

Yet as Ehrenreich points out, social class, like race and gender, are central and sometimes tragic parts of each person's story; leaving its imprint on both body and soul:

It leaves its imprint on the personality: a questing, expansionist outlook goes well with trust funds and recreational travel; an aggrieved and narrower view better suits the paycheck-to-paycheck way of life, the cramped apartments and indifferent schools. It leaves deep marks on the body too: bad teeth; chronic, uncorrected health problems; blackened lungs; and ruined backs. And it can be, in all kinds of ways, a determinant of early death.[40]

If groups are to understand each other, they need to know "stories" like the above and keep them in mind.

Getting to know other groups' stories means making them visible and giving them "voice," particularly in relation to their most salient and painful experiences.

Silence threatens others' welfare, preparing the way for tyrants. Silence is the response of the bystander, and it bespeaks denial, irrelevance, and non-concern. What frightened Jewish columnist A. M. Rosenthal, for example, was not German unification per se, but the omission of words like "Jew," "Holocaust," and "crematorium" from the speeches that celebrated it. The young German generation, he says, needs to know about it, not for the purpose of accepting the guilt of their parents, but rather to understand and remove the fears that "are as real as torn flesh still bleeding."[41] What disturbed him sometime later was not so much the vicious anti-Semitism expressed by Farrakhan aide Khalid Abdul Muhammed, but the silence of the black intellectuals who heard him speak.[42] Silence for many Jews carries the threat of a repeated history—hence their sense of partial comfort when several black leaders subsequently condemned the speech unequivocally.[43]

Telling others' stories from the speaker's perspective alone is another form of silence. For black educator James Banks, a "mainstream centric" curriculum is a "silent" curriculum, for while it may tell stories about ethnic groups, it tells them from the mainstream American or European point of view. A multiethnic curriculum, says Banks, focuses on a given social or historical event and teaches it from the perspective of many different groups, including the mainstream culture.[44] For example, Columbus and the early white settlers may be heroes to European Americans, but they represented cruelty and displacement to Native Americans and Hispanics. The story of black slaves told from the European perspective may focus on their passivity and helplessness; black Americans may choose to emphasize their courage and strategic survival techniques in the face of overwhelming odds. Failure to allow others to tell their own stories implies devaluation and delegitimization.

Failure to recognize their own cultural biases and to give others voice helps explain why many well-intentioned people respond inappropriately. Sixties activist Michael Lerner, who now edits the progressive journal *Tikkun*, apparently had something similar in mind when he tried to explain why the left of the sixties left little of a sustainable legacy for the eighties. From the left's perspective, drugs, alcoholism, and religious escapism were merely manifestations of Americans' self-indulgence and ideological delusion. Had they been willing to listen, implies Lerner, they would have understood the sense of isolation, despair, and lack of purpose which underlay Americans' behaviors of that time and proposed a different agenda.[45]

Yet even as understanding a group's common pain and central experiences helps promote understanding, so does recognition of others' variability. Not all group members share the same point of view, nor do they all necessarily even share identical experiences. On the one hand, giving others voice means acknowledging the group's common experience. On the other, it means acknowledging the variability of individuals within the group.

"In cross-cultural talk," says Jack Shaffer, professor of cross-cultural counseling, "keep information about the group in the background, but assume great variability in the foreground."[46] In other words, keep in mind the setting from which the individual comes, but above all remember that the person you're talking to is an individual. Ostensibly obvious, this advice is rarely honored in practice. While people are conscious of subtle variations in their own group, they tend to see those outside it as largely homogeneous.[47]

Groups themselves sometimes encourage perceptions of homogeneity, particularly when pursuing political goals. Such was the case, for example, when Chicano studies first began to penetrate the university. Developed primarily out of the struggle for equal rights and justice in the 1950s and 1960s, says Professor Ramon A. Gutierrez, political militancy fed "a scholarship that was very nationalistic" and "defined the Chicano community as more homogeneous and unified than it really was."[48] Rather than having their differences attended to, Chicanos were projected as uniformly working-class, victims of white society, racially distinctive, and dominated by men.

Feminist scholars were among the first to challenge this prototype, says Karen Winkler, resulting in some major reinterpretations of women's roles in Chicano culture. For example, Dona Marina, the Mayan princess who befriended Hernan Cortes, has traditionally been portrayed as a traitor to her people or a passive victim of colonial male power. Calling on new sources and reexamining old ones, feminist scholars portrayed her instead as a woman who sought to build a new society, venturing outside traditional female roles and cultural exclusivity. Once the myth of homogeneity was shattered, other scholars followed suit. Scholars now concede the multiplicity of the Hispanic experience, among whom Mexican Americans, Puerto Ricans, and immigrants from Central America, for example, differ not only from other Hispanics but also among themselves.[49]

Learning about the ways group members define their identity can be helpful in recognizing variability, but experiences with individuals from diverse groups can be more enlightening. Direct observations of individuals behaving contrary to expectations can be a powerful means for promoting perceptions of variability within groups.

Julia Anderson, past coordinator of the Perkins Project with Industry,[50] contrived such opportunities in her efforts to find employment for the visually impaired. Employers are generally reluctant to hire them, because they perceive them as less able to do the job and because they view them as excessively dependent. Statistical presentations of their variability—their success, failure, and promotion rates on the job are similar to those of the sighted—rarely persuade employers to take the risk. Anderson's major task often consisted of managing to get an interview which allowed prospective employers to see an impaired person acting contrary to their expectations.

She describes a job interview she managed to arrange for Russell, blind since the age of two. Although Russell had been trained as a computer programmer by the Perkins Project and had five years of experience as a customer service representative with a government agency behind him, the telephone company division managers who agreed to the interview were skeptical of his ability to perform the job. Their reservations were not only related to the skill he purportedly offered, but to his ability to maneuver generally. "What if there were a fire?" asked one. "How would he find his way to the restroom?" asked another. They offered him the job only after actually observing him perform:

Russell demonstrated a device attached to a computer that allows the information on the screen to be read in braille on a tactual display. While he talked about his research in adaptive devices, he wrote a program to perform a simple data sort and then inputted the names of his interviewers. As the screen displayed the sorted material, Russell read it aloud by means of the attached display.

Intrigued, the managers showered him with questions about debugging programs and the comparative versatility of braille and speech in accessing visually presented information. He answered them readily while he broke down the equipment and packed it up. As he left, Russell offered to show them "a piece of the most impressive technology every developed," and in one motion he snapped his folded cane into extension.[51]

Russell was persuasive because he understood his interviewers' apprehensions and had carefully selected the view of himself he needed to present. Had his interviewers seen him in his own home or at school, they would have quickly disabused themselves of their stereotypic conceptions without the need for such careful orchestration on Russell's part. People are more likely to perceive others' variability when they can observe them in their own settings, in their ordinary living conditions.

The story of John Miller, nature writer and teacher, illustrates this point. When his student, Craig, invited him to come see his pigeons in Harlem, Miller accepted the invitation with trepidation. When he stepped out of the taxi at 114th Street and Eighth Avenue, he was scared:

A stray German shepherd barked from the third-floor window of an abandoned building. Three men and a woman, sitting on kitchen chairs outside one of the few inhabited tenements, stared at me. I waited, regretting I had let the cab go.

Then shadows of pigeons raced up my side of broken sidewalk. Five stories up and leaning dangerously over the building cornice, Craig waved at me. Craig emerged at street level and escorted me past his seated friends, who now looked at me less suspiciously. As we climbed the steps of the tenement, he explained: A white face in Harlem means an undercover cop after a drug dealer. Craig said he had cleared me by the telling the neighborhood I was the pigeon trainer for him and his partner Junior.[52]

What John discovered for his efforts was a spectacular natural world and two experts with much to teach him. On Craig's tenement rooftop, amid pigeons coops lined with cubbyholes, John learned how to observe and study pigeons, their habits, how they pair and when to fly them, and how to recruit new ones. When the flock they had carefully launched brought in a wild all-black red-eyed pigeon, a type they had never seen before, John watched in awe as the wild pigeon marched "lock-step with the others" through the trapdoor. "I felt as if they had taken me on an expedition to some wide ocean when all the while I had been standing less than a mile from my Manhattan apartment," he observed.

Had Craig not invited him, had he not overcome his apprehensions to visit him on his own "turf," John says he might never have learned that natural scientists can be found even among inner-city minority students who rarely see trees or grass and who complain when they are pushed "to write a more-than-one-page paper."

Recognizing the importance of observing others in their own communities as a way of overcoming stereotypic homogenization, Ralph Fabrizio, superintendent of the Community School District 20 in Brooklyn, organized a special program. When Yusuf K. Hawkins, a black teenager from East New York was shot by a group of whites in Bensonhurst, an Italian-American neighborhood, Fabrizio had children spend six days during the year in each other's schools. Of all his efforts to overcome the heightened stereotyping ensuing from Hawkins' murder, this one, he says, was most successful.[53] Because the opportunities for observing variety in natural settings increase substantially, each group could see students from the other group acting much like students in their own—some friendly, relaxed or playful, others angry, stressed or serious. Students were thus able to see each other as diverse individuals, defying expectations of negative uniformity.

Just as direct observations contrary to expectations help people see individuals rather than groups, so do dialogues. A dialogue not only gives voice to the other, but is an exchange based on the presumption that each participant has something meaningful to give. It communicates not only content—a denotative message—but a relationship, what Gregory Bateson calls a metacommunication.[54] Successful dialoguers communicate a relationship of equality. They avoid patronizing, derogatory comparisons, and self-righteous indignation.

Had the managers interviewing Russell helped him maneuver himself out of the chair or offered to show him a better way to display his skills, the message would have been a caring and generous one. The metamessage would have been "You are an unfortunate victim of circumstances, and I am more competent than you." Patronizing messages are framed in just this way.

Because its message is care and concern, patronizers are often astonished when instead of the anticipated gratitude, they are confronted with anger and rejection. Rather than comforted, lesbian poet Susan Abbott felt oppressed when her mother insisted on feeling sorry for the life she had chosen. If *Rubyfruit Jungle* made her mother feel sad, Susan insisted on seeing its humor. If her mother thought she understood what lesbians were all about, she was sadly mistaken. When her mother insisted upon feeling sorry for her, saying that she felt depressed for the oppression she would experience, Susan rejected the sentiment and told her mother harshly:

Your equation that oppression = depression: feeling *sorry* for *me* so you say, because I'm oppressed, is downright oppressive. The sooner you stop feeling sorry for me, the sooner that oppression will begin to disintegrate. Also, who you kidding? You ain't going around feeling sorry for anybody but yourself. So get over it.[55]

Psychologists might call Susan's reaction overly defensive, an excessive reaction to what was not really an attack. While she may have shared with other lesbians the very sentiments her mother was expressing, she could not tolerate them from her "straight" mother not only because of its patronizing tone, but also because it implied some derogatory comparison. If her mother felt depressed at her choice, it implied that Susan's choice was inferior.

A similar view was expressed in very different circumstances by Liu Zongren, a visitor from China to the United States. Although treated with kindness from many people and acutely aware of the shortcomings in his own country, he was highly sensitive to even casual remarks from Americans which suggested unflattering comparisons:

Now that I was in a foreign country, I realized that I might become somewhat defensive—if Americans were to say critical things about China. Back in Beijing, my colleagues and I had raised many criticisms of the Chinese government and expressed them openly. But when Mrs. McKnight would occasionally make jokes about the backwardness of China, I reacted with resentment. Once, when they were having a problem with mice in their kitchen, I set traps and caught seven of them in succession. In praise of my heroic deed she said, "You have a billion people in China. How many mice do you have?"

I flared up. "You should not make fun of my country. You hurt my feelings when you joke about China."

She apologized and told me she was trying to make me feel better. But how could I enjoy such jokes? I was very sensitive on such matters, and viewed any disparaging remark about China as a personal affront.[56]

Although he never grew to like it, Liu says he eventually came "to understand and accept" such "kidding" from Americans as "something they generally reserved for people they liked." Rather than remaining self-righteously indignant and expecting Americans to adjust, Liu eventually assumed he would need to change. Had he not been willing to grant the possibility that such comments were Americans' way of indicating affection, many of his conversations would have been prematurely terminated.

Like unconscious derogatory comparisons, self-righteous indignation can stifle dialoguing, marking the other as unethical or immoral. How this can occur even in the most well-intentioned setting is suggested by writer and television producer Paul Wilkes, who describes just such an event. The setting was a program called "Seminarians Interacting." Sponsored by the National Conference of Christians and Jews, it included some sixty men and women, Conservative, Reform, and Reconstructionist Jews, mainstream and evangelical Protestants, Catholics, Eastern Orthodox, blacks and whites. As the long silences below suggest, a dialogue cannot be sustained for long when participants claim the moral high ground as their exclusive possession.

We sat in a ground-floor lounge on the campus of General Theological, an Episcopal seminary in New York, for one of the discussion groups. Before the group leader, an NCCJ staff member, could begin to try to direct the discussion, a Lutheran looked at a Jew and said she wondered why Jews would even want to talk with Christians, when Christians had been responsible for so many atrocities against Jews. The staff member tried again to get the discussion started. A female student . . . interrupted . . . "Look around you at the male authority pictures in this room. Were there no women in this church? My church! I'm uncomfortable here. I'm offended." The group members peered up sheepishly at the paintings of some of General Theological's most celebrated teachers and presidents . . .

Halfway through the session the talk turned to what members of the clergy uniquely provide as counselors, and how they can prevent personal burnout. David Krainin, of Jewish Theological, spoke of a course he was teaching that dealt with trying to help people through times of crisis, and noted that his instructor had come up with what to him was an apt analogy. "Don't let people stick to you like you were a tar baby. If you're really going to help them, that's not going . . ."

"Tar baby" rang the racist bell in the head of the EDS student who had spoken up earlier, and she would have none of that kind of talk. What was a word that could be substituted for "tar baby" she asked. The lounge was quiet once more . . . Krainin's look was at once kindly, amused, and slightly amazed.[57]

It can of course be argued that the group needed sensitization to some of the issues which their irksome colleagues raised. But it also illustrates the difficulties of sustaining a dialogue when participants attempt to stake claim to the moral high ground.

A dialogue should be a means for seeking and creating ethical values rather than imposing or appropriating them.[58] When groups have a vested interest in maintaining their values rather than in creating them, dialoguing can be a dangerous enterprise, as two Catholic nuns of the Sisters of Notre Dame discovered. Talking with the poor women whom they were committed to serve led Barbara Ferraro and Patricia Hussey to revise their positions on abortion. Having chosen to listen to the women whose pregnancies often resulted from bikers' initiation rites and gang rapes and whose children could not be supported when their marriages fell apart, they signed an ad appearing in *The New York Times* under the headline: "A Diversity of Opinions Regarding Abortion Exists Among Committed Catholics." When the Apostolic Pro-Nuncio in Washington offered to "dialogue" with the sisters, what he really had in mind was something else. "But I must insist," he said, "that after our time together you must put in writing that you support and adhere to the Roman Catholic teaching on abortion." Faced with the choice of retraction or dismissal, they resigned.[59]

For the Apostolic Pro-Nuncio, a dialogue did not mean an exchange of understanding, but a reaffirmation of unmodifiable positions determined by the superiors in a hierarchial and male-dominated structure. As he rightfully understood, a true dialogue might begin a journey whose terminal point could not be known in advance. The sisters had already discovered the perils of dialoguing, and for them there was "no turning back."

By way of contrast, Cummins Engine Company of Columbus, Indiana, was ready to venture into the unknown when it began a dialogue with aroused citizens concerned about the relocation of its headquarters into the downtown area. The consequence, as described by then CEO and chairman

Henry B. Schacht and vice-president of public policy Charles W. Powers, was years of enduring trust.

With a workforce of some ten thousand people in a city population of about thirty thousand, Cummins was the largest employer. When the company decided to relocate its headquarters to the downtown area, people became greatly concerned about its scope and nature. Would it be a Cummins facility only or part of a large complex? Would historic landmarks be disturbed? And how would it affect small businessmen, property values and public works projects? Although preoccupied internally with the complexity of the task and far from having made its decisions, Cummins's executives became aware of the community's anxieties, which already were generating many discussions. As Schacht and Powers tell it, they decided to do the following:

> In the summer of 1977, as we began to clarify our thinking, community discussion began to increase. The people of Columbus knew that they had a stake in our decision and wanted to know what the decision was. A host of internal management issues remained to be resolved, but it became clear to us that community interest was likely to turn to speculation and suspicion. Rather than fend it off, we decided to call together a full spectrum of community leaders, not merely to tell them the unsettled state of our plans but conscientiously to ask their views on the role that a new office building could play in the community's evolution and on how that role could be enhanced. Representatives of our top management, along with our architect, listened for 3 days. The discussion was open and open-ended. We focused many of our own questions on those issues (almost all of which were yet to be decided) on which we perceived the community impact of our building would be greatest.
>
> The sessions were extremely instructive. Many of our perceptions changed; the architect, Kevin Roche, incorporated a wide variety of the community's suggestions into his plans.[60]

What marked this as a dialogue was the company's acceptance of the community as legitimately coinvested in the company's decisions and the company's genuine openness to accommodation. What the executives learned was that they had more choices than had previously occurred to them.

Dialoguing with and learning about diverse others increases choices—the consequences of which may be overwhelmingly positive, as apparently was the case for Cummins, or perilous, as Ferraro and Hussey learned. Choosing to deviate from a group's conventions and values may leave one never feeling a secure and loved member of any group. When Richard Rodriguez chose to become a scholar of English literature, he became alienated from his parents' Mexican roots, was called a brown Uncle Tom by fellow ethnics, and felt not entirely at home in Anglo culture. The rewards were real, but so was the grief.

Julius Lester, the son of a southern black Methodist minister, experienced similar feelings when he converted to Judaism. Formerly admired by many blacks, he is now considered a renegade. And learning how to deal with those fellow Jews who might reject him keeps him on edge:

I did not know what to expect. As much as I love Judaism, it was still not easy for me to venture into the world of Jews. Many of them have mixed feelings about converts and some are not shy about expressing those feelings.

The comment I hear most often is "Didn't you have enough problems being black?" The remark startles me because what the person is really saying is that he has problems being Jewish. I generally respond by saying, "Being Jewish is a joy for me."

There was a woman who said sweetly, "Oh, you're like Sammy Davis, Jr." I said, "I wouldn't know. I never met him." Rabbi Lander told me that I was too polite. "You should've said, 'Oh, and you're like Mrs. Portnoy.' "

I was not polite to the woman who said to me, "Well, you're not really Jewish, you know." I looked at her with Grandmomma's eyes and said angrily, "How dare you!" Many Jews (and Gentiles) feel that if you're not born Jewish, then you aren't *really* a Jew.[61]

Straddling cultures is a painful negotiation if groups insist on maintaining firm boundaries between "us" and "them" and controlling those who venture outside or inside them. For writer David Morse's father, straddling cultures was more of a liberating game than a stressful transaction. Of somewhat dark hue, Morse's father Wil could have passed for Indian, but his one-eighth or one-sixteenth Indian heritage did not entitle him to be so labeled by the Bureau of Indian Affairs. Firmly established as a white lawyer, he nonetheless pulled out his Indian identity whenever it suited him:

He was . . . savvy enough to use his Indian identity as a vehicle for advancing his political agenda, casting his belief in socialized medicine and racial equality, for instance, as old Indian principles.

During the McCarthy era, when others wrapped themselves in the flag, my father wrapped himself in his Indianhood, keeping himself free of other labels. Adopting that Indian identity was a way of maintaining a private identity apart from the mainstream culture. I also think that it offered him some escape from the rationalism of his legal training—and for that matter the rationalistic assumptions of Western civilization.[62]

Refusing to accept an assigned identity, Rodriguez, Lester, and Wil insist on choosing their own. Their attitudes should be of particular comfort to the approximately five million American children and adolescents who are the products of mixed racial marriages.[63] Often described as particularly confused because physical appearance may lead others to assign them one group identity while their experience may lead them to identify with the other, they too can choose their own. Or they may decide instead to take Joslyn Segal's advice. A psychotherapist of mixed heritage (one parent is a Russian-Romanian Jewish musician and the other is an African-American Native American jazz dancer), Segal says that the important thing is to be everything that you are, "rather than 'this' or 'that.' "[64]

The critical issue is not whom we choose to identify with or how we create our own identities, but whether our identity connects us to diverse others or alienates us from them.[65] Diversifying implies seeking connections through understanding, and the new experiences it brings increase choices. Herein lie both the potential pangs of possible renunciation of familiar bonds, and the potential joys of liberation from constricted identities imposed on us by others.

NOTES

1. Arthur Miller, *Timebends: A Life* (New York: Harper & Row, 1987), 23–26.

2. Erving Goffman, *Stigma: Notes on the Management of Spoiled Identity* (Englewood Cliffs, N.J.: Prentice-Hall, 1965).

3. Judith Porter, *Black Child, White Child: The Development of Racial Attitudes* (Cambridge: Harvard University Press, 1971) found that black children as young as two and one-half were aware of their own racial characteristics as well as those of others.

4. Rather than call this unconscious, which implies something not realized but potentially neutral, the term "dysconscious" which Joyce King has applied to racism seems more apt in describing this kind of thinking. Dysconscious racism, she says, is an "impaired consciousness or a distorted way of thinking about race," one that "tacitly accepts dominant White norms and privileges" (Joyce Elaine King, "Dysconscious Racism: Ideology, Identity, and the Miseducation of Teachers," *Journal of Negro Education* 60:2 [Spring 1991]: 133–146, 135).

5. This helps explain why industrial consultants Suresh Srivastva and David L. Cooperrider believe it is fundamental for success in business (Suresh Srivastva and David L. Cooperrider, "Introduction: The Urgency for Executive Integrity," in *Executive Integrity: The Search for High Human Values in Organizational Life*, eds. Suresh Srivastva and Associates [San Francisco: Jossey-Bass, 1988], 1–28).

6. Stuart W. Cook, "Motives in a Conceptual Analysis of Attitude-Related Behavior," in *Nebraska Symposium on Motivation*, vol. 17, eds. William J. Arnold and David Levine (Lincoln: University of Nebraska Press, 1969), 179–235.

7. Leon Festinger, Stanley Schacter, and Kurt Back, *Social Pressures in Informal Groups: A Study of Human Factors in Housing* (New York: Harper & Bros., 1950); Wesley R. Burr, *Theory Construction and the Sociology of the Family* (New York: John Wiley & Sons, 1973); Alvin M. Katz and Reuben Hill, "Residential Propinquity and Marital Selection: A Review of Theory, Method, and Fact," *Marriage and Family Living* 20 (1958): 237–335.

8. Gordon W. Allport, *The Nature of Prejudice* (Reading, Mass.: Addison-Wesley, 1954); Yehuda Amir, "The Role of Intergroup Contact in Change of Prejudice and Ethnic Relations," in *Towards the Elimination of Racism*, ed. Phyllis A. Katz (New York: Pergamon, 1976), 245–308; Elizabeth G. Cohen, "The Effects of

Desegregation on Race Relations," *Law and Contemporary Problems* 39 (1975): 271–99.

9. The Survey, completed in 1988, was conducted by the Los Angeles County Commission on Human Relations and the Los Angeles County Office of Education. Of the 956 schools of all 1,570 public elementary and high schools in the county which responded, 37 percent reported a total of 2,256 incidents, among which racial slurs and name calling were the most prevalent, followed by physical violence and graffiti (Peter Schmidt, " 'Hate Crimes' Are Called 'Serious Problem' in L.A.," *Education Week*, November 15, 1989, 7).

10. William Damon, *The Chronicle of Higher Education*, May 3, 1989, B1.

11. According to the ADL Report, 122 such incidents occurred on 81 campuses in 1993 as compared with 114 at sixty campuses in 1992 (Anti-Defamation League, 1994). The Report also notes that speakers known for their anti-Semitic rhetoric, such as Khalid Abdul Muhammed and Louis Farrakhan, continue to be popular with black student unions around the country as well as some Black Studies faculty.

12. Cited in Juan Williams, "Integration Turns 40: The New Segregation," *Modern Maturity*, April-May 1994, 24–34. Williams, a Washington Post correspondent, is the author of *Eyes on the Prize: America's Civil Rights Years 1954–1965* (New York: Viking, 1987).

13. Ethel Simon-McWilliam, ed., *Resegregation of Public Schools: The Third Generation* (Portland, Ore.: Network of Regional Desegregation Assistance Centers and Northwest Regional Educational Laboratory, 1989); Percy Bates, "Desegregation: Can We Get There From Here?" *Phi Delta Kappan* (September 1990): 8–17.

14. Brunetta Reid Wolfman, President of Roxbury Community College in Massachusetts, interviewed by Robert M. Hass, "Spotlight on Alumni: An Advocate for Women and Minorities," *Educator* 4:3 (Fall 1990): 42–44, 43.

15. Simon-McWilliam; Percy Bates.

16. James E. Banks, "The Canon Debate, Knowledge Construction, and Multicultural Education," *Educational Researcher* 22:5 (June-July 1993): 4–14; Peter Erickson, "Multiculturalism and the Problem of Liberalism," *Reconstruction* 2:1 (1992): 97–101; Toni Morrison, *Playing in the Dark* (Cambridge and London: Harvard University Press, 1992); Catherine Cornbleth and Dexter Waugh, *The Great Speckled Bird: Multicultural Politics and Education Policymaking* (New York: St. Martin's Press, 1994).

17. Janet Ward Schofield, *Black and White in School: Trust, Tension or Tolerance?* (New York: Teachers College Press, 1989), 157.

18. Schofield, 165.

19. Schofield, 165.

20. Schofield, 166.

21. Schofield, 167.

22. Schofield, 159.

23. Simon-McWilliam describes three generations of desegration efforts: the first was aimed primarily at ending physical segregation; the second tries to address the inequalities within schools, and the third is attempting to create the achievement of equal learning opportunities and outcomes for all students. To accomplish the aims of the latter two, relationships between teachers and students and students with each other need to change significantly.

24. Whereas older definitions of culture, such as that of Clyde Kluckhohn (*Mirror*

for Man [New York: Whittlesey House, 1949]) included material components, contemporary anthropological definitions emphasize ideas. Robert LeVine defines it "as a shared organization of ideas that includes the intellectual, moral, and aesthetic standards prevalent in a community and the meanings of communicative actions" (Robert A. LeVine, "Properties of Culture: An Ethnographic View," in *Culture Theory: Essays on Mind, Self, and Emotion,* eds. Richard A. Schweder and Robert A. LeVine [New York: Cambridge University Press, 1984], 67–88, 67). Anthropologist Pat Wenger includes both ideas and behavior in his definition: "Culture," he says, is the "structured and idiomatic forms of behavior and thought that a person learns as a result of membership in society" (personal communication). As we use the term, we refer both to ideas and behavior in a society as a whole or within subgroups in the society that a person learns as a result of membership in that group. Because boundaries between culture are highly permeable, and people are usually members of several groups, the thoughts and behaviors of individuals are rarely the consequence of one type of cultural experience alone. Nonetheless, the term culture is useful as a way of describing patterned ideas and behaviors that emerge as a consequence of socialization within a particular group.

25. Roger Harrison, "Quality of Service: A New Frontier for Integrity in Organizations," in *Executive Integrity,* eds. Srivastva and Associates, 45–67, 64.

26. Raymonde Carroll, *Cultural Misunderstandings: The French-American Experience* (Chicago: The University of Chicago Press, 1987), 11.

27. Deborah Tannen, *You Just Don't Understand: Women and Men in Conversation* (New York: William Morrow, 1990), 26–27.

28. Tannen, 48.

29. While much of the evidence for this is based on studies of animals, J. Philippe Rushton claims that humans manifest the same tendency and presents as evidence the similarity between human spouses and friends with respect to such characteristics as race, socioeconomic status, ethnic background, and levels of education (J. Philippe Rushton, "Genetic Similarity, Human Altruism, and Group Selection," *Behavioral and Brain Sciences* 12 (1989): 503–553.

30. Vamik Volkan, *The Need to Have Enemies and Allies: From Clinical Practice to International Relations* (Northvale, N.J.: Jason Aronson, 1988).

31. Robert Coles, *The Moral Life of Children* (Boston: The Atlantic Monthly Press, 1986), 217–218.

32. Gordon W. Allport, *The Nature of Prejudice* (Reading, Mass.: Addison-Wesley, 1954), 172.

33. Steven A. Chin, "Minority Lawyers Quitting in Droves," *San Francisco Examiner,* September 30, 1990, A–7.

34. Fox Butterfield, "Arab-Americans Report Increase in Death Threats and Harassment," *The New York Times* National ed., August 8, 1990, IV, 24.

35. Patricia G. Devine, "Stereotypes and Prejudice: Their Automatic and Controlled Components," *Journal of Personality and Social Psychology* 56:1 (1989): 5–18.

36. Laura Mansnerus, "Worlds Apart: Schools Take Time Out for Lessons in Tolerance," *The New York Times: Education Life,* August 5, 1990, 28.

37. Louise Derman-Sparks and the ABC Task Force, *Anti-Bias Curriculum: Tools for Empowering Young Children* (Washington, D.C.: The National Association for the Education of Young Children, 1989).

38. Robert L. Crain, Rita E. Mahard, and Ruth E. Narot, *Making Desegregation Work: How Schools Create Social Climate* (Cambridge, Mass.: Ballinger, 1982): 247.

39. Patricia Nelson Limerick, "Some Advice to Liberals on Coping With Their Conservative Critics," *The Chronicle of Higher Education*, May 4, 1994, B1–B2, B2.

40. Barbara Ehrenreich, "You Lived Through the 80's and Forgot to Get Rich," review of *The Imperial Middle: Why Americans Can't Think Straight About Class*, by Benjamin De Mott, *The New York Times Book Review*, October 14, 1990, VII, 9.

41. A. M. Rosenthal, "On My Mind: Germany: Hidden Words," *The New York Times*, February 4, 1990, E, 23. Several Jewish feminists have accused feminists of a similar silence with respect to Jewish women. Evelyn Torton Beck, for example, notes that feminist texts rarely include writings *about* Jewish women, and that feminist multicultural events and discussions of minority women generally exclude Jewish women and their culture (Evelyn Torton Beck, "The Politics of Jewish Invisibility," *NWSA Journal* 1:1 [1988]: 93–102).

42. A. M. Rosenthal, "On My Mind: On Black Anti-Semitism," *The New York Times*, January 11, 1994, A, 21.

43. They included Harvard professors Louis Gates and Orlando Patterson, and Princeton professor Cornel West (ADL, *Report*, 1994).

44. James A. Banks, *Teaching Strategies for Ethnic Studies* (New York: Allyn & Bacon, 1987).

45. Michael Lerner, "Looking Forward to the Nineties," *Tikkun*, November/December 1989, 39–41.

46. Personal conversation, December 10, 1990.

47. David A. Wilder, "Predictions of Belief Homogeneity and Similarity Following Social Categorization," *British Journal of Social Psychology* 23 (1984): 323–333; George A. Quattrone, "On the Perception of a Group's Variability," in *Psychology of Intergroup Relations*, 2d ed., eds. Stephen Worchel and William G. Austin (Chicago: Nelson-Hall, 1986), 25–48.

48. Cited in Karen J. Winkler, "Scholars Say Issues of Diversity Have 'Revolutionalized' Field of Chicano Studies," *The Chronicle of Higher Education*, September 26, 1990, A-4+, A-4.

49. Winkler.

50. The Perkins Project with Industry is a federally financed project to expand job opportunities in New England for people with visual disabilities.

51. Julia Anderson, "How Technology Brings Blind People into the Workplace," *Harvard Business Review* (March-April 1989): 36–38, 36.

52. John W. Miller, "Birdmen of Harlem," *The New York Times Magazine*, November 19, 1989, 49+, 49.

53. Laura Mansnerus, "Worlds Apart: Schools Take Time Out for Lessons in Tolerance," *The New York Times: Education Life*, August 5, 1990, 4A, 28.

54. Gregory Bateson, "A Theory of Play and Fantasy," in *Steps To an Ecology of Mind* (New York: Ballantine Books, 1972), 177–193.

55. Letters exchanged between Susan Abbott and her mother Miriam, 1980, in *Between Ourselves: Letters Between Mothers and Daughters, 1950–1982*, ed. Karen Payne (Boston: Houghton Mifflin, 1983), 310–322, 320.

56. Liu Zongren, *Two Years in the Melting Pot* (San Francisco: China Books, 1984), 23, 24.

57. Paul Wilkes, "The Hands That Would Shape Our Souls," *The Atlantic* 266: 6, December 1990, 59–88, 88.

58. Srivastva and Cooperrider make this cogent observation in the introduction to their book on executive integrity (Suresh Srivastva and David L. Cooperrider, "Introduction: The Urgency for Executive Integrity," in *Executive Integrity*, eds. Srivastva and Associates, 1–28, 7).

59. Anna Quindlen, "The Nuns' Story," *The New York Times*, November 9, 1990, E23. Barbara Ferraro and Patricia Hussey have written a book about their experience called *No Turning Back: Two Nuns' Battle with the Vatican over Women's Right to Choose* (New York: Poseidon, 1990).

60. Henry B. Schacht and Charles W. Powers, "Business Responsibility and the Public Policy Process," in *Corporations and Their Critics: Issues and Answers to the Problems of Corporate Social Responsibility*, eds. Thornton Bradshaw and David Vogel (New York: McGraw-Hill, 1981), 23–32, 29, 30.

61. Julius Lester, *Lovesong: Becoming a Jew* (New York: Henry Holt, 1988), 240.

62. David Morse, "About Men: Gray Wolf's Choice," *The New York Times Magazine*, January 21, 1990, 12–13, 13.

63. The 1980 Census gave this as an approximation. What is clear is that the numbers are increasing.

64. Cited in Sonja Rothkop, "Mixed Heritage Jews Share Stories About their 'Double Lives'," *Jewish Bulletin*, April 1, 1994, 27+.

65. For an elaboration of this idea, see Ervin Staub's discussion of embedded, relational, and disconnected selves (Ervin Staub, "Individual and Group Selves, Motivation and Morality," in *Morality and the Self*, eds. W. Edelstein and T. Wren (Boston: The MIT Press, in press).

CHAPTER 7

Networking

Sitting nervously in the public health clinic that Friday before Labor Day in 1986, awaiting word on his AIDS test, Pacific Bell repairman Dave Goodenough already half knew what he would be told: he had AIDS. He'd suspected as much for seven months, ever since he first noticed the markings on his chest. His doctor dismissed them as bruises picked up at work, but when the purplish markings started showing up all over his body, Goodenough sought another opinion. It had taken the second doctor only moments to identify the symptoms as "KS"—Kaposi's sarcoma, a type of cancer frequently associated with AIDS—and the test results confirmed that diagnosis.

Suspicions of AIDS are one thing, certainty something very different. "I was wiped out," Goodenough recalls. As he began to sort out the implications of the news, one question kept recurring: Would he—could he—go back to work?

To Goodenough, confirmation of AIDS only reinforced how important it was to him to stay on the job. "If I left the job," he recalls thinking, "it would be like putting a limit on the amount of time I have to live."[1]

Fortunately for Goodenough, his disease was diagnosed in 1986, by which time Pacific Bell's policy on AIDS was in the midst of radical revision. Hence, he was able to keep his job. Had the year been 1973, when company policy precluded employing "manifest homosexuals," or even the early eighties, when some empathic employees had begun to challenge the company's traditional hostile stance toward the gay community, the story would likely have had a very different resolution. By 1988, the company had not only pioneered innovative medical insurance for employees with AIDS and new forms of treatment, but had also organized support groups and an extensive AIDS education program within the company and outside it. Pacific's efforts eventually earned it a presidential citation and an image as a model of an enlightened company.

Yet given its conservative past, a company which had traditionally confined its community activities to organizations like the Rotary Club, few could have predicted this alliance with the gay community. Pacific Bell's story, as told by public policy professor David Kirp, tells us much about the process of networking.[2]

Networking, as we define it, means the deliberate search for new social linkages for the purpose of expanding resources in developing and implementing common goals. Like diversifying, networking implies crossing social and cultural boundaries. Unlike diversifying, whose purpose is merely to understand others, networking implies pooling resources and services in pursuit of a common agenda. While the motivation is usually self-interest, a sense of care is often the consequence.

We focus here on specific conditions that promote successful networking—not only certain procedures and principles, but also a new way of thinking about problem solving. We conclude by comparing the process of networking in the business context, where its potential is being increasingly realized, with local communities marked by fragmentation. The Pacific Bell story, with which we begin, illustrates some of the conditions and procedures necessary for successful networking.

Pacific Bell began its formal association with the gay community under duress. Early policy at the company had prohibited hiring gays and the policy was rescinded only after an employee successfully challenged it in a suit which reached the California Supreme Court. The Court ruled that the state's human rights law prohibited public utilities from refusing to hire gays, and Pacific Bell wound up paying $3 million dollars as part of a negotiated settlement reached in December 1986.

When the idea of making Pacific Bell a leader in AIDS education and medical treatment began to surface as a serious undertaking, many corporate executives viewed the company's zeal as dangerous and excessive. As they saw it, linking the company with AIDS in the public mind threatened it with a risky image; one which suggested drugs, contagion, and homosexuality. Such an image, they argued, could potentially alienate customers and creditors and inhibit hiring qualified employees.

Why then did Pacific eventually support it? Without economic motives, says Kirp, Pacific would not likely have embarked on such a potentially hazardous course of action.

After the AT&T breakup in 1984, Pacific found itself in a fiercely competitive telecommunications market. A record of consistent poor earnings and an ongoing feud with the California Public Utilities were among the reasons *The New York Times* called it one of most risky investments of all the Bell regional holding companies. Regaining the competitive edge, claimed some of Bell's analysts, required among other things overcoming its backward image by demonstrating responsiveness to its new political constituencies. As Kirp explains:

A big part of becoming competitive was learning about the state's shifting political environment, and that meant becoming more socially conscious . . . in the 1980's, California's shifting coalitions of interest groups—blacks, Hispanics, consumer-oriented organizations—increasingly wielded political power. Pacific had long treated these groups as if they were the enemy. Now, however, these same groups were major purchasers of telecommunications services, and they had the ear of the most aggressive state Public Utilities Commission in the country. For the phone company to prosper on its own, it somehow had to co-opt these groups—to reach a mutually workable level of understanding and accommodation.[3]

To help co-opt these interest groups, Pacific hired Steve Coulter as director of consumer affairs. Since minority hiring and multilingual services were among the primary concerns for minorities, Coulter began negotiations with the NAACP and HACER (a consortium of some of California's major Hispanic groups organized by Pacific). When the AIDS issue surfaced, Coulter was among the first to see its possibilities as a vehicle for cementing relations with these groups. Had he not persuaded the company of its political astuteness, they would undoubtedly have chosen a safer social issue.

Both Pacific Bell and AIDS victims benefited from this strange alliance. The company achieved the new image it needed, and involvement in AIDS also turned out to be a sound business practice; one which kept Pacific's employees working without increasing medical insurance costs beyond those normally associated with employee health issues and also changed its relationship to powerful elements in the community and the Public Utilities Commission.

But as AIDS was a vehicle for Pacific Bell to achieve its interests, the company was a vehicle for AIDS victims to promote theirs. It meant the protection of jobs and the assurance of a plan for medical coverage and treatment—one that would become a model for other companies to follow—as well as the promotion of a social climate in which fellow employees and individuals outside the company might accept them without undue fears of contagion and negative moral judgment.

As the Pacific case demonstrates, networking begins with the recognition of a problem which can best be solved by working with others. If groups were self-sufficient, that is, if they could depend on their own resources alone to satisfy their goals, they would have little motivation to network with others. The primary motivation for networking is thus enlightened self-interest, which makes it appear as remote from care as any other type of market exchange based on utilitarian transactions. Yet because pooling resources empowers each group to achieve its goals and the welfare of each group depends on satisfying the other's as well, a sense of care often accompanies successful networking.

But as the Pacific case also demonstrates, need alone cannot ensure successful networking. It also requires some networking skills, one of which is knowing with whom to work.

Each group that participated in Pacific's program had a stake in it. An essential component of successful networking is to identify the "stakeholders" and to choose those with whom one might develop a common agenda.

Who exactly are "stakeholders"? Stakeholders are commonly defined as all those people who are affected by or can affect an organization's objectives.[4] Potentially, this might include anyone from the local to the international arena. Igor Ansoff, who pioneered both the concept and theory, makes the concept more useful by distinguishing between primary and secondary stakeholders.[5]

Groups that have a direct and necessary impact on an organization, affecting its core activities, Ansoff calls primary stakeholders. In Pacific Bell's case, as in any business context, primary stakeholders included owners, employees, suppliers, and customers. In the educational context, primary stakeholders include teachers, students, administrators, and state governments. In a family, they might include all the adults and children who share legal responsibilities for one another and/or strong enduring emotional ties.

Since no group could function without them, primary stakeholders should be an organization's first order of concern. Yet at Pacific, they showed little initial enthusiasm for the AIDS program. Corporate executives had to be convinced of its economic merit before supporting it. And employees generally feared contagion from afflicted coworkers besides believing AIDS to be a minor health concern (compared with heart disease and cancer for example). Yet as they began to witness more friends die and mourned with their families, many became persuaded of its moral merit. By the time the AIDS program was fully launched, compassion had overcome anxieties, and involved primary stakeholders included field workers, supervisors, nurses, mid-level management personnel, lawyers, and corporate safety staffers. They attended conferences, organized volunteers, served as advisers, and initiated and participated in educational and support group activities. Management contributed money to the program and also provided released time and other resources for employees to carry on these diverse activities.

But without the support of external stakeholders, Pacific could not have carried the program on its own. Groups that are external to the organization and not directly involved in its core activities, but nonetheless can affect it or are affected by it, Ansoff calls secondary stakeholders.

Secondary stakeholders are far more numerous than primary ones; they also vary depending on the political and local context. In business, they may

include financial institutions, government, local communities, assorted political groups (e.g., environmental and consumer), competitors, educational
institutions, and families of employees. Business, on the other hand, is a
secondary stakeholder for schools, as would be parents, religious groups,
community agencies, and political groups. Analogously, schools and business are secondary stakeholders in relation to families, as would also be
government, public agencies, and so on.

Choosing which external stakeholders to concentrate on depends on the
group's goals. Above all, Pacific Bell wanted to improve its economic picture; achieving it meant making new alliances with minority groups. Pacific
also had some secondary goals. It needed to provide continuing medical
coverage for its AIDS employees while keeping its costs tolerable; achieving
this required working with insurance groups and the medical community.
And the company wanted to satisfy its customers, some of whom objected
to AIDS employees servicing them in the field because of their fears of
possible contagion. This meant an educational campaign in which the expertise of the San Francisco AIDS Foundation became vital. External
stakeholders who wound up participating in Pacific's program eventually
included all the above in addition to mid- and high-level representation from
other corporations, equally concerned about the growing numbers of employees with AIDS. Union representatives and community volunteers eager
to do something about a problem that was afflicting increasing numbers of
people also became involved.

Why not call these groups "affected" or "influential parties" rather than
stakeholders? As business theorist R. Freeman suggests, "words make a difference in how we see the world" and the word "stakeholder" connotes an
appropriate and rightful interest. Business employees, teachers, or children
who are expected to do what they're told and not ask questions are being
treated as though they have no justifiable right to know more than their
superiors determine. Similarly, community groups whose inquiries and requests are ignored also receive the message that they have no rightful claims.
What Freeman says about the consequences of such behavior to businesses
applies as well to schools, families, or community institutions:

"Stakeholder" connotes "legitimacy," and while managers may not think that certain
groups are "legitimate" in the sense that their demands on the firm are inappropriate,
they had better give "legitimacy" to these groups in terms of their ability to affect
the direction of the firm. Hence, "legitimacy" can be understood in a managerial
sense implying that it is "legitimate to spend time and resources" on stakeholders,
regardless of the appropriateness of their demands.[6]

Had Pacific Bell not recognized employees with AIDS as having rightful
demands on them for medical coverage, or had they decided to ignore the
demands of minority groups, the fate of the company would have been

jeopardized even though their immediate costs might have been reduced. Had they not recognized that other companies and the San Francisco community (which included a large number of gay people) had a legitimate interest in their policies, they would have been deprived of valuable support they needed to protect their long term interests. While this may seem obvious in the aftermath of a successful networking effort, it is not the way organizations have traditionally looked at either "insider" or "outsider" groups.

But stakeholders, whether primary or secondary, rarely share identical primary goals. Networking requires that they find common goals, goals sufficiently important to each to rally their collective energies.

Successful networking requires developing a common agenda among groups whose primary goals are likely to vary considerably. Minority groups and the Public Utilities Commission, for example, had little interest in Pacific's finances or well-being. Working with them demanded identifying some important goal all could share and from which each could derive benefit, and the AIDS issue provided it. Successful networking depends on finding a superordinate goal which all stakeholders can willingly accept.

A common goal brings groups together, helping them cooperate even if their previous contacts have been competitive or even belligerent. As psychologists Muzafer and Carolyn Sherif proposed more than thirty years ago, competition encourages hostility, negative stereotyping, social distancing, firm boundaries between "us" and "them," and an inflated evaluation of "us." Conversely, cooperation for the sake of some superordinate goal promotes mutual trust, diminishing stereotypic thinking and "us/them" boundaries. What really happens is that each group, which formerly excluded the other, becomes part of a new "us."[7]

Journalist Randy Diamond reports a story about Gerard Papa which demonstrates how a superordinate goal can overcome even a hostile environment. Papa coached a basketball team in Bensonhurst. Team players were predominantly Italian, as were Bensonhurst residents themselves. When Papa invited some black boys from the nearby Marboro City Housing project to join the team, he had nothing but winning in mind. Bensonhurst residents, however, didn't like it at all:

"I just wanted to win some basketball games," said Papa. "I knew there were some good basketball players in the projects."

Other people had other ideas.

Black students walking a block and a half from the Marboro projects to a local church's gym were attacked by mobs of white teenagers.

The tires of Papa's Lincoln were slashed, his mother's house was pelted with eggs and Papa was bluntly reminded by more than one white Bensonhurst resident that it would be hard to coach basketball from a hospital bed.

"It was World War III," Papa admitted.[8]

But the boys on the team also wanted to win and got along right from the start. When their team won the Catholic Youth Organization's league championship in 1978, they got along even better. As Papa explained to Diamond: "Basketball is a great unifier . . . To win a game, you have to learn to get along with your teammates. The kids learn teamwork."

Working as a team in order to win accomplished many of the things the Sherifs proposed. As twenty-year-old black Flames player Ron Williams explained to Diamond, both whites and blacks began with shared stereotypes about each other. The white players felt the blacks were "all muggers on welfare," while the black players felt that the "whites had it easy" and that their families had given them everything: cars, a house, even jobs. Both Ron and Papa agree that stereotypes were significantly reduced among team players. And as several observers noted, racial tensions subsided among their parents and the community as a whole. The experience was successful enough to warrant an expanded program, in which three hundred youths ranging in age from eight to twenty, from Bensonhurst and nearby Coney Island, now participate in thirty interracial Flames teams. What began as nothing more than a wish to have a winning team thus wound up with many "winners."

A shared superordinate goal helps explain similar success for an increasingly popular teaching strategy called cooperative learning.

Traditional teaching favors competition; each student vies with others for the best grades only a few will achieve. Cooperative learning shifts the focus from the individual to the group, and success depends on collectively completing the task the group has been assigned. To make sure that the effort is really cooperative and that students learn to work with others rather than compete with them, each individual group member must contribute to the whole. Additionally, groups must be heterogeneous; that is, deliberately chosen so as to vary in terms of ability, ethnicity, gender, and so on. More than five hundred studies have been reported about the effects of cooperative learning, leading researchers to conclude it has both cognitive and affective benefits.[9] Students learn more, become more friendly and kind toward each other, and feel better about themselves and their classmates.[10]

Successful networking depends on yet another task; stakeholders need to be linked together. This task usually requires what is sometimes called "boundary spanners." In fact, boundary spanners not only link groups together, but also help identify and work with stakeholders to develop a common goal.

Gerard Papa played the boundary-spanner role for the interracial Flames team. He was the person who identified which groups could help the team win and then recruited them. But his was a simple task compared with that of Steve Coulter and Michael Eriksen, who played the same roles at Pacific Bell. Hired as director of consumer affairs, Coulter and preventative medicine and health education director Erikesen deserve the credit for envisioning the AIDS program and creating the network that made it possible.

Boundaries mark the perimeters that separate one group or place from another; spanners bridge the boundaries, connecting bounded groups. Boundary spanners serve their groups or organizations; yet with a foot in several other groups, they operate as it were at its borders. They gather information and interact with primary and secondary stakeholders, interpreting each group's interests and behaviors to the other. Business professor Donna J. Wood captures the subtleties of their role in the following passage:

Like the double-faced Roman Janus, boundary spanners look both ways—inside and out. They are watchful for signs of change, conflict, emerging needs, and incongruities. They are skilled in identifying and responding to emergent threats and barely visible opportunities. They are the information and action link between the company and its environment.[11]

Wood claims no business could function without boundary spanners; the same may be said of any social institution or group, whether family or school, welfare agency or church. But people who perform this role rarely bear the title "boundary spanner." Management and public relations personnel typically carry it in business, but numerous others may perform it unofficially. An adult usually bears it in families, but school-age children sometimes play this role too.

The more difficult a task is, the greater the need for skilled boundary spanners. A dramatic example of skilled unofficial boundary spanning is offered by several of the rescuers we studied. Without such skills, they would never have been able to succeed.

One Polish rescuer, for example, estimates that saving a single Jew required the support of at least ten people. As the following story suggests, linking them together required taking advantage of what Wood might describe as barely visible opportunities. As the only link between a doomed Jewish child and any person or group who might have a stake in her survival, this rescuer, like Wood's "double-faced Roman Janus," was constantly looking inside and out, ever watchful and responsive to emergent threats and opportunities.

It started with news brought by E. C., with whom we worked in the Relief Committee. E. C. reported . . . [that] help was immediately needed for an eleven-year-old girl, Anna. By some miracle she had been smuggled out of the house while the Gestapo was already there . . . It was imperative that we take the child away and find a safe place for her, get her an "authentic" birth certificate, and so on. I immediately called our reliable friend, S. K. Together we went to Father M., who was the priest in Saint Norbert convent. I knew him from our common illegal work—sending packages to camps—in which I participated as a representative of the Democratic Party. Father M. started examining the parish registers of those born eleven years ago, and—

incredible luck—he came up with just the right person. I'll never forget the moment—he slapped his thighs with glee. He had found the name of a maid who had given birth to an illegitimate child eleven years ago and had subsequently died. She thus became the mother of our child.

Anna's father wanted her to be converted to Catholicism. I don't know whether he wanted this out of conviction or just to save her. I wanted it because as a Roman Catholic she would be entitled to live. So together with S. K., we went to the bishop's place with a letter of recommendation. I found the priest, and while speaking with him, I noticed his lips were trembling. With the cruelty of which only the very young are capable, I said to him: "Father, you must be scared stiff. How can you do missionary work? Do you imagine that you are in some remote place where cannibals are waiting to put their teeth into you?" What a bitch I was! He agreed to perform the ceremony.

Then we had to send the child out of Cracow to some other place. Dr. S. helped— he signed the document certifying that someone was to accompany her to the Kostow orphanage. And Mr. B., who worked for the Warsaw Relief Committee Branch and was in constant touch with Cracow Headquarters, accompanied her. She was taken to a school run by nuns at Kostowiec.[12]

Less dramatic but impressively consequential were the unofficial boundary spanner roles played by a school principal, a pediatrician, and two obstetricians in an incident related by Lisbeth Schorr. They wound up spearheading school programs that significantly reduced adolescent pregnancy and school absenteeism. Like rescuers, they knew how to take advantage of barely visible opportunities, becoming the information and action link between groups. But they had no idea of this in the beginning.[13]

Their story begins at St. Paul's Mechanics Arts High School in the early seventies. An inner city school, with a 40 percent minority enrollment, it claimed the highest absenteeism and fertility rate among fifteen- to seventeen-year-olds in the city, and double the average dropout rate.

But these matters were not on the principal's mind when he called the public hospital, St. Paul-Ramsey, located two blocks away. What he wanted to know was whether the hospital could provide day care services on the school grounds for teachers and students.

In response, the chief of pediatrics, Dr. Homer Venters, consulted with the chief of obstetrics, Dr. Erick Hakanson. Hakanson, already frustrated by the hospital's teenage family clinic in which adolescents appeared in their ninth month of pregnancy only to return pregnant again nine months later, consulted with Dr. Laura Edwards. Edwards, an obstetrician whom Hakanson had appointed two years earlier to head the hospital's federally funded maternal and infant care project, was appalled at the high rate of teen pregnancy in St. Paul.

The three quickly agreed that transferring the clinic to the high school might be the way to overcome their sense of futility. Hence, when they called the principal back to say yes, they made it conditional; in return, he would help them develop a center at the high school that would combine day care with health care, birth control information, and services for pregnant girls.

Opinions about the proposed center were hardly unanimous. For the next two years, teachers, parents, school board members, and religious groups debated its merits. Some feared the center would give the school a bad reputation; prenatal care for pregnant students and information about contraception might suggest endorsement of teenage sex. Others feared that the clinic would divert resources from the classroom. Students worried that parents would be notified about birth control counseling, and parents worried that they would not be. Finally, in February 1973, the school board voted to give the clinic a one-year tryout, with the condition that contraceptives would not be dispensed in the school but would be available at the hospital two blocks away.

The program was so successful—absenteeism and fertility rates at the school decreased dramatically—that even though Mechanics Arts High was torn down a few years later, clinic centers were established in four of St. Paul's six high schools. Childbearing has decreased by more than half in these high schools and nine out of ten students who have babies now graduate. The cycle which threatens these adolescent's children also shows promise of being reversed. Pregnant students receive prenatal care while still in school, learn parenting skills, and work with children in the day care center.

What made it all possible, however, was happenstance; the chance presence of several caring professionals who were flexible, willing to try ideas and accept responsibilities outside their traditional domains. Had the school principal not entertained the idea that child services might be an appropriate school service for both staff and students; had he not happened to think of the nearby hospital as a possibly interested party; or had he resisted calling, clinic and school would never have networked. Had the doctors he reached not been equally flexible and concerned enough to see their project through, or had they not involved all the constituencies that had investments in the outcome, the school clinic would not have materialized.

Is successful boundary spanning then dependent on particularly gifted individuals who happen to be at the right place at the right time? Or can boundary-spanning skills be taught? We believe they can and should be taught as a routine approach to problem solving.

Competent boundary spanners approach problems holistically rather than fragmentedly. They begin by identifying stakeholders but go on to consider the interrelations among stakeholders. Solving the problem often requires changing those relationships.

Edith M. Freeman and Marianne Pennekamp call this approach "ecological thinking," and they teach social workers to solve problems in just this way. To illustrate how holistic thinking differs from conventional thinking and how it can actually resolve problems, consider the case of Ms. Lucas and her social worker, Susan, as Freeman and Pennekamp tell it.[14]

Ms. Lucas came to the attention of Child Protective Services when a neighbor called to complain that her three young children, ages three to eight, were frequently left alone. Once more left without adult supervision this past Saturday, said the neighbor, three-year-old Jimmy cried hysterically after falling down the steps and biting his tongue, and eight-year-old Anita, unable to cope with the situation, became similarly distressed.

How would a social worker receiving the complaint normally respond? According to Pennekamp, she would have called Ms. Lucas and reported the neighbor's complaint. Ms. Lucas would then most probably have explained that she had to work that Saturday, and because her aunt who usually supervised the children was unavailable, she had to leave them alone. The social worker would then most likely have reminded her that the law demanded that children be supervised at all times and that another complaint would require further investigation. And she probably would have concluded with a veiled threat—something to the effect that she just hoped the department would not be forced to take action.[15]

Ms. Lucas's assigned social worker, Susan, took another approach, one which we call "holistic" and what Freeman and Pennekamp call "doing social work in an ecological context." Rather than depending on a phone call, Susan arranged to visit Ms. Lucas at home. What she learned is worth telling in some detail because it illustrates how complex problems can be, even when ostensibly simple, and how solving them requires addressing their complexity.

Twenty-seven years old and a single parent, Ms. Lucas worked as a relief telephone operator three six-hour days a week to supplement her AFDC funds (Aid to Families with Dependent Children) and occasional child support from her ex-husband. Unable to pay for child care, she was dependent on family and friends during work hours; when the latter were unavailable, she left the boys in eight-year-old Anita's charge. John, the five-year-old, was difficult to manage at home and at school; his teacher complained frequently. Jim, the three-year-old, got upset every time he went to the child care center and was frequently sick. Unable to afford taking time off from work, Ms. Lucas had not responded to their teachers' requests for a meeting.

Anita, on the other hand, was a fine student; the school had informed Ms. Lucas that she was eligible to enroll in a special program for talented youngsters. Anita's gifts only posed another problem for Ms. Lucas:

It makes me feel good to know that she is such a good student, but it makes it hard for me when she would as soon keep her nose in her homework or a book when I need her to help with the dishes and to watch the kids. To tell the truth, if Anita were in this talented program, there might be trouble if I keep her home to babysit when Jimmy is sick and can't go to Child Care. Now, the teachers don't seem to pay much attention when she misses school, but if she were in a special program, they might get mad at me for keeping her home. I know it is wrong to use Anita as a babysitter, but what else can I do? I only get paid when I work. I have no benefits and no sick leave since I work less than half time. Nobody seems to understand!

If it weren't for Anita, sometimes I wonder how I would make it. Then I worry about her, too. She is missing out on her childhood and lately, she is getting awfully quiet.[16]

At first glance, all Ms. Lucas needed to solve her problems was to find child care while she was at work. Yet child care alone would not have resolved Ms. Lucas's sense of isolation and despair or her children's school problems. The real issue was to find a way to break the cycle so that Ms. Lucas could begin to help herself and her children.

What did Susan do? She began by diagramming what Freeman and Pennekamp call an "ecomap": a chart of the varied people and programs with whom Ms. Lucas and her children had some relationships. All told, these included some twenty stakeholders. Helping Ms. Lucas to help herself and her children, concluded Susan, depended on remedying the stressful relationships, calling on the positive ones to help her do so if possible and linking her with new sources who might be of help.

Ms. Lucas and Susan worked out a cooperative plan of action. Ms. Lucas would invite her aunt and a friendly neighbor—potential sources of help—to meet with Susan the following week. Susan would visit the children's schools to find out concerns and potential resources, and Ms. Lucas would follow up later. Susan would also try to find child care alternatives for John with the local Child Care Council (a child care coordinating agency) and some adult support for Ms. Lucas herself.

At the next week's meeting, the aunt offered to coordinate her calendar so as to better meet Ms. Lucas' baby-sitting needs and volunteered to recruit another family member to help. The friendly neighbor offered to play the role of "peacemaker" with the complaining neighbor who had called the Child Protective Services. As a consequence of Susan's visit to the school, the school social worker (Evelyn) began to intervene directly with the children's teachers, encouraging Anita's teachers to pay particular attention to her progress and helping John's teacher assume more of the responsibility for managing him while demanding less of his mother. Eventually, too, Evelyn became the person who found a neighborhood day care program. As for Ms. Lucas herself, Susan helped her locate an already formed adult group: people in situations similar to her own who could provide help and counsel and become a source of new friendships.

In short, what had begun as a "no exit" scenario began to have promise. Had Susan not understood the relationships among the stakeholders who impinged on the Lucas's family life, nor intervened to change some of them, that promise would not have emerged. Instead, frustrations among all would likely have increased, each one perceiving the other as uncaring and blame-worthy. Pressures on both mother and children would have mounted, Ms. Lucas would have continued feeling impotent to solve them, and before long the situation would have been labeled hopeless and chronic.

Susan, who played the boundary spanner in the above scenario, learned to think holistically as a consequence of her training. Donna Wood proposes detailed procedures whereby business managers can do the same.[17] If professionals, as well as others, learn to approach problems in this way, they may well find what Ms. Lucas did: impotence might yield to agency and insoluble problems might become surmountable, even if not completely resolvable.

Just as it requires a different way of thinking, successful networking also depends on a different way of relating, one which is implied in several of the above scenarios as well as the concept of "stakeholder" itself. Participants in a successful network become partners rather than members of a hierarchy.

The prestigious MIT Commission on Industrial Productivity highlighted this point after studying more than two hundred U.S., European, and Japanese companies in eight major sectors of the economy. The Commission, chaired by economist Michael Dertouzos, included social scientists, economists, business management theoreticians, biologists, as well as nuclear, aeronautic, and electrical engineers. The failing American economy, they concluded, was largely due to a pervasive faulty organizational and managerial model, one which emphasized hierarchy, compartmentalization, and adversarial and litigatious relationships both internally and externally. To regain its productive edge, businesses needed to incorporate the practices of the best performance companies. What were these practices? The best performance companies, they said, were distinguished by integrated linkages and cooperative partnerships with both internal and external stakeholders. According to the MIT Commission, companies need to relate to both primary and secondary stakeholders as partners.[18]

What does partnership imply? For one thing, it implies *joint planning*. For business, this means joint planning at the strategic, professional, and production levels as Rosabeth Kanter observes.[19] Fernando Bartolomé, professor of management at Bentley College, describes how joint planning helped a small South American conglomerate overcome both some bad feelings and low productivity. For years, the conglomerate's founder and CEO treated each of the six divisions within it as independent groups, making secret deals with each of the vice-presidents and keeping others in the dark about his arrangements. The strategy worked reasonably well until the company grew:

But now times were tougher, the company was bigger, and he began getting complaints from his VPs about resource allocation. None of them was satisfied with his own division's share, but none was in a position to consider the needs of the company as a whole.

At this point, the CEO recognized that his way of managing was part of the problem, did an abrupt about-face, and created an executive committee comprising himself and his six VPs. They all took part in setting priorities, allocating resources, and planning company strategy. Conflicts remained, of course, as each vice president fought for resources for his division. But trust increased substantially, and for the first time there was communication between divisions and a willingness and opportunity for the company's leadership to work together as a team.[20]

Partnership also implies *sharing information* rather than hoarding it. Competitors hoard information to protect themselves and preserve their power. Sharing information can help groups to focus on superordinate goals, and feel better about each other.

Sharing information within the company may be a good idea, say some corporation executives, but they argue that doing so with outsiders can be detrimental to the company's interests. According to some business executives, however, sharing information with external stakeholders, including the public at large, is equally important.

While laws require companies to share some information with the public, A. W. Clausen, president and chief executive officer of BankAmerica Corporation, believes this is not enough. He advocates "voluntary disclosure," a policy which BankAmerica Corporation has adopted. Voluntary disclosure means telling various external constituencies more than the law requires and doing so in an anticipatory mode, in advance of external pressures. It has reciprocal benefits, says Clausen, serving both the public and the company's interests. Affected as it is by company activities, the public has a right to know. The company, in turn, benefits by creating a more trusting relationship with its constituencies, one consequence of which can be early knowledge about problems it can address internally before they become severe.[21]

Partnership also implies *acting as though relationships will be long-term rather than temporary*. When people expect their relationships with stakeholders to be long-term, they treat them differently. The difference is suggested by this Digital manager describing how his company's relationships with suppliers have changed:

We have suppliers who deal with fifty different sites. In the past, Phoenix would call and say, "Hey, we want to give you more business—thank you," and then the Boston plant would call and say, "The quality of this last shipment stunk, get your acts straight." Now we meet quarterly with our major suppliers and say, "Here's what the report card says and this is how you have done for Digital. Let's talk about why you haven't done well in these areas." In many respects, it is a two-way street now. We may say, "The quality on 50 percent of your lots is 80 percent and we want 100 percent. What is going on?" Whee, they may say, "Wait a minute, Digital, how you spec the piece parts is not clear. We interpret that 20 percent as per your spec." We are both working together toward an ultimate goal of saving money.[22]

In other words, when Digital's relationships were conventionally hierarchial, managers would simply have told suppliers what they wanted and expected them to conform. If they failed, the company would have terminated the relationship and sought other suppliers. Instead, they now presumed that they would have a continuing relationship with their suppliers, working with them to solve supply problems. Suppliers had become partners who shared a common goal.

Reciprocity is the cornerstone of the partnership concept, alluded to by the Digital manager when he says "in many respects, it is a two-way street now." Often used synonymously with the term "exchange," reciprocity simply means the return by one person or group for a service done by another.[23]

Rather than being less desirable than altruism, where one side performs a service for another without return, some psychologists believe reciprocity may be the optimal human relationship; one which is best suited to promote enduring positive feelings.[24] Receiving more than one returns incurs a sense of indebtness. Instead of feeling appreciative, recipients may feel guilty or resentful, choosing to avoid their benefactors whose very presence reminds them of their debt.[25] Reciprocal benefactors, on the other hand, view each other as equals; equally worthy and competent, equally dependent and needy. This may help explain why people generally prefer reciprocal relations to asymmetrical ones in the long run. Even the most needy are no exception: disabled people, for example, regardless of age, sex, social, or economic class, prefer to maintain reciprocal relationships rather than those which cater to them.[26] Like others, they prefer relationships which confirm their self-worth and sense of competence to those which emphasize their dependence and inadequacies. The norm of reciprocity is so powerful in human interactions, wrote Alvin Gouldner more than thirty years ago, that both intimates and strangers prefer and expect it.[27]

Networking depends on reciprocity, a matter of particular importance when boundary crossings involve groups who have traditionally related to each other as unequals. Reciprocity helps explain the success of the Urban Outward Bound program, for example, which routinely brings diverse ability, age, and ethnic groups together. One such group brought together for the first time five white adult women and men, and seven black inner-city youth between the ages of fourteen and seventeen. Reporter Tom Seligson describes how it worked and what the effects were.

Each adult was paired off with one or more of the boys and the entire group spent a weekend together: hiking through Wall Street, camping out in New York City, spending time with homeless men, climbing rock cliffs in a city park, and crossing a rope bridge one hundred feet in the air. The underlying assumption of the program was that positive feelings depended on creating a sense of mutual dependence in overcoming obstacles new to all the participants.

The rope bridge crossing in particular made interdependence essential for mutual survival. Participant Tom Seligson described what happened to him and his teenage partner, Byron, as follows:

We were asked to cross an 80-foot rope suspended between the masts of the *Peking*, a 1911 German bark moored at the South Street Seaport. Earlier, we had been taught the basics of balancing on a rope. We also had been told that, with our elaborate harnesses, it was impossible to fall. However, we *could* slip. And since we were tied to our partner, one's misstep was also the other's.

I watched as other adult/teenager teams lost their balance, then struggled to right themselves, some eventually returning to the mast in defeat. Their obvious difficulty made me even more apprehensive about going up.

"Do I really have to do this?" I asked.

"Don't worry about it," Byron said. "We'll do it together."

Which is exactly what we did. Using a system whereby one steadied the rope while the other inched forward, we started across. Eyes locked, we gently guided each other's steps. It required the ultimate teamwork, and when we finally made it across after what seemed like hours, we'd achieved so much mutual dependence that when an instructor told us how to get down from the mast, we were both reluctant to obey her. We trusted only each other.[28]

For Calvin, one of the young people, the consequence was increased self-confidence. As he explained afterward, he was "real scared" when climbing the rocks, but felt so proud of himself when he completed it, that he was ready to take on "a bigger mountain." For Byron, Tom's youthful partner, it was a changed perception of white adults: what he had learned, he said, was that they could be interested in him. And for Robin, a suburban mother of four, it was a changed perception of urban youth generally. Whereas they had previously frightened her, they now seemed more "familiar" and she was "definitely more relaxed" around them.

What these adults and young people exchanged was not only mutual services but status: a sense that each had something vital to contribute to the other which in effect mitigated or obliterated previous advantages or liabilities. Relationships and productivity at school and the workplace, including desegregated ones, would likely be considerably enhanced if they were designed to include just such reciprocal exchanges.

Are we becoming more of a networking society united by common interests? Or are we becoming an increasingly fragmented society, torn apart by diverse and competing claims? Optimists say that we are rapidly becoming a networking nation, joining with disparate groups in pursuit of shared goals. Pessimists claim that we are increasingly becoming a segmented and alienated society, evidenced in higher rates of crime, drug usage, and child abuse. Both are right: the realities differ depending on the level and locale in which one lives.

One such optimist, William E. Halil, claims that information technology, which makes ever broadening and interlocking linkages possible, lies at the heart of what he calls a "second American Revolution." More than any other, the economic sector is spearheading it, not out of altruism, but rather out of concern for survival.[29]

Two themes characterize this second Revolution, says Halil: democratic principles and avoidance of capitalistic exploitation. Accompanying it is a whole new conception of what capitalism is all about, about economic survival and the role of corporate executives in relation to society.

Business survival requires accommodating to new values and a more complex environment. In place of materialism, diverse groups—environmentalists, women, varied ethnic groups, the aged—are demanding services that improve the *quality* of life, such as better health, more effective education, better human relationships, and more meaningful work. Satisfying these demands requires a holistic view, one which recognizes business linkages to other societal institutions, all of which in turn are intermeshed with each other.

This intermeshing pattern of interorganizational networks already exists, says Halil, making it difficult to tell where one organization begins and another stops, and information systems will expand them:

There are estimated to be some 1.3 million corporations in the United States today, 90,000 schools and universities, 330,000 churches, and myriad other miscellaneous institutions, all interacting with one another to weave a rich tapestry of social structure. Some of these links were always in place, of course, but now they are expanding as information systems increasingly connect organizations into working relationships that constitute the organic structure of the economy and society itself.[30]

To take advantage of these linkages, businesses need to become "open systems" rather than bounded ones; that is, organizations ready to become partners with rather than adversaries of other groups. In that context, says Halil, the powerful autocratic corporation executive determining the best means to make a profit has no place. Open systems businesses require instead executives who will evolve into "economic statesmen," integrating disparate interests into a larger economic community via a type of "social contract" whose goal is "social wealth" as much as financial wealth. All that is required, he says, to make this vision a reality, is to encourage all people—customers, citizens, politicians, and investors—to pursue their enlightened self-interests.

While not everyone shares Halil's optimistic view of the benevolent effects of these increasingly intermeshed institutional coalitions,[31] he is not alone. Even as businesses are contributing to social and environmental destruction, for example, some see them as having the greatest power to heal human relationships with each other and with the earth.[32] But the information technology that is helping business form increasingly broader cooperative national and international networks is having little effect on local communities.

At the local community level, particularly in urban centers, groups and institutions are largely "closed systems," competing with others rather than cooperating with them to achieve shared goals. If integrative networks are expanding in the economic sector, non-integration and fragmentation characterize most inner cities. The consequences for the young have been especially tragic.

The impact of fragmented communities was highlighted in a study of adolescents by Francis Ianni. While pathologies, such as juvenile delinquency, drug and alcohol abuse, and teenage pregnancy, are commonly attributed to parental failures and sometimes to television or the absence of religion in schools, Ianni locates their source in the relationships of local institutions.[33]

Ianni and his associates observed and interviewed thousands of adolescents over a ten-year period in ten U.S. communities: rural, affluent, and urban inner-city areas. They studied them in a variety of settings: in families, schools, the workplace, juvenile detention facilities, and in mental health facilities. When these institutions shared overlapping common goals and acted on them, they concluded, adolescents either coped adequately or did not experience the traumas associated with this transitional period. Conversely, when these institutions failed to support each other or acted in opposition to each other, adolescents were left to their own devices in reconciling their competing ideologies, often with disastrous aftermaths.

In some locales Ianni studied, convergence among these institutions occurred in an almost natural manner, without apparent effort. Such was the case in Sheffield, a small, affluent suburb of approximately ten thousand people. What unified this community and all its social institutions was neither religion nor ethnicity, but overlapping and superordinate goals.

Preparing their children for a future like that of their parents was Sheffield's unifying value. Most parents worked at jobs requiring college education, and family, educational, and religious institutions were united in their goal of helping prepare youngsters for college and careers. Parents regarded Sheffield's schools as first rate, and many had moved to Sheffield for just that reason. They began shaping their children's goals early and continued directing them until they left home.

Schools shared parents' values and welcomed their involvement. Parents helped children with their schoolwork and played an active role in the schools, serving on committees and organizing sports and extracurricular activities. Churches, too, supported family values and made efforts to join parents with children in activities which included both—such as family out-ings and youth clubs where parents acted as advisers. Knowing the community's shared investment in their children's future, even the police cooperated by keeping youngsters in line through means other than the courts or correctional agencies. If they apprehended a youthful offender, most commonly they sent him or her back to the family or a community agency—school, church, or social service agency—for help. Revoking the offender's driving privileges was one of the most extreme sanctions they applied; they used it, with family and community approval, for a wide range of offenses, including incorrigibility at home, school truancy, or possession of small amounts of marijuana. As Bruce, one adolescent youngster, expressed it, Sheffield is "like a big family."

Such congruence among families, schools, religious institutions, and the justice system provides youngsters with a firm and dependable external structure. When young people are guided throughout their developmental process toward an achievable model of adulthood, they can resist excesses which might threaten their life chances. If they make a mistake—neglect their studies, smoke some "pot," drink too much, or even become pregnant, a variety of people—families, friends, parents, schools, and social agencies—will reach out to redirect them.

Southside, however, another community Ianni studied, presents a very different picture. An urban inner-city area of a major eastern metropolis, Southside is polyethnic, poor, and crowded. There are Chinese and Hispanic immigrants from Puerto Rico, the Dominicans, and Cuba; southern blacks, West Indians as well as a few Africans; some pockets of Ukrainians, Eastern European Jews, and Italians; growing numbers of new Chinese immigrants from Hong Kong and mainland China, and some gays and "yuppies." Over 250 thousand people live in this two-square-mile area, marked by massive public housing projects and aging tenements. Single-parent families are common, and drugs are the major underground economy product.

As Sheffield is an example of integrated community institutions, Southside's social institutions are atomized and dissonant. In Sheffield, school goals are congruent with jobs students will seek; in Southside, academic school requirements have little relevance for the dead-end, low-paying jobs available to most adolescents. Parents, in similarly restricted jobs and lifestyles, can offer little guidance. Burdened by poverty and stress, uncomfortable in an academic setting and generally rejected by teachers as incompetent, parents stay away from their children's schools. The professionals who staff the schools and community agencies might be able to help, but living outside the community themselves, they are at best visitors whose lives are only remotely linked with the youngsters they service. Rather than working with parents and schools, community social service agencies frequently ignore both. The juvenile justice system is flooded with youthful offenders, and the courts lack the resources to attend to them adequately, even to assign them to appropriate diversionary programs. Whereas Sheffield residents see the police as an extension of the community, Southside residents regard them largely as a hostile, alien force.

What happens to adolescents in Southside is significantly different from what happens to them in Sheffield. Sixteen-year-old Josie Delgado is a good example.

Josie moved to Southside from the Dominican Republic when she was seven. The youngest of ten children, she lives with her mother in a three-room apartment. Her father abandoned the family some years ago. Several of her married siblings live in the same tenement or nearby. Josie is fond of her family; she feels warm and comfortable with them. But while her sisters encourage her to "make something of herself," something other than they have of their lives, an invisible sorting system is already at work, precluding options and alternatives.

The sorting system begins in Josie's family, none of whom can quite envision what an alternative besides early marriage and children looks like. It continues at the local high school which Josie attends along with forty-five hundred other students, reflecting the neighborhood's diversity in similar proportions. Neither school teachers nor classmates pay much attention to Josie. On any typical day, she interacts almost exclusively with a very restricted group of like Dominican adolescents:

Up before 7:00 A.M. on school days, Josie begins her day early. She dresses, applies some makeup (usually eyeliner), and eats breakfast in time to meet a girlfriend or two and walk to school by 8:30. Most of her girlfriends are also Dominican.

Arriving at school a few minutes early, she smokes a cigarette with her friends outside the school in a location where other Dominican students hang out. Nobody has ever said that she or other Dominicans have to congregate here, just as no one has ever said they all have to live on the same block or in the same building. But ethnicity, not wealth or talent or even interests, is the primary source of social identity in Southside, where it structures peer group formation in the school just as surely as it does residence.

When Josie enters the school building at about 8:35 she goes immediately to the third floor stairwell, which is the gathering place for her friends in the section of the building that is the Hispanic gathering place. She finds herself a niche on the steps . . . where she sits and talks (in both Spanish and English) to her closest friends. Then she goes to her first-period gym class and begins the round of classes for which she is scheduled.

Mr. Katz, a young Jewish teacher wearing a yarmulke, fills the front board with the cryptics of mathematics, earnestly emphasizing the points with the tip of his chalk, but Josie and her friends seem unimpressed. There is a low but constant stream of chatter among the Hispanic students. In this class, as in most others, Josie sits with her fellow Hispanic students, just as most Chinese and black students sit with their ethnic peers.[34]

Josie's chances for success at school are slim, as they are for thousands of other youngsters in Southside. Not inherently differently endowed from average youngsters in Sheffield, they fail, says Ianni, because they live in a fragmented, non-supportive, competitive, and hostile environment. In this context, youngsters are left to their own devices, dependent on themselves to create alternative lives and futures. If the entire community is like a family for Bruce, says Ianni, the family and a small circle of friends are all the community sixteen-year-old Josie Delgado of Southside has. Hence, it is not surprising that most simply re-create the lives of their parents. As for adults around them, ethnicity, rather than achievement, becomes the primary means of identification. Like the adults around them, ethnic youth groups compete for power and resources, their common unifier factionalism and fear. Caught in the cracks between incongruent or conflicting social structures, with no common goals to relate all youth to each other or varied institutions within the community to each other, most youngsters, like Josie, simply give up.

Yet Josie is lucky. She does not belong to the growing numbers of children who suffer parental physical, sexual, or emotional abuse; neither she nor her family uses drugs and no one has yet been the victim of neighborhood violence. While numbers of her peers are already in the streets, she has a warm home. While her future may be limited, she does not appear to be a likely candidate for what Lisbeth Schorr calls "rotten outcomes."[35]

"Having children too soon, leaving school illiterate and unemployable, and committing violent crimes" are the "rotten outcomes" that afflict a significant number of American adolescents, says Schorr. The group most at risk is America's underclass—the class that has disproportionately high percentages of school dropouts, welfare recipients, female heads of household, and working-age males only intermittently employed. They live primarily in the inner cities, and while the majority of them are probably black, they also include other minorities and whites. More than a third of them are estimated to be children. Representing approximately one percent of the total population, they include some two and a half million people. Some among them will ultimately become self-supporting, productive adults, but many will remain welfare dependent and unemployed, perpetuating the cycle among their children.

Money alone cannot solve the cycle of disadvantage, says Schorr: "After twenty years of vastly increased social spending more children are poor, more children are growing up without stable families, and more young people are out of work."[36] The reason they have failed, says Schorr, is not that people prefer a "handout" to resolving their own problems, but that their problems have been tackled in a piecemeal fashion. Programs often focus on a single issue—such as employment skills, raising test scores, counseling pregnant unwed teenagers, or providing adequate nutrition for children. Rather than cooperating with each other, such programs compete with each other for resources. If they are to succeed with more than a few, they need to merge their efforts on behalf of a superordinate goal, namely overcoming the inter-related environmental conditions in which urban problems fester.

Remediation, in other words, requires an ecological approach, looking at the whole rather than the part. Providing options for alternative futures requires addressing all the social institutions which impinge on them. It means changing possibilities and relationships within the family, among peers and the whole school, in addition to changed relationships between families, schools, religious institutions, the workplace, and social service agencies. Empowering people to change their lives requires networking— forming shared agendas developed cooperatively among all stakeholders, along with the resources to act on them.

These principles underlie hundreds of documented successful programs with high risk youth across the nation, which Schorr describes. They are beginning to shape the practices of some educational institutions: in "restructuring," which means students, teachers, parents, and business working together, and in "school-based management," where teachers working together with administrators, rather than superintendents or boards of education alone, make decisions about curriculum, allocation of funds and teaching assignments. And as we have seen, they are becoming part of the training for some professionals, such as business managers and social service workers.

Yet it would be naive to underestimate the challenge the networking concept poses. It can only occur among mutually open individuals and systems, which is not the way our society normally operates. Nor can we be certain that integrative systems will use their power for good. But change often begins with alternate visions, and the networking concept offers one.

NOTES

1. David L. Kirp, "Uncommon Decency: Pacific Bell Responds to AIDS," *Harvard Business Review* (May–June 1989): 140–151, 140.

2. Kirp.

3. Kirp, 145–146.

4. R. Edward Freeman defines business stakeholders as "any group or individual who can affect or is affected by the achievement of the firm's objectives" (R. Edward Freeman, *Strategic Management: A Stakeholder Approach* [Boston: Pitman, 1984], 24).

5. Igor Ansoff, *Corporate Strategy* (New York: McGraw-Hill, 1965). For an excellent summary of how the stakeholder concept can be applied to the business context, see Donna J. Wood, *Business and Society* (Glenview, Ill.: Scott, Foresman/Little, Brown Higher Education, 1990), chap. 3.

6. Freeman, 44–45.

7. Muzafer Sherif and Carolyn W. Sherif, "In-Group and Intergroup Relations: Experimental Analysis," in *Social Psychology*, Muzafer Sherif and Carolyn W. Sherif (New York: Harper & Row, 1969), 221–288. The Sherifs' proposals have come to

be known as "a functional theory of intergroup relations." See also Robert R. Blake and Jane S. Moutin, "Reactions to Intergroup Competition Under Win-Lose Conditions," *Management Science* 7 (1961): 420–435; Robert R. Blake and Jane S. Moutin, "The Intergroup Dynamics of Win-Lose Conflict and Problem-Solving Collaboration in Union-Management Relations," in *Intergroup Relations and Leadership*, ed. Muzafer Sherif (New York: John Wiley & Sons, 1962), 94–140; Muzafer Sherif, *Group Conflict and Co-operation* (London: Routledge and Kegan-Paul, 1967).

8. Randy Diamond, "In Brooklyn, Bigotry Yields to Basketball," *San Francisco Examiner*, April 5, 1990, A8.

9. David W. Johnson and Roger T. Johnson, *Cooperation and Competition: Theory and Research* (Edina, Minn.: Interaction, 1989).

10. Robert E. Slavin, *Cooperative Learning: Theory, Research, and Practice* (Englewood Cliffs, N.J.: Prentice-Hall, 1990); David W. Johnson et al., *Circles of Learning: Cooperation in the Classroom* (Alexandria, Va.: Association for Supervision and Curriculum Development, 1984); S. Willis, "Coop Learning Shows Staying Power," *Association for Supervision and Curriculum Development Update*, March 1992, 34, 1–2.

11. Wood, 495.

12. Samuel P. Oliner and Pearl M. Oliner, *The Altruistic Personality: Rescuers of Jews in Nazi Europe* (New York: Free Press, 1988), 99.

13. Lisbeth B. Schorr with Daniel Schorr, *Within Our Reach: Breaking the Cycle of Disadvantage* (New York: Doubleday, 1988), 48–50.

14. Edith M. Freeman and Marianne Pennekamp, *Social Work Practice: Toward a Child, Family, School, Community Perspective* (Springfield, Ill.: Charles C. Thomas), 1988.

15. Marianne Pennekamp, personal communication.

16. Freeman and Pennekamp, 25, 26.

17. Wood, 495.

18. Michael L. Dertouzos et al., *Made in America: Regaining the Productive Edge* (Cambridge, Mass.: The MIT Press, 1989).

19. Rosabeth M. Kanter, *When Giants Learn to Dance: Mastering the Challenge of Strategy, Management, and Careers in the 1990's* (New York: Simon & Schuster, 1989), 138.

20. Fernando Bartolomé, "Nobody Trusts the Boss Completely—Now What?," *Harvard Business Review* (March–April 1989): 138.

21. A. W. Clausen, "Voluntary Disclosure: An Idea Whose Time Has Come," in *Corporations and Their Critics: Issues and Answers to the Problems of Corporate Social Responsibility*, eds. Thornton Bradshaw and David Vogel (New York: McGraw-Hill, 1981), 61–70.

22. Kanter, *Giants*, 138.

23. Peter Blau, credited with developing the most systematic and comprehensive theoretical approach to what sociologists call "exchange theory," defines social exchange as "voluntary actions of individuals that are motivated by the returns they are expected to bring and typically do in fact bring from others" (Peter M. Blau, *Exchange and Power in Social Life* [New York: John Wiley & Sons, 1964]).

24. M. S. Clark and H. T. Reis, "Interpersonal Processes in Close Relationships," in *Annual Review of Psychology* 39, eds. Mark R. Rosenzweig and Lyman W. Porter

(1988): 609–672; J. D. Fisher, A. Nadler, and S. Whitcher-Alagna, "Recipient Re-
actions to Aid," *Psychological Bulletin* 91 (1982): 27–34; Toni C. Antonucci and
James S. Jackson, "The Role of Reciprocity in Social Support," in *Social Support:
An Interactional View*, eds. Barbara R. Sarason, Irwin G. Sarason, and Gregory R.
Pierce (New York: John Wiley & Sons, 1990), 173–198.

25. Martin S. Greenberg, "A Theory of Indebtedness," in *Social Exchange: Advances in Theory and Research*, eds. Kenneth Gergen, Martin S. Greenberg, and Richard H. Willis (New York: Plenum, 1980).

26. Antonucci and Jackson.

27. Alvin W. Gouldner, "The Norm of Reciprocity: A Preliminary Statement,"
American Sociological Review 25 (April 1960): 161–178.

28. Tom Seligson, "To Survive, We Must Trust," *Parade*, October 8, 1989: 10–
12, 12.

29. William E. Halil, *The New Capitalism* (New York: John Wiley & Sons, 1986).

30. Halil, 143.

31. Herbert Schiller, for example, sees it as nothing more than a mask for corporate dominance of public life (Herbert Schiller, *Culture, Inc: The Corporate Takeover of Public Expression* [New York: Oxford University Press, 1989]).

32. Willis Harman and John Hormann, *Creative Work: The Constructive Role of
Business in a Transforming Society* (Munich: Schweisfurth Foundation, 1990); Marjorie Kelly, "Revolution in the Marketplace," *Utne Reader*, January-February 1989,
54–62.

33. Francis A. J. Ianni, *The Search for Structure: A Report on American Youth
Today* (New York: The Free Press, 1989).

34. Ianni, 32, 114.

35. Schorr with Schorr.

36. Schorr with Schorr, xxiv.

CHAPTER 8

Resolving Conflicts

What do they want? Well, they're not primarily interested in contributions that various groups have made to our history. They want to make
sure minority students get told nice stories about themselves . . . And
the authors also want to make sure everybody gets equal time.

The ramifications are clear . . . when you think about the number of
minority groups that will be competing to get their share of the curricular pie. If Chinese and Japanese, why not Thai? Why not Koreans? Why
not Vietnamese? Why not any group that can put enough pressure on a
school system—and the school had better get the time allotments right.

All this might or might not lead to improved self-images among minority students. But cultural sound bites, multiplied as many times as a
district has vocal minorities, will obviously lead to a badly fragmented
curriculum. And it's doubtful that it will lead to a better understanding
of the other guy. In fact, kids are more likely to lose heroes than to gain
them—"Abraham Lincoln is *my* hero, not yours." "That's all right. I
have Martin Luther King—but how come the teacher spent more time
talking about Lincoln?"[1]

Albert Shanker, president of the American Federation of Teachers, made the
above retort in January 1990 to the Task Force authors of the controversial
Sobol Report. Charged by New York State's commissioner of education
Tom Sobol, to make recommendations regarding ways to promote equity
and excellence in education, the Task Force issued a strong indictment of
educational materials and practices. While improvements had occurred over
the last several years, they said, curriculum materials remained systematically
biased "toward European culture and its derivates." African and Asian
Americans, Puerto Ricans, Native Americans, and Latinos, they wrote, have

"all been victims of an intellectual and educational oppression that has characterized the culture and institutions of the United States and the European American world for centuries." Excluded from mainstream history, minority students suffered a lack of self-esteem, which contributed to their poor academic performance. The curriculum, the Task Force concluded, needed to more "adequately and accurately reflect the pluralistic nature of our society."[2]

Shanker has no problem with the report's basic recommendation; "Clearly," he says, "the more people know about each other, the better able they will be to live together in harmony." His concern is with what it considers "adequate" and "accurate." Just how inclusive can a curriculum be, he asks, without becoming trivial and shallow? How "accurate" can content be if each group is presented from a positive point of view only? And how many varying perspectives can a curriculum present without destroying adherence to the common democratic culture upon which our society is based?

Shanker's questions are not easily answered. They stem from a fundamental conflict among diverse groups regarding the function of education, core American values, and how they can be reconciled with claims of diversity. Conflicts of this nature have been common in American history: Catholics objected to what they perceived as the Protestant school culture, labor found fault with its "big-business" perspective, and globalists were often appalled by its patriotic chauvinism. Each has in turn demanded that their points of view not only be included, but that they be presented in only the most favorable light. What distinguishes the current conflict is the sheer number of groups seeking inclusion.

Herein lies the problem! As diversifying and networking increase the possibilities for inclusion and cooperation, so do they also increase the potential for conflict. And while many people acknowledge the value of cooperation, only a few perceive anything positive in conflict.

Webster's International Dictionary captures the prevailing negative view of conflict—clash, competition, antagonism, disharmony, incompatibility, irreconcilability, contention with or against one another in strife or warfare. This view has long historical roots. Plato, Aristotle, Hobbes, and Locke believed conflict threatened order, essential for the good society. Utopian visions, Biblical and otherwise, commonly fantasized worlds without conflict: consensual communities where principles of care and justice reigned without challenge.[3]

An emerging view gaining credence takes a radically different position; rather than being inherently destructive, it argues that conflict is potentially productive. Darwin led the way for this kind of thinking; the "survival of the fittest" thesis suggested that contest and struggle were necessary for change, development, and growth. Spencer, Hegel, and Marx believed that the good society could only evolve from conflict. And twentieth century sociologist Georg Simmel advanced the revolutionary idea that rather than destructive of relationships, a certain amount of conflict was necessary to maintain them—in society at large as well as in intimate relationships.[4] Lewis Coser elaborated on this idea extensively, maintaining that conflict potentially has many productive functions.[5]

Along with Simmel and Coser, contemporary analysts agree that conflict can result in either destructive or productive outcomes. Destructive conflicts isolate and alienate individuals and groups, energizing them toward ever escalating expressions of mutual hostility and the development of exclusive moral norms. Productive conflicts, on the other hand, promote creativity and needed change by integrating diversity and embracing more inclusive moral norms.[6]

Our purpose here is to suggest means and procedures for making conflicts *productive*. We begin with conflict resolution procedures and how to regulate conflict, then go on to describe the evolution of many real-life conflicts and the conditions often necessary for their resolution. We conclude by considering how conflict resolution relates to care, justice, and peace.

One way to resolve conflicts productively is through a process which persuades people that despite their differences, they can interact cooperatively to resolve mutual problems. That process is called conflict resolution.

The assumptions underlying resolving conflicts differ substantially from those involved in settling or solving them, and they lead to different conceptions of appropriate strategies for dealing with them.

Traditional thinking presumes that conflict needs to result in winners and losers.[7] Conflict resolution theorists reject this premise. They argue that conflicts are not really settled unless both sides win, and that a "win-win" consequence is not only possible but essential for enduring results.

Traditional strategies for settling conflicts depend on assertions of power (personal or legal authority, war), compromise, negotiation, or arbitration where third parties frequently impose solutions. Conflict resolution rejects coercion generally and violence summarily. It also rejects any strategy which implies giving up something—as implied by terms such as compromise or negotiation—or any form of externally imposed solution.

The conflict resolution process depends on a strategy which aims to transform disputants into cooperative problem solvers and adversaries into allies. To do so, it avoids any direct confrontation of values and ideologies, concentrating instead on changing behaviors. It also requires that the disputants themselves work on solving the problem, although external people may facilitate the process.

To illustrate some general characteristics of the strategy as well as its wide applicability, consider what happened in two vastly different conflict situations. One occurred between neighbors in a modest suburban area of Delaware County; the other at the roundtable discussions in Poland in 1989 when the fate of the nation depended on negotiations between Solidarity and the ruling Communist government.

The narrators of the neighbor story are two mediators at the Community Dispute Settlement program (CDS) in suburban Philadelphia. Initiated in 1976 by the Friends Suburban Project, a Quaker group, CDS seeks to resolve community disputes through mediation rather than the legal process. Contacted by the young mother in the dispute after she had received a summons and a demand for $300 to be paid to her elderly neighbors, two CDS mediators describe their interview with her:

"Every morning, I wake up and think, 'I've got to face this again today,' " the woman said. It was a hot day. She stood on her small front porch, looking over the fence at her neighbor's house. "Whenever my kids play outside, he curses at them. He steals their balls. My Mom has had to take my kids most days. I can't keep them indoors all the time, can I? Half the time I'm scared to answer the door for fear it's going to be him or the police again."

She wasn't finished. "You know, we don't have much money but we paid for this house. All I want is to live in peace."[8]

Not surprisingly, the neighbors, an elderly couple, had a very different view of events:

The husband was eager to talk. "Don't let her fool you. That woman lies through her teeth! To hear her, you'd think her kids were floating around with a couple of halos. Look where they smashed our fence. They run all over our vegetable garden. Once my wife told them to get out, and she says, 'Oh, Jimmy, don't listen to that old bag.' So he sticks out his tongue . . . They're like animals, those people."

His wife spoke up. "We've lived here for 24 years and never had trouble like this, ever. Every weekend it's loud parties, cars in and out till all hours . . . We don't want trouble. I call the police and let them take care of it." Her face had been expressionless but now her voice caught. "We just want to be left alone to live out our last years in peace."[9]

The ensuing mediation session took two hours. At its conclusion, the neighbors signed a simple written agreement: "Everyone would speak to each other politely. The mother would come over to retrieve any balls." This apparently simplistic resolution to a conflict which had been serious enough to warrant police intervention was accompanied by hugs and kisses:

Everyone shook hands. The two women kissed each other. As she was leaving, the old woman took the mediator's two hands in hers, tears in her eyes. "Thank you so much," she said, still trembling. At the door, her husband turned. "We just want to live our last years in peace."[10]

What had occurred in a two-hour mediation session to make this resolution possible? Researcher Jennifer Beer, the source for the above anecdote, says the typical session proceeds along six carefully structured stages with reasonably predictable responses.

The first three stages basically allow the disputants to ventilate their feelings safely. The mediator begins with an *opening statement*, welcoming the disputants and making them feel at ease, clarifying the purpose of the session, describing what will occur at each subsequent stage and promising confidentiality. During the second stage, called *uninterrupted time*, the mediators ask each person to explain what is happening and how she or he feels about it. The objective is not to ascertain the facts, but rather to allow each person to state her or his point of view with minimal interruptions and with no fear of attack. Emotions tend to run high during this stage. *The exchange*, the third stage, is the time when disputants respond to questions and accusations. Although intended to allow all parties, including mediators, to get the information they think they need, disputants frequently simply repeat familiar fight scenarios. Mediators allow it to occur within tolerable limits and for a limited time.

It is during the last three stages that the real work of resolving the conflict occurs. By the time the fourth stage is reached, the *building agreement* period, a few issues have surfaced repeatedly. The mediator checks for their accuracy and completeness, then asks whether these are what people want to work on. If they agree, the mediators do not propose solutions themselves; rather, they solicit ideas and alternatives from the disputants. They then try to work out the specifics: what people will do, and when and how they will do it. Based on what the disputants say, the mediators draw up a tentative written agreement. That latter becomes the focus of the the fifth stage, *the agreement*. The mediators read back the points of the agreement and ask each person to suggest changes. At its conclusion, each person signs the revised agreement. During the final stage, called *the closing*, the mediators thank everyone, and review their progress.[11]

In sum, the strategy provides a controlled environment where the adversaries have an opportunity to ventilate their feelings, identify the major issues of dispute, and agree about the specific behavioral changes each requires. The strategy is unlikely to work, however, unless both parties agree beforehand that they want to resolve the conflict peaceably and that each understands that neither is bound in advance to honor the outcome.

Community oriented mediation programs like CDS deal with small-scale disputes only. In the case of Poland, the dispute was a large-scale political conflict. Nonetheless, as described by participant-observer Janusz Reykowski, a social psychologist who cochaired the political table at the Round Table negotiations, the eventual peaceful resolution—an agreement between two sharply divided adversaries, the ruling Communist coalition and the political opposition, Solidarity—was the product of several similar techniques.[12]

By 1988, Poland confronted a grave crisis; violence seemed imminent. Efforts by the state leadership at economic reform had failed; educated workers and the intelligentsia, and most particularly young people, challenged not only the regime's legitimacy but the political system upon which it was based. The state, however, still commanded military power and Solidarity leaders feared that should they choose the path of violent confrontation, they would fail to get the support they needed. State leaders also preferred to avoid violence and made some conciliatory gestures. In August 1988, the Interior Minister, General Kiszczak, publicly proposed that Solidarity and state representatives meet to resolve the issues; but the secret talks that followed ended in a stalemate. In December 1988, the ruling party discharged some of the hardliners from the highest leadership echelons while simultaneously recruiting outsiders known for advocating political reform and conciliation with the opposition. A few weeks later, it declared itself ready, under certain conditions, to prepare the ground for political pluralism, including legalization of Solidarity. This set the stage for the ensuing Round Table negotiations.

The first meeting, conducted in secrecy, took place at the end of January 1989, when ten official representatives from each side confronted each other in a small villa in Magdalenka, not far from Warsaw. It began warily, says Reykowski. Carrying their traumatic pasts with them, neither side trusted the other:

Both sides tended to regard the other as the "enemy." The government saw Solidarity as imposters, trying to snatch power through any means, while perceiving itself as the only legal authority. Solidarity, on the other hand, saw the government as an evil regime who had grabbed power illegitimately, and itself—the only legitimate representative of the society—as the retriever of some of the state's power to make sure that societal rights would be respected. Thus, both sides tended to see the major goal of the negotiations as a *containment* of the adversary.[13]

The first task, says Reykowski, was to transform the concept of the other side from "enemy" to "partner," as someone equally interested in improving the situation but having different images of what this might mean. One of the first successes of this endeavor—a minor one—was a linguistic change. Solidarity forces preferred describing themselves as representing "the society" while labeling the opposition, "the regime"; the ruling coalition, on the other hand, favored the label "legal authorities" for itself and "the illegal opposition" for its adversary. Both sides eventually abandoned these charged labels, settling on the neutral terms "governmental coalition vs. Solidarity-opposition."

Equally important, says Reykowski, was transforming traditional notions of negotations with which many representatives on each side began. Anticipating that they would have to bargain and compromise, some on each side initiated the talks by making excessively high demands. Those who had a better idea of the conflict resolution process tried to shift the focus from demands to a shared problem. Arguing that it was in Poland's best interest to abolish autocracy and build a democratic order without destabilizing the state, they emphasized the need to work together. Eventually, they persuaded others that finding the best strategy for change was the issue which needed their concentrated and cooperative attention. The seating arrangement—a "roundtable" where people sat side by side facing each other—was an effort to promote this psychological attitude in a physically concrete way.[14]

Controlling destructive confrontations presented another challenge. Since past events had inflicted considerable suffering and trauma on participants, harshly aggressive outbursts were common. Recognizing their potential for bringing the negotiations to a rapid halt, some participants proposed that arguments about the past be prohibited. While the rule was not always honored, it did serve to contain emotions while not suppressing disagreements. The latter in fact proved useful, says Reykowski; they helped clarify the limits of each side's position and the points beyond which shared common ground could not be found.

Finally, says Reykowski, the group had to devise a strategy for confronting what he calls "critical moments," periods of impasse when positions became so polarized that fruitful discussion was impossible. At such points, postponement frequently helped; withdrawing from the situation allowed participants time to reformulate the problem and try again.

What did the Round Table discussions share in common with the CDS mediation process? Before answering this question, let's look at their differences, as important as their commonalities.

The CDS conflict was basically a single issue, a dispute between neighbors on the behaviors of children. In Poland, however, the conflict was multi-issued and deep; adversaries viewed each other as fundamentally opposed on political, economic, religious, and nationalistic issues. The rules and structures were set up in advance in the former, and the participants understood from the beginning what they were; in the latter, many of the rules and structures evolved as creative responses to immediate situations. The mediators in the CDS conflict were outsiders; in Poland, mediators were themselves participants in the conflict. The resolution of the conflict was a matter of concern to the negotiating parties alone in the CDS case; in Poland, it was a major concern for the society at large, making the entire process more complex and vulnerable to charges of "sell-out" by outside hardliners. It took but two hours to resolve the CDS conflict; the Round Table discussions took several months and the agreement to begin them several years to evolve. But most important of all were the differing consequences. Neither social change nor institutional modifications followed the CDS resolution. The Polish resolution, however, introduced radical political change; the parliamentary election the parties agreed to hold in June 1989 made Solidarity the new political power.

Despite their major differences, the motivation and strategies whereby resolution was achieved had much in common. Adversaries in both cases preferred a peaceful resolution, and both agreed to participate with the understanding that they had no obligation in advance to honor its outcome. Face-to-face meetings between adversaries occurred in both situations. In both cases, a deliberate effort was made to create a safe environment—a place where people could express their disagreements and angry feelings, but deliberately controlled so as to minimize aggression. Skilled conflict managers helped guide events in both cases, appointed mediators trained in conflict resolution skills at CDS, and individuals with considerable expertise in social psychology and intergroup communication who voluntarily assumed these roles at the Round Table discussions. In both cases, mediators focused most of the discussions on the future, not the past, and in both cases negotiations ended with a signed agreement.

The critical similarities—those which made both examples of conflict resolution rather than conventional settlement models—were the roles mediators and disputants played and their goals. Rather than trying to bring the demands of adversaries closer by asking each to give up something, mediators focused on an identified shared problem which they asked disputants to resolve cooperatively. Rather than proposing solutions themselves, mediators elicited proposed solutions from the disputants. Rather than accepting imposed solutions, disputants developed their own.

While bargaining and negotiating in the traditional sense,[15] or even simple recourse to authority, are often the most expedient and efficient ways of solving conflicts, conflict resolution has its own distinct advantages. Without preconditions imposing obligations, adversaries are more likely to agree to participate. Participation of itself implies recognition and legitimation of the other and face-to-face talk often promotes trust. Since adversaries themselves do the work of resolution, they learn new skills, which they presumably can transfer to new conflict situations. Without threats to their self-esteem— more likely to occur when external parties impose solutions—disputants can feel better about themselves and each other and are more inclined to accept responsibility for their behaviors. Finally, the very process of cooperative problem solving holds the promise of transforming the relationship among participants from adversaries to allies and partners. When adversaries concentrate on resolving a shared problem for their common interests, they become members of a new superordinate group. As a consequence, each side tends to minimize formerly exaggerated ideas of its own group's similarities and its differences with their adversaries, resulting in less biased views of each other.[16]

All of the above presumably add up to a more long-lasting stability, one in which conflicts are really settled rather than left to simmer only to erupt on another day. In Poland, stability may be short-lived. Participants at the Round Table discussions purportedly acted on behalf of the society at large, but the latter were not themselves parties to the process. While the relationships among participants may have changed, they have not necessarily changed among non-participants. Rather than a resolution of the conflict, the agreement is perceived by many of Poland's citizens as an imposed solution, one which does not address their issues. Reacting to job purges at the hands of the new regime, as well as threats of more serious reprisals, including investigations of criminal behavior, large numbers of the old regime feel they were duped by the policy of reconciliation. Should the opportunity arise, observes Reykowski, they may well "become soldiers of the 'counter-revolution.' " What has thus begun in Poland as a productive conflict may yet become a destructive one.

Among other things the Polish case points to is that large scale and deeply rooted societal conflicts cannot be resolved via short-lived transactions attended only by representatives to the conflict. Long-standing enmities do not evaporate speedily, and the temptation to use newly gained power to vanquish former enemies may be too attractive to resist. Yielding to it means perpetuating the cycle of hostility with its attendant social threats. Breaking the cycle requires adopting conflict resolution strategies as an ongoing widely diffused routine mode of social behavior—in intimate relationships as well as institutional life. If this appears difficult in Poland, it may be only somewhat less so in western democracies where "win/lose" strategies commonly govern relationships.

Overcoming conventional social habits presents a formidable challenge, yet efforts at making conflict resolution strategies more routine are occurring in the United States as well as abroad. One such effort involves American elementary and secondary schoolchildren, many of whom are learning conflict resolution strategies as part of their curriculum. Two representative lessons from a workbook by Fran Schmidt and Alice Friedman illustrate how youngsters learn to apply such techniques to solve typical student conflicts.

One lesson presents students with common school experiences—someone pushes you, calls you a name, steps on your foot—and students are to say what they would do if they saw themselves as the offender's enemy and what they might do if they were the offender's friend. Asking youngsters to declare their potential responses based on different perceptions of their relationships is a way of helping them see that changing beliefs about offenders can de-escalate crises.

In the other lesson, best friends Tammi and Lori become angry with each other at a Valentine's Day dance when Al, a boy they both like, ignores Lori while repeatedly asking Tammy to dance:

The next day at lunch, Lori sat with some girls at another table, away from Tammy. They were giggling, with their heads close together. Tammy stormed across the room with her hands on her hips. She demanded to know what Lori was telling the girls about her.

Lori laughed and replied, "It's for us to know and for you to find out." With her fist clenched, and eyes glaring, Tammy moved toward Lori. Lori shook her fist and called Tammy a name. The other girls at the table were all laughing. One of the girls whispered, "Don't let her push you around Lori." Tammy lunged forward and shoved Lori.[17]

"What was the original conflict?" asks the text; "What actions escalated it and how could either friend have changed its direction?" Students are thus led to analyze the source of conflicts and consider alternatives they themselves have the power to implement. Teachers who have used such techniques claim that students not only change their behaviors in school as a consequence, but also transfer their newly acquired skills to resolve conflicts outside it—among family members as well as friends.[18]

Similar efforts are also occurring in universities and organization-sponsored workshops around the world, where a wide variety of people, including leaders in industry, education, and international relations, are learning to be "conflict managers."

Consistent with the view that conflicts can be productive, managing conflicts commonly means neither preventing them nor eliminating them, but regulating them. Conflict management theorists generally agree that conflict can benefit any organization, providing there is neither too little nor too much of it.

Too much conflict is easier to detect than too little, observes organization and community researcher David Brown. A high degree of tension, resistance, grievances, sabotage, and violence are among its symptoms. Each side blames the other, seeing itself as the victim and the other as a malignant oppressor; each side attempts to control the other through coercive means. While energy levels are high, information is usually distorted, resulting in poor and often harmful decisions, and relationships continue to deteriorate as antagonisms escalate.[19]

Obviously, "too much" conflict can hurt an organization, but how can "too little" be anything but beneficial? It can hurt, Brown suggests, when its absence more accurately reflects avoidance and suppression rather than nonexistence.

Common avoidance techniques include refusing to discuss problems, resisting challenging others, assuming others have common interests, insisting on premature cooperation, or actually withdrawing from the field. Common ways of suppressing conflict include concealing feelings, denying the fact that differences exist, refusing to collect or disseminate information that might reveal problems, and attacking those who expose them. Avoidance and suppression lead to similar consequences, says Brown: low energy and commitment, perpetuation of unchallenged traditions and myths, poor decisions based on inadequate information, and "fragile relations that cannot face the challenge of changing circumstances."

When conflict is too high, good managers seek to de-escalate it, using such measures as debunking stereotypes regarding one's own virtue and others' incompetence, improving the quality of information flow, identifying goals that require cooperation, rotating personnel across departments, and altering the organizational structure to compel cooperation between departments. When conflict is too low, good managers seek to heighten it, using such measures as increasing communications, surfacing differences, expanding controversial exchanges, relaxing rules, and altering the organizational system so as to reward such behaviors.

The objective in either case is to promote productive conflict. Productive conflict leads to an expanded understanding of the issues, recognition of differences as well as commonalities, mobilization of energies and resources toward problem solving, and the possibility for future stable relationships. In short, says Brown, the consequence of productive conflict is increased efficacy.

Good conflict managers can presumably detect problems early and avoid their excesses, using techniques such as Brown suggests. Many typical conflicts, however, begin with too little and escalate to too much before managers even notice them. When managers intervene, their efforts often appear clumsy and haphazard rather than considered. Yet, if they manage to provide the necessary conditions for finding creative solutions, the conflict may nonetheless be resolved.

This was the case, for example, in a medical laboratory conflict Brown describes. While it eventually concluded satisfactorily, the path toward resolution appeared to be largely hit or miss. As we shall see, it provided conditions necessary for the conflict to be resolved. And as we shall also see, the responses of all concerned reflected a pattern which commonly accompanies the rocky road toward conflict resolution.

South Side Hospital, a medical facility of National Health Care in a large midwestern city, served many minority clients. Initially intended to handle routine laboratory work only, the hospital employed a small number of temporary technicians when it opened. Most of the technicians had no more than high school degrees, and most were black, including their supervisor, Ms. Grey. When National Health Care decided to expand and improve the laboratory's services in 1973, the hospital hired a young white laboratory technician, Ms. Williams, to head the project. Persuaded that the best way to improve the laboratory's services was to recruit more highly trained personnel, Ms. Williams hired new technologists, most with college degrees and all of them white. The conditions for conflict were ripe:

By 1976 the Laboratory had expanded to a staff of fifteen, which was split into two antagonistic groups. One group, led by the original supervisor, Ms. Grey (black), included the original staff and other minorities (six blacks, a Polynesian, and a first-generation Jewish immigrant). All the members of the "Old Guard" were technicians, with less professional training than technologists. The other group was led by Ms. Williams, and included the five newly hired white technologists. The Old Guard believed that the New Hires owed their positions to racial prejudice rather than superior qualifications.[20]

During that same year, an event occurred which confirmed the Old Hires' belief that Ms. Williams was motivated by racial prejudice. To upgrade and make them consistent with other National Health Care facilities, laboratory jobs were reclassified. As a consequence, the New Hires wound up receiving more pay and responsibilities, while the Old Hires' job titles and responsibilities remained unchanged.

The situation became critical in 1977. Performance had declined badly, and two Old Guard employees had filed suits with external agencies, charging Ms. Williams with racial and religious discrimination. National Health Care decided to settle these out of court, yielding to most of the employees' demands. The reason they did so was that they feared serious repercussions from the Equal Employment Opportunity Commission (EEOC); they had not yet complied with their agreement with the EEOC, made several years earlier, to promote minority personnel and institute systematic performance reviews.

Settlement of the suit, however, did not resolve the problem. Elated by their victory, Old Guard employees pressed for firing Ms. Williams, and the union steward recommended this to management. Management saw this as neither fair nor potentially effective in resolving the productivity issues. They hired two consultants to mediate the situation—one male and one female, and both white. Unable to gain credibility among the Old Guard, who viewed them with suspicion, the consultants in turn invited yet a third mediator—a black male. He, in turn, developed good rapport with the Old Guard, but alienated the New Guard and eventually the other two consultants as well.

Simultaneously, upper management had activated the personnel department to begin training managers to implement regular employee performance appraisals as per their agreement with EEOC. At this point, management and the consultants themselves began pressuring Ms. Williams' immediate supervisor, Ms. Thomas, to develop standards and procedures for appraising the performance of employees at the laboratory. Ms. Thomas, who had heretofore remained aloof from the problem because she wanted to appear unbiased in the eyes of the union and the EEOC, agreed. Her behaviors in the next several weeks contributed significantly to the resolution:

Ms. Thomas began to attend meetings of the Laboratory staff to discuss the development of the new appraisal system. She agreed to develop standards and procedures for appraising the performance of Laboratory employees, provided they would participate in that process so the resulting system would be relevant to them and their jobs.

Over the next several months, Ms. Thomas spent considerable time in the Laboratory. She discussed job definitions and performance criteria with the Old Guard and New Hires, and she and they together developed standards for assessing employees' contributions. She agreed to participate in appraising employee performance with Ms. Williams, and to join her to discuss appraisals with each employee.[21]

As it turned out, performance standard appraisals were the critical issue, and by involving both Old and New Hires in developing them, Ms. Williams helped facilitate its resolution. The interaction script changed from a win-lose black-white confrontation to finding a way to resolve the performance issue so that the interests of all were safeguarded. While this may or may not have changed racial assumptions generally—Brown does not say—it did apparently persuade both groups that they could work cooperatively in resolving an issue of mutual concern despite their differences. As a consequence, overt conflict diminished, laboratory performance improved, and threats of new suits did not materialize.

Not only did management fail to recognize the problem early, but much of what they did subsequently appeared to be no more than trial and error. Nonetheless, their efforts served a vital function; they provided the conditions for creative thinking. Productive resolutions of conflict require creative thinking, and while creativity by definition is innovative and uncharted, the conditions that promote it often share a pattern very much like the above. Morton Deutsch sketched its general format in his pioneering work on conflict resolution some years ago.[22]

Creative problem solving, said Deutsch, begins in an experience which promotes the recognition of the problem and arouses the motivation to resolve it. Commonly, efforts to resolve it through routine means follows. Should this fail, tension and discomfort increase, often followed by a temporary withdrawal from the problem. Withdrawal allows for some new perceptions, reformulation of the problem, and new insights. A tentative solution emerges, usually accompanied by feelings of exhilaration. An elaboration of the solution typically comes next, accompanied by some "reality checks" to assess its workability. If the solution seems viable, it is then communicated to relevant parties.

Deutsch added a critical caveat. Unless three critical psychological elements accompany the process, he said, resolution is unlikely. The three critical elements include arousal of optimal motivation to resolve the problem, conditions which permit the reformulation of the problem once an impasse has been reached, and the concurrent availability of enough diverse ideas to do so.

What constitutes optimal motivation? Neither smugness nor despair, said Deutsch. Smug people may be temporarily aroused by a crisis, but they will not be sufficiently motivated to persist at resolving it in the face of frustrations or impasses. Despair leads to a sense of helplessness and passivity rather than action. Optimal motivation, said Deutsch, "presupposes an alert readiness to be dissatisfied with things as they are and a freedom to confront one's environment without excessive fear combined with a confidence in one's capacities to persist in the face of obstacles."[23]

What kinds of conditions permit the reformulation of a problem once an impasse has been reached? The best conditions, said Deutsch, provide an environment that encourages innovative ideas and keeps people alert without threatening them. Threat makes people defensive rather than open to new and unfamiliar ideas; rather than feeling free to explore the novel without censure, they are likely to become rigidly protective of their original views.

How many concurrent ideas need to be available? At least enough of sufficient diversity and flexibility so that they can be combined in new and varied patterns, said Deutsch. This requires people with a creative bent and social conditions that allow them to exercise it. Creative problem solvers enjoy ideas; they value diverse and novel experiences, like to play with ideas, are able to make remote associations, and are generally intelligent and independently minded. Conditions that facilitate creativity include opportunities to communicate with a wide range of people with relevant but unfamiliar ideas (such as impartial outsiders and experts), a social atmosphere that values innovation and encourages the exchange of ideas, and an optimistic social tradition holding to the view that with time constructive solutions to problems can be found.

The medical laboratory story illustrates Deutsch's general pattern as well as conditions for creative resolutions of conflict. Had management adhered to their agreement with EEOC, they would have advised Ms. Williams to retrain and promote from within the Old Guard before seeking new hires. As long as services continued to improve, they remained detached. Only when confronted with a suit did they acknowledge the problem, and once having settled the suit, they again withdrew, hoping that routine procedures would take care of the rest of it. When productivity continued to decline and threats of additional suits followed, they became sufficiently aroused to take further action. Recognizing their own limitations, but not overpowered by them, they solicited new ideas by hiring outside consultants and activating a heretofore uninvolved internal resource, namely Ms. Thomas. By the

time Ms. Thomas began her meetings, many new approaches toward resolution had surfaced, most of which had proven non-viable. Involving the
disputants themselves in developing new appraisal standards overcame the
impasse and provided an ongoing "reality check" for the new ideas being
proposed by the group that was going to be most affected by them.

While the medical lab story illustrates a typical conflict resolution sequence
and the conditions often required for resolution, it also raises an important
question—a question equally applicable to neighbors and to Poland. In each
of these situations, conflict escalated to a crisis before a creative productive
process was begun. Does a crisis then constitute a precondition for its
evolution? If by "crisis" we mean a perception on the part of decision makers that a critical conditions exists, there is reason to believe it does. In fact,
intervening to resolve a problem before decision makers perceive it as critical
is likely to prove futile.

A case of too early intervention occurred in Miami, Florida, in 1980.
Warned by the Community Relations Service that Miami was facing a crisis,
the Dade County Police refused to acknowledge it. Gilbert G. Pompa, director of the Service, describes the conditions which led him to believe that
a riot was impending, how he tried to avoid it, and why he failed:

In the 1980 Miami riots, we tried over a period of time to involve the Dade County
Metro Police in a series of symposiums on the use of force. We held one in St.
Petersburg and another one in Fort Lauderdale. They were attended by most of the
police jurisdictions from around those areas. Dade County did not attend. They did
not have a crisis as far as they were concerned and took a very strong position that
they did not have to be present. Our assessment had been that the city of Miami
was definitely heading towards a riot.

I sent a report to the Attorney General two days before the riots began. There had
been an intrusion into the home of a black, Nathaniel Lafleur, by mistake. The police
went into his house and physically attacked him. Then there was the indictment and
conviction of a black school superintendent in Dade County and the assault and
killing of Arthur McDuffie. McDuffie was on a motorcycle, pursued by police for a
traffic violation. Eventually he was overtaken and beaten to death. In these three
incidents involving blacks, one was beaten, one killed and a third indicted, prosecuted
and convicted.

Consequently, a perception developed in the black community that the adminis-
tration-of-justice process worked when a black was the accused, but did not work
when a black was the victim and sought redress. The situation came to a head when,
after a trial of those accused of killing Arthur McDuffie, the five police officers in
question were acquitted. On the day of the acquittal, a Saturday, "all hell broke
loose" in Miami.[24]

What the Dade County episode illustrates is the subjective dimension of
a crisis: its existence depends on the perceptions of beholders. While both

the black community and Pompa perceived a crisis, the Dade County police did not. What it also illustrates is that in conflicts between powerful and powerless groups, the perception of the former is the cogent one in promoting change. Only the Dade County Police could decide whether to change their tactics; as long as they believed no crisis existed, they had little motivation to do so despite the fact that in the black community's eyes, the situation was critical indeed.

Why had the Dade County police failed to define the situation as a crisis? Poor communication with the minority community, the lack of cultural sensitivity, and lethargy born out of resistance to change no doubt contributed to it. Equally likely, they failed to perceive a crisis because they overestimated their power to control events.

When one side feels it can dictate terms and impose its will, it generally has little motivation to resolve a conflict. As a consequence, conflict resolution strategies are rarely used when adversaries are marked by sharp differentials in power. In the Community Dispute Settlement program's (CDS's) experience, for example, landlords or school principals rarely agree to participate. In Poland, both sides agreed to negotiate only after each became persuaded that it could not determine the outcome alone.

The situation changes dramatically when a powerless group has caused a condition which the powerful define as a crisis. Under such circumstances, they have not only acquired a tool to force the adversary to negotiate, but can also now negotiate from strength. Strength facilitates a redistribution of power in their favor, without which an ensuing agreement is likely to be short-lived.

Responding to defined crises only and redistributing power as a consequence of intervention underlie the work of the very successful Community Relations Service agency. Established as a conflict resolution agency in 1964 under Title X of the Civil Rights Act, it initially involved itself in disputes relating to the voluntary integration of educational institutions and public facilities (such as hotels and public beaches). The agency abandoned its original conflict resolution approach only after it became persuaded that it was largely ineffective in changing discriminatory practices.

The agency came to believe that discriminatory practices based on race, color, or national origin, could not be satisfactorily resolved unless the dispute resolution strategy attacked the fundamental problem of discrimination. The powerlessness of the victims was the primary problem, and it precluded a resolution which would benefit them. Disputes would not be resolved in the victims' favor unless they first acquired some strength.

How could the agency best determine if victims had acquired such strength? The best signal, they decided, would be a declaration by powerful community elements that a crisis had occurred. Only under such circumstances, says Director Pompa, can they negotiate a settlement that will generally be to the benefit of both sides but in particular to the minority community.[25] Consistent with this view, the agency now responds to crises only and has helped resolve several major national crises, including the one at Kent State (where several students were killed), at Skokie (where more than ten thousand people were prepared to confront American Nazi Party marchers), and at Wounded Knee (which the American Indian Movement occupied and where three Indians were killed, one FBI agent was wounded, and a federal marshal shot).

In the Community Relations Service (CRS) agency's case, violence or its threat are most commonly defined as crises. Fortunately, crises are often provoked in alternative and less dangerous ways.

A crisis represents an acute situation, and any situation deemed sufficiently threatening to prompt a new course of action can be construed as a crisis. Self-interest often determines perceptions of crises, as is the case, for example, with businesses that have modified their practices when threatened by serious economic losses, such as those involved in strikes and boycotts, or wide dissemination of investigative reports by consumer groups. But moral sensibilities alone can cause people to perceive a crisis, leading them sometimes to behaviors which threaten their very lives, as was the case for some civil rights protesters and rescuers of Jews. The latter offers a hopeful message: if we can manage to teach moral values adequately, so that people recognize and respond to transgressions early, we may be able to avoid those crises which provoke violence and despair.

Moral principles can help people recognize and react to moral crises, but they play little or no direct role in the conflict resolution process itself. The essential principle underlying the conflict resolution process is that both sides need to "win." In that context, moral principles have little place in the conflict resolution proceedings; invoking them may do more harm than good.[26] But notions of morality do hover around the periphery of conflict resolution, one of which has more to do with relationships than it does with matters of moral principles.

Successful conflict mediators confine themselves to limited issues—central issues, to be sure, and not so small that real change is impossible, but restricted in scope and clearly defined. Conflict management theorists agree that only the latter are amenable to resolution.

Principles contribute little to conflict resolution because adversaries commonly have widely divergent ideas about them. Views of justice, for example, vary sharply depending on culture and historical experiences. Prevailing western notions emphasize its rational and universal character; competing views argue its historical and contextual relativity. Vitally concerned about justice, Socrates, Lincoln, and Martin Luther King had widely different views about slavery, notes Laurence Thomas: "Socrates was more accepting of slavery than Lincoln, who was more accepting of it than King, who was against not just the peculiar institution of American slavery, but all forms of slavery."[27] While this might be dismissed as the product of different histor-ical periods, the experiences of contemporaries also vary widely. "Specific modes of thinking and holding values arise from from transaction within contexts," says Charlene Haddock Seigfried, and contexts differ for different people—men, women, minorities, and nationalities.[28]

Seigfried's point is highlighted in the story of Gene Woodley, Jr.; his experiences as a combat Vietnam veteran and a black man shaped his view of justice. From his point of view, justice has more to do with relationships than abstract rational principles, a view which the conflict resolution process supports.

Eighteen years old when he enlisted in 1968, Woodley was persuaded that America's cause was just:

"I didn't ask no questions about the war. I thought communism was spreading, and as an American citizen, it was my part to defeat the Communist from coming here. Whatever America states is correct was the tradition that I was brought up in. And I, through the only way I could possibly make it out of the ghetto, was to be the best soldier I possibly could."[29]

Returning one year later, after having served as a combat paratrooper in the 173rd Airborne Division, he describes himself as "an animal" who "scared" even his own mother. When he was honorably discharged in Jan-uary 1971—with five Bronze Stars for valor—he could deal neither with school nor people. By the time he was ready to go back to school, he could not afford it; without skills, he was still unemployed more than ten years later. The injustice of it all hit him one day when buying some groceries at a neighborhood store, he discovered that a Vietnamese from An Khe, the very village in which he was stationed, owned it.

He's got a business, good home, drivin' cars. And I'm still strugglin'. I'm not angry 'cause he Vietn'ese. I don't have anything against the Vietn'ese. Nothin'. Not a damn thing. I'm angry with America. When the Vietn'ese first came here, they were talking 'bout the new niggers. But they don't treat them like niggers. They treat them like people. If they had gave me some money to start my life over again, I'd been in a hell of a better situation than I am right now. We went to war to serve the country in what we thought was its best interest. Then America puts them above us. It's a crime. It's a crime against us.

This country . . . lied. They had us naive, young, dumb-ass niggers believin' that this war was for democracy and independence. It was fought for money. All those big corporations made billions on the war, and then America left.

I can't speak for other minorities, but living in America in the eighties is a war for survival among black folks. And black vet'rans are being overlooked more than every-body. We can't find jobs, because nobody trust us. Because we killers. We crazy. We went away intelligent young men to do the job of American citizens. And once we did, we came back victims.[30]

Justice for Woodley means a particular relationship with the American government: one in which he performed as a soldier to his best understanding of what was required of him and in which the American government, in return, takes care of him by providing him with a job at least equivalent to the Vietnamese he fought. While western rational conceptions might judge this level of moral reasoning quite low—analogous to "I'll scratch your back if you scratch mine" mentality—Woodley nonetheless makes a point which conflict resolution theorists generally endorse. Relationships, they would agree, are critically important to a peaceful society. Like Woodley, the conflict resolution process is more concerned with relationships—ongoing harmonious relationships—than with matters of abstract justice.

In fact, argues Anthony Cortese, justice itself *is* about relationships. Rationality, he argues, can provide us with a "concept of justice, but not justice itself." Justice, he says, "must always refer to some type of relationship; justice is meaningless without its application to relationships. If we do not comprehend the social fabric of our relationships with others, then justice is merely a set of empty mathematical, reified formuli."[31] Rationality can help people construct elaborate justifications for their behaviors based on abstract notions of equity and fairness, even as their behaviors themselves destroy positive connections to others.

Cortese's analysis helps explain why solutions which ignore relationships while attending to principles may in fact exacerbate conflict. Ruth Wynn makes this very point in her evaluation of current legislation regarding the custody of children in the event of divorce. Whereas women were previously awarded the custody of children—particularly very young children—on the assumption that they were better suited to care for them, fathers' rights advocates successfully challenged this doctrine on the basis of equality. Women were no more genetically suited to parent than men and, given their increasing participation in the work force, could no longer claim superior parental fitness because they were home. Current legal interpretations, says Wynn, have affirmed the equality of parental claims and in adjudicating custodial claims, have invoked the "best interests of the child" as the criterion. This, she says, "has transformed disputes into an intractable problem." What is really in the best interest of the child is a situation free of parental conflict and dispute. Rather than end it, court decisions now often protract and exacerbate conflict following a divorce as parents battle over visitations, child support, and quality of care; in some cases, even resulting in kidnapping children. When chronic mistrust and hostility between parents exists, she observes, mediation does not work. Unless their relationship is repaired—not likely to occur unless they change the way they interact with each other—parents cannot be compelled to cooperate, and children will suffer.[32]

Improving and maintaining a long-run peaceful relationship, rather than adherence to principles, is a fundamental tenet of conflict resolution strategies. Hence the importance of continued respectful relationships. "Once you have achieved a particular objective," advises conflict management expert Robert Heath, "do not ignore those with whom you have worked." Heath offers this advice in the context of managing conflicts in the business sector, but it applies with equal vigor to all conflicts. As he points out, "tomorrow's issues may be even more important than today's" and making new coalitions to resolve them may well depend on treating your adversaries respectfully.[33]

If relationship supersedes principles, does this then mean that moral concerns are entirely irrelevant to the conflict resolution process? Yes . . . and no.

To the extent that it concerns itself neither with right nor wrong, nor with deciding that the "good" shall be winners and the "bad" losers, issues of justice are essentially irrelevant to the conflict resolution process. Above all, conflict resolution is practical—the "art of the possible" in pursuit of peaceful relations. For this reason, critics charge it with "pacification," a means for promoting resignation to the status quo rather than systemic social change. The latter, they say, can only come through changing laws and recourse to the courts. To illustrate its validity, Beer relates a rumor regarding one mediation program in which the wife agreed not to nag and to have supper ready on time while the husband promised not to beat her again. Mediation put the issue back into the family, notes Beer, whereas women's rights advocates are fighting to have the law treat abuse as criminal behavior.[34]

While Beer ascribes the above incident to rumor, Alexander Abdennur believes this posture is characteristic of those who value peaceful relations above all. Most of them, he says, are characterized by a "conflict resolution syndrome" personality: one which seeks to avoid conflict at all costs. As a consequence, they are strongly tolerant of others' views, including oppressive practices and institutions. Preferring instead to respond to serious social issues through compromise, appeasement, neutralization, and avoidance of conflict, they in fact catalyze conditions which ultimately lead to violence.[35]

While Abdennur may legitimately be accused of overstating his case—the evidence he provides to substantiate it is weak—and confusing those who seek to resolve conflicts with those who seek to avoid it, he does make the essential point that *peace does not necessarily reflect morality.* Rather than care and social integration, it may simply reflect detachment.

An ethnographic study of a suburban town by M. P. Baumgartner supports this view. Underlying Hampton's pervasive tranquility and civility, says Baumgartner, is a deep aversion to conflict of any kind:

In Hampton, the most basic component of this system is a strong conviction that conflict is a social contaminant; something to be prevented if at all possible and to be ended quickly once begun.

This orientation expresses itself in various ways. For one thing, it is associated with a considerable degree of embarrassment and discomfort evident in the town's residents whenever interpersonal tensions arise and with an eagerness to conceal these tensions from others . . . Related to the negative assessment of conflict is the attitude that the exercise of social control is dirty and unpleasant work. This extends not only to aggressive tactics such as violence—which is felt to be extremely distasteful—but also to many efforts simply to reach a peaceful accommodation with an offender.

People generally avoid those viewed as contentious . . . Common sense in the suburbs dictates that "normal people will see the advantages of avoidance for the prevention and containment of conflict."[36]

Rather than manifesting social integration and concern for one another, says Baumgartner, this avoidance of conflict actually reflects indifference. If people avoid contest with others, they simultaneously reject caring obligations toward them except in the most superficial ways. He calls this normative code "moral minimalism":

Moral minimalism entails a considerable degree of indifference to the wrongdoing of others. In fact, in settings where moral minimalism dominates as it does in the suburbs, this is only one dimension of a larger indifference that is found. If people in such places cannot be bothered to take action against those who offend them or to engage in conflicts, neither can they be bothered to help those in need.

To an extent in families, but especially among friends and neighbors, assistance is restricted to casual actions that entail few costs.

Moderation thus prevails in both positive and negative behavior alike. In this sense, weak social ties breed a general indifference and coldness, and a lack of conflict is accompanied by a lack of caring.[37]

Conflict resolution is not intended to endorse a morally minimalist orientation; rather than avoid conflict, it seeks to approach it in a new way. Adversaries do listen to each other, and as they can reject an agreement as well as influence its terms, conflict resolution offers the opportunity for moral outcomes although it cannot ensure it. And unless they feel that the outcome is indeed fair and attends to their interests, adversaries are unlikely to honor the agreement. Hence, although moral principles are not directly addressed in the process itself, they are an essential by-product.

Nor is conflict resolution intended to replace protest or recourse to the courts as they may be necessary to establish more just principles. It is entirely inappropriate in the face of clearly immoral adversaries; in that case only a win-lose strategy will do. Since few conflicts are matters of clear right and wrong, conflict resolution is a way of avoiding the perils of losing.

While the process itself does not address moral issues directly, it does so indirectly. The Quakers argue, for example, that because it empowers victims to create their own futures, it liberates them. Since it attends to multiple voices and divergent points of view, the process invites a more inclusive morality.

The central moral framework of conflict resolution—one that we believe best describes its moral orientation—is *care*. Care means attending to the needs of others, and such attention initiates the process, sustains it, and ultimately resolves it. The process begins with people who are having difficulties meeting their respective interests, values, and needs; its strategy focuses on them and seeks a resolution which gives heed to them. While its objective is peaceful relations, principles of care are integral to its concept of peace.

Michael Banks elaborates on the connections between conflict resolution, care, and peace in an article addressing international conflicts. There are four kinds of conceptions of peace, says Banks. One, the *peace as harmony* vision, "describes people, individually and collectively, as living in a state of self-absorption, enjoying a mystical existence" in a society in which not only violence, but even disagreement is unknown. This vision is both unrealistic and dangerous; the former because competing values and clashing interests are inevitable among people; the latter because by ignoring the realities of conflict, it in fact generates and escalates destructive conflict.

The second vision, *peace as order*, values above all a relatively predictable and stable social order. Conservatives who hold this view (Banks calls them "structural realists") emphasize that peace depends on power, and they resist anything that interferes with the reigning power-political mechanisms. Liberals "tinker" with the system, advocating reform through evolution. Neither side, says Banks, can conceive of a future substantially different from the past or present.

The third view, *peace as justice*, means different things to different people: human rights, conformance with constitutional principles, retribution for past offenses, absolute equality of treatment, or inequality based on some principle of proportionality. No advocate of moral relativism, Banks acknowledges that justice claims—poverty, oppression of ethnic groups, and group identity claims—must be attended to for peace to occur. But peace, he says, does not consist of submitting "to the demands of IRA hit men, Shi'ite suicide bombers or Sikh murderers of innocent tourists." Justice claims alert us to what is wrong with the system, but they cannot provide the framework for peace itself.

The fourth concept, *peace as conflict management*, sees peace as a "network of relationships full of energy and conflict which is nevertheless kept under societal control." It begins with the needs and values of ordinary people: the activities they like and the possessions they hope to own, the relationships they cherish and the protection of the groups with whom they identify—in short, what they require for physical survival and spiritual fulfillment. Conflicts revolve around such needs; conflict management is a way of attending to them before they become pathologically malevolent.[38]

In Banks's view, as in our own, peace is thus not tranquility but managed conflict; rather than a condition, it is a process. While it cannot ensure justice, it is a manifestation of care. In that context, the school conflict with which we began—the belief that the curriculum needs to be modified so as to remove its European bias as opposed to the view that the curriculum needs to stress a common democratic culture—can at best be regulated but probably never quite concluded. At its best, it will unleash creative energies to find new resolutions that more adequately attend to the needs of heterogeneous cultures while improving the relationships among them. Few groups, however, will be completely satisfied; new charges of exclusion and injustice will be leveled, and the cycle will begin anew. Such is the nature of a dynamic, managed peace in which contest, as much as consensus, is a valuable commodity.

NOTES

1. Albert Shanker, "Where We Stand: The Sobol Report," Advertisement under the auspices of the New York State United Teachers and the American Federation of Teachers, *The New York Times,* January 28, 1990, E7.

2. Thomas Sobol, "Understanding Diversity," *Educational Leadership* 48 (November 3, 1990): 27–30. Sobol, New York commissioner of education, appointed the "Task Force on Minorities: Equity and Excellence" which submitted their report to him in July 1989.

3. William M. Kephart, *Extra-ordinary Groups: Sociology of Unconventional Life-styles* (New York: St. Martin's Press, 1982); Benjamin Zablocki, *Alienation and Charisma: A Study of Contemporary American Communes* (New York: Free Press, 1980).

4. Georg Simmel, *Conflict*, trans. Kurt H. Wolff (Glencoe, Ill.: Free Press, 1955).

5. Lewis Coser, *The Functions of Social Conflict* (Glencoe, Ill.: Free Press, 1956).

6. Building on Coser's work, contemporary conflict analysts have tried to develop a more neutral and elaborate definition of conflict—one which neither binds it to images of violence nor aberration alone, and while recognizing the varied conditions which may lead to conflict, locates its basic source in beliefs and perceptions. James Laue's definition captures most of these elements: Conflict, he says is merely "escalated . . . competition" and competition is "natural." Adversaries may seek to injure or destroy one another, but they may also be content with gaining some advantage or simply neutralizing the other. While conflict flourishes in conditions of "scarce resources, power and prestige," Laue maintains that the real source of conflict lies in the beliefs adversaries have about each other; each believes that the goals of the other are incompatible with his own (James Laue, "The Emergence and Institutionalization of Third Party Roles in Conflict," in *Conflict Management and Problem Solving: Interpersonal to International Applications*, eds. Dennis J. D. Sandole and Ingrid Sandole-Staroste [New York: New York University Press, 1987], 17–29). Ronald Fisher also emphasizes the critical role of perceptions: Conflict, he says, is "a social situation involving perceived incompatibilities in goals or values between two or more parties, attempts by the parties to control each other, and antagonistic feel-

ings by the parties toward each other" (Ronald Fisher, *The Social Psychology of Intergroup and International Conflict Resolution* [New York: Springer-Verlag, 1990] 6).

7. Anatol Ray Rapoport, *Fights, Games, and Debates* (Ann Arbor: University of Michigan Press, 1960); Thomas C. Schelling, *The Strategy of Conflict* (Cambridge: Harvard University Press, 1960); John W. Burton, *Resolving Deep-Rooted Conflict: A Handbook* (New York: University Press of America, 1987); Fred Edmund Jandt with the assistance of Paul Gillette, *Win-Win Negotiating: Turning Conflict into Agreement* (New York: John Wiley & Sons, 1985). From the perspective of game theory, traditional views see conflict as competitive "zero-sum" games: one wins and the other loses.

8. Jennifer E. Beer, *Peacemaking in Your Neighborhood: Reflections on an Experiment in Community Mediation* (Philadelphia, Pa.: New Society, 1986), 1.

9. Beer, 1.

10. Beer, 233.

11. Elise Boulding, "Foreward," in Beer, iii–vi.

12. Janusz Reykowski, "Resolving Large Scale Political Conflict: The Case of the Round Table Negotiations in Poland," Paper presented at the 1990 Texas A&M Symposium on Group Conflict, College Station, Tex., April 1990.

13. Reykowski, 20.

14. As Fisher and Ury observe, it reinforces "the mental attitude of tackling a common problem together" (Roger Fisher and William Ury, with Bruce Patton, eds., *Getting to Yes: Negotiating Agreement Without Giving In* [Boston: Houghton Mifflin, 1981], 64).

15. Conceptions of these terms in current literature often bear greater similarity to the conflict resolution idea than traditional views. "Bargaining" as used by Lawrence Susskind and Jeffrey Cruikshank (Lawrence Susskind and Jeffrey Cruikshank, *Breaking the Impasse: Consensual Approaches to Resolving Public Disputes* [New York: Basic Books, 1987]) and "negotiating" as used by the Harvard Negotiation Project (Fisher and Ury) are two such examples.

16. David A. Wilder, "Social Categorization: Implications for Creation and Reduction of Inter-Group Bias," in *Advances in Experimental Social Psychology*, vol. 19, ed. Leonard Berkowitz (New York: Academic Press, 1986): 293–356; Ronald J. Fisher, *The Social Psychology of Intergroup and International Conflict Resolution* (New York: Springer-Verlag, 1990).

17. Fran Schmidt and Alice Friedman, *Creative Conflict Solving for Kids: Grades 4–9* (Miami Beach, Fla.: Grace Contrino Abrams Peace Education Foundation, 1983), 34.

18. Susanne Wichert, *Keeping the Peace: Practicing Cooperation and Conflict Resolution with Preschoolers* (Philadelphia, Pa.: New Society Publishers, 1989); Priscilla Prutzman et al., *The Friendly Classroom for a Small Planet: A Handbook on Creative Approaches to Living and Problem Solving for Children* (Philadelphia, Pa. and Santa Cruz, Calif.: New Society Publishers, 1988).

19. L. David Brown, *Managing Conflict at Organizational Interfaces* (Reading, Mass: Addison-Wesley, 1983), 8.

20. Brown, 180–181.

21. Brown, 188.

22. Morton Deutsch, *The Resolution of Conflict: Constructive and Destructive Processes* (New Haven: Yale University Press, 1973).

23. Deutsch, 361.

24. Gilbert G. Pompa, "The Community Relations Service," in *Conflict Management and Problem Solving: Interpersonal to International Applications*, eds. Dennis J. D. Sandole and Ingrid Sandole-Staroste (New York: New York University Press, 1987), 130–142, 137.

25. Pompa, 130–142.

26. By way of contrast, principles play a critical role in The Harvard Negotiation Project. While it too focuses on problem solving rather than bargaining, the method requires that the negotiator insist on fair standards—the latter to be determined by some objective criteria such as market value, expert opinion, equality of treatment, or law. In this approach, relationships are secondary (Fisher and Ury with Patton).

27. Laurence Thomas, *Living Morally: A Psychology of Moral Character* (Philadelphia: Temple University Press, 1989), 5.

28. Charlene Haddock Seigfried, "Pragmatism, Feminism, and Sensitivity to Context," in *Who Cares: Theory, Research, and Educational Implications of the Ethic of Care*, ed. Mary B. Brabeck (New York: Praeger, 1989), 63–83, 65.

29. "Vietnam Veteran Arthur E. 'Gene' Woodley, Jr., Combat Paratrooper, 5th Special Forces Group, 173rd Airborne Division, U.S. Army, An Khe, November 1968–December 1969," in *Bloods: An Oral History of the Vietnam War by Black Veterans*, Terry Wallace (New York: Random House, 1984), 243–265, 245–246.

30. "Vietnam Veteran, Woodley," Wallace, 263, 264.

31. Anthony Cortese, *Ethnic Ethics: The Restructuring of Moral Theory* (Albany: State University of New York Press, 1990), 158.

32. Ruth L. Wynn, "Custody Disputes and the Victims," in *Intractable Conflicts and Their Transformation*, eds. Louis Kriesberg, Terrell A. Northrup, and Stuart J. Thorson (Syracuse, N.Y.: Syracuse University Press, 1989), 83–92.

33. Robert L. Heath and Associates, *Strategic Issues Management: How Organizations Influence and Respond to Public Interests and Policies* (San Francisco: Jossey-Bass, 1988), 197.

34. Beer.

35. Alexander Abdennur, *The Conflict Resolution Syndrome: Volunteerism, Violence, and Beyond* (Ottawa, Ont.: University of Ottawa Press, 1987).

36. M. P. Baumgartner, *The Moral Order of a Suburb* (New York: Oxford University Press, 1988), 130–131.

37. Baumgartner, 131, 133, 134.

38. Michael Banks, "Four Conceptions of Peace," in *Conflict*, eds. Sandole and Sandole-Staroste, 259–274.

CHAPTER 9

Making the Global Connection

Managing a salvage yard is a great way to make a living because there is so much waste in this culture . . . Basically what we have now in the cities is a system designed to manufacture garbage . . .

Even if we started building everything to last, the old things would still be good and they'd be lower priced because they are old. That's another aspect of recycling and salvage. There's an egalitarian access, ultimately, for everybody.

My salvage yard in Berkeley, Urban Ore, provides an outlet for imagination . . . Certain people who come into the yard are looking for something to spark their imagination. You can see them eyeing things, trying to discover a new use for something . . . Fraternity guys buy cracked used toilets because they just want something to fill with ice and put beer cans in. They think it's funny. Well, cracked ceramic is better for the ozone shield than Styrofoam.

There's an art contingent that comes into the yard. People will buy a piece of rusted iron because they like the way it looks. People come in and they'll say, "I'm not into recycling. I'm just cheap." . . . But a lot of people combine that bargaining spirit with a sense of ecology, a desire not to exploit the earth . . .

On the other hand, we get people who are barely surviving, probably homeless, and on a rock-bottom level in terms of their ability to survive in a city. For example, you get a guy like Jamie who calls and says he's got this pedestal sink he wants to bring in . . . When he gets here, it turns out to be this *beige* pedestal sink with good chunks of the enamel broken off and you can see the iron beneath it. It's something nobody would buy . . . So I gave the guy five bucks for the effort of doing it, and somehow that all fits into the betterment of the urban sce-

nario . . . There are a lot of people like him who have no money, yet
don't want a handout . . .
    I dislike the word recycling because it seems so antiseptic. It doesn't
have a human element to it . . . Conservation is an idea I like as "the
right thing to do." But salvage is a process. It's more alive. Salvaging
and scavenging include the elements of judgment and discrimination and
imagination and freedom. When people ask me what I do, I say, "Run
a salvage yard." . . . I'm a junk man.[1]

Salvage man Michael Helm, who expressed the above thoughts to interviewer Beth Bosk some three years ago, has little difficulty making what we
call "the global connection." Measured by ordinary success standards, his
occupation would rank near the bottom. Measured in terms of meaningful
work, Helm's conceptualization of what he does would place it nearer the
top.
    What does "global" mean? A derivative of the word "globe," "global"
means something much larger than the sphere representing the physical features of the earth. Webster's Dictionary says it means "comprehensive," "all
inclusive," "relating to or involving the whole world." More a metaphor
than a precise term, globalism implies a whole world, not merely the earth
but something beyond, in which humans are no longer the exclusive frame
of reference but part of an intricately interdependent ecosystem. Making the
global connection means personally relating to and feeling responsible for
this totality, even if understanding escapes us.
    Helm expresses some ways of relating to this totality. He is mindful of a
physical space much larger than the one he lives in: the urban scene, where
garbage collects, and the skies above, the site of the vulnerable ozone shield.
But he's also very concerned with humans and their inter-relationships. "An-
tiseptic" words, like "recycling," repel him because they have "no human
element," and he has a profound respect for particularly human attributes
such as imagination and judgment. His pleasure at being able to "buy"
something from Jamie rather than letting him feel he's getting something
for nothing suggests how much he values others' dignity. And he particularly values egalitarian relationships. He's delighted, for example, that he can
provide all people—rich and poor, the artistic and merely "cheap"—" egalitarian access" to what he has to sell. And as though to emphasize the notion
of equal merit of all people, he eschews any lofty description of what he
does—such as conservationist or recycler—in favor of the term "junk man."
    These elements and more constitute the elements of what we call "making
the global connection." It includes a deep respect for natural systems and
diverse life forms, a profound intuitive sense of human equality, a keen appreciation for those particular human attributes that can best visualize and
create more humane and balanced futures, and a pervading recognition that
peace is the essential precondition for all the foregoing to become manifest.

Two major principles underlie these attitudes: the principle of *stewardship*, which calls upon people to leave the world's human and nonhuman resources no less depleted than we now find them, and the principle of *restoration*, which calls upon people to repair and replenish the world's human and nonhuman resources. In short, the elements of the global connection are care writ large.

Our purpose here is to suggest ways to encourage making the global connection, particularly as it relates to the themes of environment and peace, and to illustrate how people in diverse contexts may and do express it. We begin first with global thinking and global talk.

Encouraging people to think globally is one means for making the global connection. Global thought is abstract; its advantage lies in keeping people focused on the larger picture even as they act locally. Global thought, in other words, can inform appropriate local action.

Not everyone agrees that global thinking is useful. Echoing thoughts we expressed earlier, prominent ecologist Wendell Berry argues that the very terms "global" or "planetary" are not only too abstract to be useful, but potentially pernicious. Abstractions, he says, are responsible for many of the world's problems and rather than helping people orient themselves in a larger whole, they actually remove them from the only context in which they can have any impact—the local context.[2]

Alan AtKisson, editor of the environmentalist journal *In Context*, offered a persuasive rebuttal to Berry in an article he wrote in 1990. "Understanding *in the abstract* that the sum of our individual actions has an effect that is planetary" is useful, said AtKisson, because it helps us "reach as far as we can." Without the pull to extend themselves, which abstractions provide, people may well "withdraw their antennae," looking "only at the precious piece of earth under [their] noses."[3]

Like Berry, we agree that abstractions can be dangerous, and like AtKisson we also believe they can deepen understanding and inspire benevolent visions. Toward that end, we need appropriate global abstractions.

Global thinking requires an appropriate language. Encouraging people to think globally requires global talk: a deliberate and conscious effort to use concepts and metaphors which express global themes. It includes words like equality, diversity, respect, peace, and care applied universally. Global talk is difficult, yet the effort itself can change entrenched attitudes and ways of relating.

David Gershon, ecological and peace activist, offers a good example of how even the most enlightened find global talk difficult. A creative visionary, he, along with his partner Gail Straub, organized the first Earth Run, a metaphoric event intended to promote the idea of global responsibility for peace. Relay teams around the world carried a lit torch, making sure that the light did not become extinguished at any point. The torch represented the light of peace, and in order to encircle the planet with peace, each community within each country had the responsibility for moving the light through their part of the planet. An inspired idea, the Run was eminently successful, involving thousands of people around the world.

Ironically, however, Gershon could not resist using war metaphors in regard to another project he organized, the Gaia Leadership Project. Describing the difficulties in getting people to work cooperatively on behalf of transformational change, he said "It's as though we have to fight a battle," where "all these different generals need to go out together in concert." As for himself, "I sometimes like to think of what I'm doing as the 'spiritual warrior school.' "[4]

The problem with such language is not necessarily the speaker's intent—Gershon is conscious of the battle metaphor he's using—but their impact. Warrior crusades make death alluring: martyrdom becomes a way to achieve heroic status, as evidenced by the label "ecomartyr" bestowed on Brazilian activist Chico Mendes when he was murdered in 1988. Peace language needs to embrace terms like "struggling with" rather than "battling against," growing rather than winning, and living rather than dying, as feminist and peace educator Betty Reardon points out.[5] We need to find ways to make such language as appealing as war images.

Religious talk offers yet a more complex example of the difficulties of global peace talk. Yet as it is developing, it also illustrates the usefulness of abstract thinking in creating new understandings and relationships.

All major religions of the world espouse peace, yet each has also justified war in particular historical circumstances. Religious differences have contributed significantly to some of the world's bitterest confrontations, each side claiming justice as its own and God on its side.[6] Yet as religion can divide and promote group hatred, so can it reconcile groups, even encouraging heroic altruism on others' behalf. Religion is both a wedge and a bond, declared the United States Institute of Peace in 1989: a vehicle for mobilizing bloody warfare as well as one "that lifts tensions and promotes reconciliation, and a force that drives people to disregard personal welfare and follow the directives of their faith."[7]

Impeding the reconciliation process is one of the self-defining characteristics of many religious groups; the sense of the absolute correctness of their truth claims and the fundamental error of all others. Ecumenism, a twentieth century movement, is the concept which has helped launch some religious groups towards acceptance of diversity and the notion of pluralism. Yet ecumenical talk poses continuing problems, even for the benevolently inclined.

Ecumenism began as a Protestant movement, and initially confined itself to intra-ecclesial unity among Protestants. Its proponents hoped to achieve a universal Christian fellowship through conferences designed to promote mutual understanding and cooperation among Christians on common missionary tasks. No longer the province of Protestants alone, ecumenism is beginning to mean an acceptance of religious pluralism and a vision of the unity of humankind.

One of the first tasks ecumenicists often undertake is to remove their pejorative "talk" with reference to other groups, a matter of considerable gravity since such talk encourages not only prejudice but fratricide. The Catholic Church, for example, launched itself on this path in relationships with Jews in the 1965 Vatican II document, *Nostra Aetate*, which absolved Jews collectively of the charge of deicide and called for the removal of the term "perfidious" from the liturgy.

While this represented a major theological shift, ecumenicity advocates soon discovered that it barely scratched the surface. For while it removed the most blatant aspects impeding the spirit of unity, it did not address the more subtle ones, those that most revealed the Church's continuing sense of singular "truth" and superiority.

An initial statement issued in 1987 by Joseph Cardinal Ratzinger (Prefect of the Vatican's Congregation for the Doctrine of Faith) illustrates how feelings of triumphal superiority can surface even when meant to build bridges. Intended to convey a new spirit between Catholics and Jews, Cardinal Ratzinger wrote that the church dialogue with Judaism "always implies our union with the faith of Abraham, but also the reality of Jesus Christ, in which the faith of Abraham finds its fulfillment."[8] Hence, while speaking of unity, the statement implied that Judaism by itself was lacking, and that only in Christianity could it find completion.

As a consequence of the criticism he received, Ratzinger issued a revised statement: the two new words he added changed the meaning dramatically. The church dialogue with Judaism, the new statement said, "always implies our union with the faith of Abraham, but also the reality of Jesus Christ, in whom, for us, the faith of Abraham finds its fulfillment."[9] No longer a statement implying Judaism's inadequacy, it implicitly acknowledges a plurality of views regarding religious fulfillment, while simultaneously maintaining that for Catholics completion of the faith of Abraham requires accepting the reality of Jesus Christ.

Yet without a sense of superiority with respect to other religions, many religious groups feel their core identity threatened. As Claude Geffré puts it: "The most difficult requirement for the Christian is that of recognizing equality among dialogue partners. What is my Christian faith if it does not concern a definitive manifestation of God? If Christ is but one mediator among others?"[10] Yet, as Geffré also notes, there can be no real dialogue and "union" if participants insist that theirs is the only religious truth.

Does ecumenicity and religious pluralism then require surrendering one's convictions and abandoning evaluation of others' moral codes? Not according to J. Paul Rajashekar. What it does require, he says, is acknowledgment of the reality of multiple religious expressions and the willingness to dialogue with the premise "that the major religious traditions of the world have something worthwhile to contribute to the enrichment of humanity and are ways of leading people to their fulfillment, however this goal may be understood and interpreted—salvation, liberation, heaven, kingdom of God, etc."[11] What the process can do, he says, is to move groups toward "understanding, corrective criticism and mutual enrichment," without "diluting the respective heritages or prejudging irreducible differences."

The spirit of mutual enrichment and religious pluralism without abandonment of their own distinct heritage and their right to assess other truths informs the "*Emet Ve Emunah*" statement of faith recently issued by the Conservative branch of Judaism. Conservative Jews, it points out, have learned much from others, and their mission is to continue to discern truths from which they can learn and to share those they have learned. And while Jewish tradition recognizes but one God, it also recognizes that "God has more than one nation":

As Conservative Jews, we acknowledge without apology the many debts which Jewish religion and civilization owe to the nations of the world. We eschew triumphalism with respect to other ways of serving God . . . Many modern thinkers, both Jewish and Gentile, have noted that God may well have seen fit to enter covenants with many nations. Either outlook, when relating to others, is perfectly compatible with a commitment to one's own faith and pattern of religious life.

Theological humility requires us to recognize that although we have but one God, God has more than one nation. Our tradition explicitly recognizes that God entered into a covenant with Adam and Eve, and later with Noah and his family as well as His special covenant with Abraham and the great revelation to Israel at Sinai. It is part of our mission to understand, respect, and live with the other nations of the world, to discern those truths in their cultures from which we can learn, and to share with them the truths that we have come to know.[12]

Of course, ecumenicity is as yet an embryonic movement whose spirit has yet to reach not only Christians and Jews in all their sectarian forms, but also Moslems and Buddhists among others in North America as well as world-wide. That we may indeed be entering a new ecumenical age is suggested by the current effort of multiple religious groups—Catholic, Protestant and Orthodox Christians, Jews, Hindus, Buddhists, Muslims, and Sikhs and Bahais—to draft a "Universal Declaration of a Global Ethic." Its endorsers hope the global ethic document, ultimately intended to be accepted by a full range of religious and ethical institutions, will serve as a minimal ethical standard for all of humankind.

The Global Ethic Project was launched at the 100th anniversary meeting of the World Parliament of Religions which met in Chicago in 1993 and included more than six thousand participants. At that meeting, the Parliament adopted a preliminary document drafted by Professor Hans Küng and titled "Toward a Global Ethic."[13] A revised version, proposed by Professor Leonard Swidler of the religion department at Temple University and titled a "Universal Declaration of a Global Ethic," has been the focus of several subsequent international meetings held in Warsaw; Washington D.C.; Seoul; and Italy.[14]

The document's assumptions and scope make it unique in the annals of religious history. It calls on all civilizations and cultures, including religious cultures, to reject the "age of monologue"—isolation, domination or absorption of others—and embrace the "age of dialogue," conversing with others for the *primary* purpose of learning from them. It also calls on all individuals and religious traditions to work for universal human rights, justice, peace, and conservation of the earth, and assume responsibilities to enhance freedom, dignity, and the valuing of all living and non-living things as such issues arise in law, conscience, relationships between women and men, property, and other related specifics.

In any attempt to embrace the meaning of ecumenism, each group will inevitably wrestle with problems of reconciling unity and diversity, pluralism and particularism, and the necessity for discernment: detecting, analyzing, and distinguishing those elements which can be mutually enriching from those which are pernicious and destructive. That such issues can arise is testimony to the power of an abstract idea in creating an alternative future.

Ecumenism is an abstract concept, a way of articulating a peaceful relationship among world religions. Without action, however, it would remain little more than a provocative thought. The ultimate purpose of global talk and global thinking is not thought itself but action. Making the global connection means acting locally on behalf of global welfare.

The "think globally, act locally" advice, a popular motto among globalists, was first offered at the First Global Conference on the Future held in Toronto, Ontario, in July 1980. Some considered assumptions about the nature of social change underlie it.

How does social change happen? Conventional paradigms postulate a "top-down" model. The model requires reformers who presumably understand the problems and how to remedy them, and who are prepared to lead the unenlightened in the appropriate direction, coercively if necessary.

Many contemporary globalists believe these paradigms are outmoded and doomed to failure, even when benevolently intended. They fail ideologically because those who presume they have the answers to problems really don't understand just how complex they are. They fail strategically because policy decisions emanating from above need to be imposed on those below, who often prove recalcitrant and suspicious.

Contemporary globalists acknowledge that they do not fully understand global problems and reject the idea that they can be solved by imposition from above alone. Change, they believe, is a creative, evolving process that depends on wide public participation, more "bottom-up" than "top-down." Since people live their lives and make decisions at the local level, and even the smallest decisions cumulatively affect the globe, "local action" is the significant arena for global solutions. As Canadian businessman and environmentalist Maurice F. Strong expresses it, the "most effectively managed scale and level of decision-making" is the local one. Elevating every issue to the global level for solution invites paralysis, for while global problems can only be fully understood and addressed in the global context, global solutions are few."[15]

But just how "local" is "local?" Like "global," it seems more a metaphor than a precise term. It depends on where and how you live, whether you are stationary or mobile and if mobile whether you choose to go somewhere, who your networks are, and how you communicate with each other. As we shall see, ordinary people act out their global impulses from their dining rooms to the international scene.

To illustrate this diversity, we focus on two major global themes: the *environment* and *peace*. In some cases, local action begins as a response to global thinking; in others global thinking plays no role. In some cases, the motivation appears to be dominantly altruistic, in yet others enlightened self-interest or what some have called "mindful opportunism" may be the central inducement. Rarely are motivations singular.

Environment issues attract many diverse people. Acting locally often means acting with neighbors and friends.

Heather Halabisky, for example, hosts home environmental parties from her dining room. She started doing this, she says, after she attended a friend's home environmental party in Canada, where she learned for the first time that her "lifestyle was contributing to the destruction of the planet":

Until then I had assumed that it was "they" who were causing all the trouble—the paper mills, the chemical plants, the politicians. It came as a shock to realize I was just as irresponsible. I assumed I was doing all I could by recycling! It never occurred to me that the products I used, the plastic bag I carried my groceries in, the car I drove and the food I chose were damaging the planet in much the same ways as the action of those I pointed my finger at.[16]

Heather now hosts her own home environmental parties to which she invites friends, neighbors, and acquaintances. She begins by allowing people to introduce themselves, then discusses the problem and moves on to some solutions, which revolve around three themes: reduce, reuse, recycle. Reducing includes selective shopping, refraining from buying unnecessary products, selecting products with as little packaging as possible and avoiding plastics. Reusing means simply using everything as many times as possible, and recycling implies converting used products rather than disposing of them.

To help her guests understand concretely what this means, Heather shows them how she does things:

I display the non-toxic cleansers I use, the cloth lunch bags, the recycled paper products, the mug and straw and utensils I carry in my shopping bag. We walk through the house and see my recycling system—simple baskets and boxes. And I take them outside to see the trench into which I throw kitchen wastes and the compost where I "cook" my garden clippings.[17]

As Heather implies, those she has hosted have modified their mindless habits, and the experience itself has proved community building as people learn to know each other and harness their energies around a common goal.

Bertha Gilkey used her energies to repair the residential center in which she lives. The results have been not only a transformed physical area, but as in Heather's experience, an enhanced sense of community. Unlike Heather, who thinks globally, Bertha just wanted to improve the heavily vandalized shabby public housing project in St. Louis that she calls home. As journalist Harry Boyte tells the story, it all began with a laundromat:

Everyone wanted a laundromat again. All of the project's previous ones had been vandalized. Bertha and her group began to organize other residents. "Let's get our laundromat locked," they said. "Locked?" Gilkey recalls, "When we took over, there were no locks. There were no doors! All the doors had been taken down."[18]

Bertha's group held a fund-raiser to buy a new lock and paint and got a new door from the city housing authority. After repairing the laundromat, they painted the hallways on each floor. As Gilkey explained: Everybody who lived on a floor was responsible for painting that floor . . . If you didn't paint that floor, it didn't happen." Parents whose floors remained unpainted were nagged by their children until they complied. Unable to help with the painting, the elderly prepared lunch.

The group organized a conduct code, establishing rules of behavior and elected monitors for each floor. "No fights, no garbage out the windows, no loud disruptions, etc." To reach the young people, they involved the schools. In the art classes, children constructed a cardboard model of what Cochran would look like with a playground and street. When the principal put it on display in a glass dome, the proud artists would point out the building in which they lived. In other classes, children wrote papers titled "What I Like About Living Here." All of this, says Gilkey, told these young people that "it's all right to live in public housing" and by gradually re-building their self-esteem, helped them concentrate on what was positive in their lives.[19]

The net result was a transformed residential center which the participants themselves created. The physical changes have been dramatic; the center now includes courtyards, tennis courts, playgrounds, a community center, and townhouses. And as is generally the case in such cooperative ventures, relationships among neighbors have improved, and those who made it happen feel an enhanced sense of potency. What makes them particularly proud is the fact that they used their own resources to make it happen, for as Bertha explains, "This goes against the grain. Poor people are supposed to be managed."

Bertha spearheaded what some might call a grassroots restoration effort, one that began with a local need and was resolved by the community most affected by it. Alan Durning of the World Watch Institute says that grassroots efforts such as these "are our best hope for global prosperity and ecology." On the rise around the world, they form what he calls a "front line in the worldwide struggle to end poverty and environmental destruction."

Like the St. Louis inhabitants, the type of grassroots groups Durning describes are also the impoverished, acting on behalf of their own community interests. To be found on all continents, including North America, they take many forms: peasant farmers unions, neighborhood action federations, tribal nations, religious study groups, and workplace co-ops. Their impact often extends beyond their modest beginnings. In Kenya, for example, the National Council of Women launched a national tree planting drive that has resulted in more than a million trees being planted since 1977, while in the Sahel of West Africa, the African federation "Naam" has organized thousands of villagers to do such things as build check dams to trap drinking and irrigation water and adopt simple farming techniques to conserve water.[20]

In an effort to encourage grassroots restoration efforts, some groups have established settlements in areas which most desperately need them. The Auroville international community in southern India is an example. As with people who begin such ventures, their spirit was altruistic and their goals unclear.

The vague desire to do something constructive led some thirty people in 1968 to Auroville, a deforested and environmentally degraded area. As described by resident Savitra (Alan Lithman), who arrived there in 1969, they were not ecology experts but rather "generalists" and "seekers" who simply wanted to do something together. Without any real sense of what they might do ecologically, it was not until three years later, following suggestions made by Huey Johnson who was then with the Whole Earth-Point Foundation in the Bay Area, that they began planting trees. Now composed of seven hundred residents from twenty-three nations, their group has transformed the area into a fertile productive forest and agricultural land.

But as Savitra describes it, the change became possible only when group members recognized their own ignorance:

At first they [the Tamil villagers] were skeptical, with so many westerners in their area and with their memories of colonial times . . . These villagers were not giving us carte blanche. They did not know what we were doing there, it didn't make sense to them. And most of us didn't have backgrounds as social workers. So we started off from where we were, with our prejudices and our misconceptions of each other. We found early on that trying to convince villagers verbally of what was in their best interests was a total failure. We'd go to the local people and say "Listen, don't cut down your trees for firewood. You're going to have no land left." But how do you stop that with words? They need to cook their food, and "afforestation" has no meaning for them. We went through a couple of awkward years while they watched us planting trees and digging these earth mounds all around our field, and they went on doing what they were doing, cutting down trees and using what land they had for monsoon agriculture.[21]

But as their forests grew and the effects started to show, the villagers began to understand, says Savitra. Now working together with the Auroville residents, they are learning the techniques and applying them to their own fields. "*Living* there," says Savitra, "not just being a one-shot project or an aid program—has made all the difference, because we have lived through our own impatience, and they have lived to see the results with us."

Having begun with the assumption they could simply tell the Tamil residents the right way to behave, Savitra and his community learned they could not succeed without addressing their needs and sharing their lives.

Some religious groups are acting locally in response to environmental concerns by incorporating environmental themes in their rituals, issuing proclamations and sometimes modifying their theologies to accord with environmental concerns.

For example, a Jewish environmentalist group calling itself Shomrei Adamah (Guardians of the Earth) recently published a book titled *Greening the Holidays*; its purpose to suggest ways of relating all Jewish holidays to environmental issues.[22] Several religious groups participate in Earth Day. And members of the clergy often make the environment a focus of their sermons, although few perhaps rival the one delivered by Pastor Christina Del Piero at St. Paul's United Church of Christ in New York's East Bronx on Earth Day 1989:

By all accounts, Pastor Christina Del Piero of St. Paul's United Church of Christ in New York's East Bronx gave an especially memorable sermon last June 11. It was their celebration of Earth Day, and to give thanks for nature's bounty, members of the congregation had brought in apples, barley and flowers to lay on the simple wooden altar. From the pulpit, del Piero praised the offerings. Then she opened a bag of garbage and scattered it around the altar. As the congregation gasped, she explained her apparent blasphemy. "We trash the earth, yet it is every bit as sacred as any place within this church."[23]

Several groups have issued proclamations indicating their concerns. The American Baptist Church and the United Methodist Church, for example, have issued a policy statement urging their congregants to pursue ecologically sound life styles, and evangelist Billy Graham has proclaimed that Christians "have a responsibility to take a lead in trying to take care of the Earth."[24] The Vatican's 1990 World Day of Peace on January 1 focused on the environment while the Jewish Theological Seminary in New York devoted its 1989 High Holy Day Message to the environment.

But one of the most significant events indicating the essential shift in consciousness occurred in 1987 when more than five hundred priests and nuns, Mennonites, Eastern Orthodox Christians, and other theologians met at the first North American Conference on Christianity and Ecology (NACCE) in North Webster, Indiana. Here, fundamentalists and liberals discussed their differing views of the Bible's environmental statements. Many may have regarded Dominican priest Matthew Fox's declaration that "the universe itself rather than the Bible is the proper starting point for spirituality" as blasphemy, but most agreed that action on behalf of the Earth was more important than theological debate. Toward that end, the NACCE coalition pledged itself to intensify its efforts to spread the message among all sympathetic religious groups.[25] Their efforts helped make possible another significant event. Asked recently to sign a Scientists' Appeal on the Environment, hundreds of religious groups representing eighty-three countries around the world did so.[26]

Ecological concerns have thus propelled many religious groups toward finding common ground and a shared arena for action, albeit expressed within the particularistic traditions of each. All of this is a far cry from some twenty-five years ago, when environmentalists generally shared the view of Lynn White, Jr., that Christianity and Judaism were primarily responsible for the ecological planetary crisis.[27] Whether in fact the attack on religion was warranted,[28] what distinguishes the current response of many Christian and Jewish clergy is the move toward making environmental issues a prominent item on the religious agenda.

Some businesses, small and big, are also responding to environmental concerns in terms of the products they manufacture and sell and the economic "wants" they are creating or responding to. Their motives, too, are often mixed, ranging from primary concerns with environmental degradation to enlightened self-interest and what some have called "mindful opportunism."

Like Michael Helm, several small business entrepreneurs are viewing what they produce and sell through an environmental prism.[29] Musician Barbara Herson, for example, has organized a project she calls "Earthtunes," which puts on programs for schools:

I put on programs designed to address the environmental concerns of a community, and offer it to schools . . . The programs focus on a variety of issues including waste disposal, air and water pollution, and energy conservation. Earthtunes helps children learn about ways to effect a positive change in their environment."[30]

Paul Hawken, chair of Smith & Hawken (a catalog and retail company specializing in horticultural products), calls small entrepreneurs like Herson "the real cultural revolutionaries" of our society. The reason they go into business, claims Hawken, is to solve problems that money alone cannot and more to become themselves than to make money.[31] In the process, many of them change the values of the society around them.

This appears to be true for Don Hayden, owner of "The Undaunted Recycler." Hayden collects used computer and bond paper from small businesses and sells it to Weyerhaeuser Company to be made into stationery, ledger paper, newsprint, tissue, and toweling. But Hayden does more than just sell the paper; he also educates: "I don't just pick up paper and sell it. I give my clients information to increase their awareness of the solid waste problem and how they can be part of the solution."[32] Apparently successful, Hayden, who employs only one other person, has managed to acquire 125 clients.

Small business concerns have been the source of many environmental innovations eventually adopted by larger companies. Recycling paper, for example, began with small businesspeople. When Ann Newkirk Niven, a commercial printer, decided to start printing on recycled paper in 1988, some people thought it was "weird"; one potential customer even told her she was filing her name on her Rolodex under "Hippie Printers."[33] By 1992, several major publishers had adopted the practice of using recycled paper and wanted their consumers to know it.[34]

Anita Roddick, founder of The Body Shop, has turned her global ideology into a successful international business. The Body Shop began as a small enterprise in England, specializing in natural cosmetics, all of them biodegradable and none costing more than six dollars. With her company now expanded to include 370 outlets in thirty-four countries, Roddick has maintained the same natural product and price structure. In addition, every franchise is expected to participate in a community project of some sort—Amnesty International, AIDS, battered women—and to pay "First World" wages even in "Third World" countries.[35]

Success has apparently not jeopardized Roddick's commitments but it has raised some fundamental issues for Ben & Jerry's Homemade Inc., another "socially responsible" business. Their story illustrates the painful value conflicts small entrepreneurs face when they lose control of the decision-making process.

Ben & Jerry's Homemade began as an ice cream producing business, which from the outset included a commitment to ecology, egalitarianism, and peace. Translated into business practices, this meant such things as using natural products (including the agricultural products from the endangered rain forests of Brazil), a salary structure that did not allow too wide a gap between executives and the lowest paid workers, and a general collegial way of making decisions. It also meant putting 7.5 percent of the company's pretax income into the Ben & Jerry's Foundation, which spends it on a broad array of causes including peace and education groups, citizenship exchange and cultural programs, and cooperative international ventures in science, business, and the arts.

Yet for Ben, one of the original partners, the problems began when the company went public. In place of a partnership, the business now became responsible to stockholders, many of whom were valued neighbors and friends. The problem was not the stockholders' values, which apparently were largely similar to Ben's, but rather the way they preferred to realize them. As many of them saw it, the company's first responsibility was "to make as much money as possible, and then spend it in a socially responsible way." Ben does not agree; in his view *how* one makes money is equally important: "I see those values as influencing the way the company does business in all facets, and influencing how it makes all its decisions."[36]

Ben has lost control, and his frustration may well reflect Hawken's point. Rather than merely to make money, small entrepreneurs go into business to become more themselves and to realize their values. When this no longer becomes possible, the venture loses its attraction.

Yet if small businesses introduce cultural innovations out of the spirit of personal values, enlightened big businesses often adopt them because of "mindful opportunism." Unlike "mindless opportunism," which is short-sighted and exploitative, mindful opportunism takes advantage of opportunities to make things better.

Mindful opportunism has increased profits for some businesses. Recycling industrial chemicals in-house has saved 3-M Corporation millions of dollars, for example, while an internal paper recycling program has saved American Telephone and Telegraph Co. 2 million dollars in disposal costs.[37] Evidence like this has led several ecologists to share an optimistic view about the future.

Ecologist Nora Goldstein, for example, says increased profits, coupled with growing consumer ecological awareness and new government regulations, may help persuade businesses that good ecological management practices are consistent with good economics and are essential for future prosperity.[38] Stanford business and law school graduate, Earth Day cofounder Dennis Hayes agrees: companies that are environmentally responsive, he asserts, will have a very substantial advantage in this decade.[39] If the United States used energy as efficiently as the Japanese, says The World Watch Institute, they would have saved $200 billion dollars in the last several years.[40] Michael Silverstein, president of Environmental Economics, ventures a grand prediction: millionaires of this decade will be the pollution "cleaner-uppers."[41]

Such optimism may be overstated even for the affluent west, where consumer pressures and government regulations are encouraging businesses to be more mindful. It seems a fantasy as applied to developing nations, where regulatory mechanisms are few and consumers overwhelmingly concerned with meeting basic survival needs. In this context, businesses find it far more profitable to "dump" products rejected by the more environmentally conscious west, including products which may be safe when used in western societies but harmful when consumed in the context of developing countries.[42]

Yet here too is some room for guarded optimism. For one thing, the environmentally safer products developed for domestic consumption may eventually find their way to less developed countries. And the media that will advertise them are likely to draw attention to their particular environmental features, thus perhaps exporting some of the west's growing environmental values and modifying Third World consumer consciousness.

For another, nations around the world increasingly realize that they have a stake in a common global environment. When the first world conference on the environment was held in Stockholm in 1972, many nations believed that environmental protection and economic development were incompatible goals. Today, says international and environmental law professor Edith Brown Weiss, "countries recognize that sound economic development must be environmentally sustainable" and their basic concern is how to finance it so as to raise living standards for the poor today and in the future.[43]

Evidence of this change is the fact that countries around the world are participating in developing international laws to regulate the economy so as to protect the environment. Some 870 such international legal instruments already exist, Weiss claims, each having "one or more provisions addressing the environment." Like other forms of international law, of course, they bind only those states that accept them as binding, and frequently even those that helped develop them subsequently refuse to accept them. They are, however, setting new international normative standards about environmental protection.

Like environmental issues, concerns about peace have also prompted varied forms of "acting locally." In fact, local action has become the heart of the "peace movement," a loosely organized grassroots effort to promote peace around the world. Its objectives generally include finding alternatives to violence, encouraging military restraint, and promoting interpersonal and international cooperation.

The central strategy advocated by peace activists is "citizen diplomacy." Diplomacy has traditionally meant negotiations between officially appointed high level nationals. Citizen diplomacy assumes that ordinary people interacting unofficially can affect world peace. They may do this by promoting positive relationships among people in various nations, thus preparing a general global culture receptive to peace. Or they may focus on relationships between adversarial nations, encouraging citizens within each to exert their influence with high level officials on behalf of peace.

The central role peace activists assign citizens stems from several beliefs about governments, one of which is that they tend to be rigid, non-creative, and inefficient. Some support for this assumption comes from developments in international humanitarian aid.

International humanitarian aid provides material help to stricken places around the globe. It presumably promotes peace by sending messages of care and by reducing the potential for violence often borne out of desperate needs. One of its major problems has been its frequent failure to reach the very people who need it most.

Increasing numbers of people attribute the problem to reliance on governments as the recipients and distributors of help. As they see it, private nonprofits are more efficient and cost effective than governments and react more quickly and impartially than governments. After having studied the problem, researcher Brian Smith argues that the belief is warranted: private nonprofits are able to carry out helping tasks that governments cannot, and the poor in developing countries are more likely to receive the aid. Moreover, because they are not constrained by public mandates, they can single out particular groups for special help and be more flexible in the types of services they can offer.[44]

This helps explain why increasing numbers of people are funneling aid through nongovernmental nonprofit organizations. In 1980, for example, North Atlantic private voluntary organizations or nongovernmental organizations transferred some $4.7 billion dollars to Africa, the Middle East, Latin America, and Asia—an increase of 68 percent over 1964. Over 4600 private groups (e.g., church-related missionary and service agencies, secular nonprofit organizations, credit and cooperative associations, foundations, and educational and labor groups) received such monies, transmitting them in turn to more than twenty thousand organizations in developing countries.[45]

Peace activists rely on ordinary citizens for yet another reason. Governments, say some of their leading spokespeople, are better suited to aggravate international hostilities than to transform them into peaceful relationships. As peace activist Craig Comstock explains:

Almost any government, even a democratic one, is structurally ill-adapted to transform hostility into peace. One of the primary duties of government is to identify and defend against enemies. As soon as a pair of countries begin to identify one another as enemies, as the U.S. and the Soviet Union did long ago, they generally take steps that confirm and amplify the initial fears, thus starting a familiar cycle. If a government fails to be vigilant in "threat assessment" or to procure weapons with which to threaten the enemy in return, it does not deserve to govern.

So who is left to create the conditions for peace? . . . We suggest that the main source of peaceful intiatives is ordinary citizens and voluntary associations or, as they are now often called, "nongovernmental organizations."[46]

Is there evidence to support the idea that ordinary citizens can in fact mitigate international hostilities? David Cortright, former executive director of SANE and president of the Fourth Freedom Forum, provides some to suggest that the Cold War came to an end not because of the arms buildup, but because of ordinary citizens who labored to achieve peace democratically and peacefully. Governmental policy, he says, favored a "peace through strength" philosophy which became modified only as a consequence of massive various grassroots efforts.[47]

Many people agree. In the course of its evolution, the peace movement developed some strikingly innovative techniques for promoting peace among adversarial nations. Prominent among them are what has come to be known as "Track II" negotiations and grassroots reconciliatory dialogues and conversations.

Track II diplomacy is the name given to networking contacts between unofficial but important high status representatives of hostile groups. Begun some twenty years ago by John Burton,[48] Leonard Doob,[49] and Herbert Kelman,[50] invited participants usually include non-government individuals who have achieved public recognition in their respective countries. The format is generally a workshop setting designed to facilitate communication. Groups commonly meet often, their intent to overcome the sense of enmity through conversation, dialogue, role taking, and simulations. The International Society of Political Psychology (ISPP), which includes more than a thousand members (psychologists, historians, economists, etc.), for example, has initiated such contacts between Americans and Russians over the years, and also between Israelis and Arabs. While former undersecretary of state David Newsom says that such efforts are marginal at best in influencing official decision makers,[51] others believe they contributed substantially in shaping central conflict resolution strategies and principles, as well as preparing the path for significant shifts in these adversarial relationships.

Track II diplomacy concentrates on high status groups, who presumably are in the best position to influence their respective governments. But as Richard Schwartz points out, without the support of their larger national and ethnic communities, even governments wanting to reconcile adversaries may find it difficult to do so. In order to overcome wide-spread animosities and potential popular resistance, Schwartz advocates what he calls "grassroots reconciliatory dialogues."

Like Track II diplomacy, a grass-roots reconciliatory dialogue, as Schwartz conceives it, is essentially a dialogue among nationals from diverse backgrounds who have opposing partisan loyalties about a conflict. Unlike Track II diplomacy, it includes ordinary people who are far removed from the scene of confrontation, usually living in other countries. Schwartz, who has participated in such efforts with respect to the Middle East, says that when successful, their positive effects radiate beyond the dialogue itself. People encourage others to dialogue and often generate creative new ideas which, if widely publicized, may reach the powerful people who actually make decisions. The big problem, says Schwartz, is getting ordinary people to participate:

The first obstacle is disbelief that ordinary people, far removed from an international conflict, can have any effect at all. Second is the concern that participation in dialogue, if it has any effect, will be harmful to one's cause. Third is the fear of personal detriment, ranging from opportunity costs to less tangible anxiety over loss of status or even personal safety. Any one of these inhibitors can be sufficient to prevent people from participating in, let alone initiating, grass-roots dialogue to help overcome remote international conflicts.[52]

Despite these obstacles, says Schwartz, some people are motivated to participate in them out of a sense of "curiosity, intellectual interest, skepticism at claims of a monopoly of virtue, an attraction to lost causes, and a need to try to do something constructive."

Some or all of these motivations may well underlie participation in other types of grass-roots reconciliation efforts, whose objective is less to promote a structured dialogue among adversarial nationals and more toward promoting personally warm interactions among them.

Earthsteward's Network, whose self-stated objective is to create a model of peaceful service in sites known primarily for ethnic/racial mistrust and fear, is one such reconciliation group. One of its projects, called Peacetrees, invites young people from around the world to work together in reforesting a denuded area, most commonly a Third World site; another includes mutual visitations between hostile nationals for the purpose of building friendships and maintaining contacts. A similar kind of endeavor underlies the International Peace Walks Association, in which representatives of adversarial nationals participate in extensive walking tours in each other's countries, conversing with people along the way.

The impact of such endeavors is often greatest on the participants themselves; many say that they have learned a great deal besides feeling that they have indeed done something constructive on behalf of world peace. Such was the case, for example, for senior citizens Pat and Ron Herson, who participated in the Soviet-American Peace Walks in 1987–1988. Russell Baker, who interviewed the Hersons in 1989, describes their recollections as Pat, wearing a T-shirt saying "Babushka Pat" (grandmother) in Cyrillic, encountered the Soviets, and when the Soviets, in turn, walked in the United States:

"The babushkas came and hugged her," recalls Pat's husband Ron, "and they were crying and they said: 'for our children, please no more war.' " . . .

They arrived in Leningrad in June 1987 for the 450-mile journey to Moscow and soon found themselves a part of history in the making. "Everywhere we went, people said 'I've never seen an American before, but you're just like us,' " says Ron.

The most surprising aspect of the walk in the United States, they say, was the way their countrymen greeted the Soviets.

"We met the most loving, giving, interesting, interested people," Ron says. "Not only the walkers, but those who housed and fed us. It was like seeing our country through fresh eyes."[53]

A similar expererience led peace advocate Herb Walters, who participated in The Listening Project, toward a new view of a group he had considered an "enemy" and a different understanding of the role of peace groups generally.

Developed by the Rural Southern Voice for Peace, the Listening Project describes itself as having one major goal: "communication between people who normally are not communicating with one another, and should be doing so." A spin-off, The Contra Listening Project was intended to communicate with the Contras in Nicaragua. As described by Herb Walters and Carol Latharus, "for most of us in the peace movement, the Contra have been the enemy." Accepting the goal of The Listening Project, they went to Nicaragua to listen to the Contras, more specifically to do in-depth interviews with Contra foot soldiers rather than leaders or commandantes. Here's what Herb Walters writes happened to him as a consequence:

The Contra Listening Project helped me develop some new understanding. There are Guardia and mercenaries and power hungry commandantes in the Contra forces. But there are also men like Hilberto Sobal and Francisco Rodriquez who receive no salary for the war they fight. They see their fight as a struggle against oppression and injustice in Nicaragua.[54]

While he has not necessarily rejected an advocacy role, the experience has led Walters to reconsider the role of peace organizations. "Is there also a place for peace organizations that could act more as mediators than as advocates for one side?" he asks. "Is there a place for organizations that could be trusted by both sides—that could find the human faces of 'the enemy' and carry that message across the battle lines?"

It's a provocative question, one that challenges peace promoters around the world and is the centerpiece of the activities we've sketched here, including the one in which Walters himself participated. It is part of an effort to create a global culture of negotiation, one that tries to avoid dualistic "us/them" confrontations and promote cooperation through conflict management.

Can the activities we've described thus far—environmental home parties, grassroots restorations, Track II diplomacy, international walking trips, or reconciliatory dialogues—really repair or restore our human and non-human resources? As singular events, not very much. But as AtKisson proposes, cumulative efforts can be powerful, and they need to be incorporated into the routines of ordinary people from all walks of life.

Routinization requires compromise; the "purist" approach that demanded absolute consistency between ideals and life-styles advocated by globalists a decade ago have largely been abandoned on pragmatic grounds. Joel Makower, for example, coauthor of *The Green Consumer Guide*[55] notes that "environmentalism 1970's style embraced a back-to-the-earth philosophy and a simple no-frills life style," the consequence of which was that it wound having almost no impact at all.[56] Donella Meadows, a leading figure in environmental studies and coauthor of *The Global Citizen*, echoes a similar theme. During what she describes as her "scarcity" stage, she rejected material things and probed each purchase and habit for its environmental impact. A royal "pain in the neck" as a result she was frequently avoided—a separation, she says, that contributed to rather than inhibited "planetary destruction." Now embracing a life style based on "sufficiency"—"enough for generosity but not waste, enough for security but not hoarding"—she is tolerant of others' compromises as well as her own, which she acknowledges with some irony, includes among other things "probably burning up 100 times as much fuel as any other family" in her town as she jets around the world to promote environmental causes.[57]

Whether directed at environmental issues or peace—two intimately interconnected concerns—globalism is a future-oriented enterprise, as much concerned with generations to come as it is with the present. Only a broadly based constituency can provide the needed imagination, hope, and wherewithal to keep it evolving.

NOTES

1. Beth Robinson Bosk, Interviewer, "Michael Helm of City/Country Miner and Urban Ore," *The New Settler Interview* 29, mid-March–mid-April 1988, 35–54, 36–39, 51–54.

2. Wendell Berry, "The Futility of Global Thinking," *Harper's* 279, September 1989, 16–22.

3. Alan AtKisson, "The Utility of Global Thinking," *In Context* 25 (Late Spring 1990): 55–57, 55.

4. Robert Gilman, "Gaian Leadership: An Interview with David Gershon," *In Context* 22 (Summer 1989): 54–55, 54.

5. Betty A. Reardon, *Comprehensive Peace Education: Educating for Global Responsibility* (New York: Teachers College Press, 1988), 52.

6. Whereas politics can be built on compromise, observes Roger Williamson, research director of the Uppsala Life and Peace Institute, battles based on religious

traditions often have "a fatal tendency to harden political confrontations into insoluble configurations" (Roger Williamson, "Why is Religion Still a Factor in Armed Conflict," *Bulletin of Peace Proposals* 21:3 [1990]: 243–253, 251).

7. *Biennial Report of the United States Institute of Peace, 1989* (Washington, D.C.: United States Institute of Peace, December 1989), 20.

8. Cited in Michael S. Kogan, "Jews and Christians: Taking the Next Step," *Journal of Ecumenical Studies* 26:4 (Fall 1989): 703–713, 705.

9. Kogan, "Jews and Christians," 705.

10. Claude Geffré, "Christian Faith and Religious Pluralism," *TD* 38:1 (Spring 1991): 15–18, 15.

11. J. Paul Rajashekar, "Dialogue with People of Other Faiths and Ecumenical Theology," *The Ecumenical Review* 39:4 (October 1987): 455–461, 458.

12. "Emet ve'Emunah," issued by the Jewish Theological Seminary of America in 1988 and cited in Kogan, 710.

13. Hans Küng and Karl-Josef Kuschel, Eds., *A Global Ethic* (New York: Continuum, 1993).

14. Leonard Swidler, "Toward a Universal Declaration of a Global Ethic," June 14, 1993 Revision.

15. Maurice F. Strong, "Preface: A Time for Action," in *Through the '80s: Thinking Globally, Acting Locally*, ed. Frank Feather (Washington, D.C., 1980), 3–4, 4.

16. Heather Halabisky, "Hosting a Home Environmental Party," *In Context* 25 (Late Spring 1990): 8.

17. Halabisky, 8.

18. Harry C. Boyte, "People Power Transforms a St. Louis Housing Project," *Utne Reader*, July/August 1989, 46–47, 46.

19. Boyte.

20. Alan B. Durning, "Grass-roots Groups Are Our Best Hope for Global Prosperity and Ecology," *Utne Reader*, July/August, 1989, 40–49.

21. Alan AtKisson, "Living Restoration: An Interview with Savitra," *In Context* 22 (Summer 1989): 48–53, 50.

22. Ellen Bernstein and Honey Vizer, *Greening the Holidays* (Shomrei Adamah) (Wyncote, Pa.: Reconstructionist Rabbinical College, 1990).

23. Betsy Carpenter, "The Greening of the Church," *U.S. News & World Report*, November 27, 1989, 66+, 66.

24. Pat Stone, "Christian Ecology: A Growing Force in the Environmental Movement," *Mother Earth News*, January/February 1989, excerpted in *Utne Reader* 36, November/December 1989, 78–79.

25. Stone.

26. Carl Sagan, "To Avert a Common Danger," *Parade*, March 1, 1992, 10–14. Sagan says that the signatories included "the general secretaries of the World Muslim League and the World Council of Churches, the vice-president of the World Jewish Congress, the Catholicos of All Armenians, Metropolitan Pitirim of Russia, the grand muftis of Syria and Yugoslavia, the presiding bishops of all the Christian churches of China and of the Episcopal, Lutheran, Methodist, and Mennonite churches in the United States, as well as fifty cardinals, lamas, archbishops, head rabbis, patriarchs, mullas, and bishops of major world cities." (14).

27. Lynn White, Jr., "The Historical Roots of Our Ecological Crisis," *Science*, 1967. Environmentalists argued that both religions shared an exalted view of man-

kind and conversely, a degraded view of all else, leading to the assumption that the universe existed for man's subjugation and exploitation. As evidence, they pointed to the first chapter in Genesis: "And God said unto them, 'Be fruitful and multiply and replenish the earth and subdue it; and have dominion over the fish of the sea, and over the fowl of the air, and over every living thing that moveth upon the earth.' "

28. Bible scholar Robert Gordis, for example, argued environmentalists had grossly distorted Judaism's attitudes, which were based on two major principles: *tza'ar ba'alei chayim*—sparing giving pain to all living creature, and *bal tashchit*—prohibition of any form of destruction. Judaism, he said, "insists that human beings have an obligation not only to conserve the world of nature, but to enhance it because mankind is the 'copartner of God in the work of creation'." As for the Genesis verse, said Gordis, its meaning was entirely contrary to the charge levied:

The opening chapter of Genesis, in which humankind is given the right to 'subdue' the earth and to 'have dominion' over all living things, does not even permit people to use animals for food. For the very next verse—Genesis 1:29—declares: "I have given you every plant yielding seed which is upon the face of all the earth, and every tree with seed in its fruit; you shall have them for food." This is surely a drastic limitation upon humankind's rights. Not until many centuries later, after the Flood, are people (in the person of Noah and his family) permitted to eat meat. And even then, all people are forbidden to eat the blood of the creatures they have used for food because the blood is the seat of life. Reverence for life dictates that the blood be poured out and not consumed. This ritual is a symbolic recognition that all life is sacred—all life, even the life of animals we kill for the sake of sustenance (Robert Gordis, "Judaism and the Environment," *Congress Monthly*, September/October 1990, 7–10, 10, originally published in slightly different form in *Congress Bi-Weekly, April 2, 1971, 8*).

29. The importance of small business practices on the economy should not be underestimated. As Paul Hawken points out, the Fortune 500 companies have lost a net of six million jobs since 1973, while during that same period, twenty-three million net new jobs were created, 98 percent of them coming from businesses with one hundred or fewer employees (Paul Hawken, "Entrepreneurs: The Real Cultural Revolutionaries," *Utne Reader*, January/February 1989, 72–73, excerpted from a speech given to the Commonwealth Club of California, October 23, 1987).

30. "Singing to Save the Earth," *In Business*, September/October 1989, 10.

31. Hawken.

32. Teresa Carp, "Wastebuster," *In Business*, Summer 1989, 28–29.

33. Anne Newkirk Niven, "Recycled Paper: A Printer's Story," *In Context* 22 (Summer 1989): 7.

34. Prominently displayed on the inside cover page of a 1992 published text by Allyn and Bacon (Ronald C. Doll, *Curriculum Improvement: Decision Making and Process*, 8th ed. [Allyn and Bacon, Boston, 1992], inside cover), for example, is an inscription heralding their environmental commitment: "A NOTE FROM THE PUBLISHER: *This book is printed on recycled, acid-free paper*. At Allyn and Bacon, we share the widespread concern for preserving the natural environment. We are proud to be among the first college textbook publishers to adopt a policy of using recycled paper for many of our books and advertisements. This commitment reflects the concern of *all* of our employees—a commitment that is further reinforced through an ongoing, voluntary paper recycling program in our corporate offices."

35. Marjorie Kelly, "At the Frontlines," *Utne Reader*, January/February 1989, 76.

36. Erik Larson, "I Scream, You Scream," *Utne Reader*, January/February 1989, 64–75, 70.

37. Nora Goldstein, "The New Reality," *In Business*, Summer 1989, 17–19, 18.

38. Goldstein, 18.

39. Chris Barnett, "Earth Day 1990," *Vis-a-Vis*, April 1990, 38–44.

40. Cited in Huey D. Johnson and Peggy Lauer, "Let's Develop a Marshall Plan for U.S. Environmental Quality," *San Francisco Examiner*, January 19, 1992, A–13.

41. Michael Silverstein, "The Joys of Environmental Employment," *In Business*, Summer 1989, 29–31.

42. The Nestlé powdered infant milk formula is a case in point; without clean water to mix the formula and sufficient fuel for sterilizing bottles and nipples, as well as no refrigeration to store unused formula or enough money to buy a sufficient supply, mothers in Third World countries actually wound up harming their infants more than if they had depended on traditional means of feeding them.

43. Edith Brown Weiss, "Global Environmental Change and International Law: The Introductory Framework," in *Environmental Change and International Law: New Challenges and Dimensions*, ed. Edith Brown Weiss (Tokyo, Japan: United Nations University Press, 1992), 3–38.

44. Brian H. Smith, *More Than Altruism: The Politics of Private Foreign Aid* (Princeton: Princeton University Press, 1990), 3.

45. Smith, 3.

46. Craig Comstock, "Going Beyond War," in *Citizen Summitry: Keeping the Peace When it Matters Too Much to be Left to Politicians*, eds. Don Carlson and Craig Comstock (Lafayette, Calif.: Ark Communications Institute, 1986), 8–13, 13.

47. David Cortright, *Peace Works: The Citizen's Role in Ending the Cold War* (Boulder: Westview Press, 1993). Cortright acknowledges, however, that "the peace movement achieved success at the margins but did not alter the core structure of the war system" (248).

48. John W. Burton, *Conflict and Communication: The Use of Controlled Communication in International Relations* (New York: Free Press, 1969).

49. Leonard W. Doob, *Resolving Conflict in Africa: The Fermeda Workshop* (New Haven: Yale University Press, 1970).

50. Herbert Kelman, "The Problem-Solving Workshop in Conflict Resolution," in *Communication in International Politics*, ed. Richard L. Merritt (Urbana: University of Illinois Press, 1972), 168–204.

51. David D. Newsom, "The Limits of Citizen Diplomacy," *Christian Science Monitor*, October 12, 1990, 18.

52. Richard D. Schwartz, "Arab-Jewish Dialogue in the United States: Toward Track II Tractability," in *Intractable Conflicts and Their Transformation*, ed. Louis Kriesberg, Terrell A. Northrup, and Stuart Thorson (Syracuse, N.Y.: Syracuse University Press, 1986), 180–209, 186.

53. Russell W. Baker, "Citizen Diplomats: 'Peace Walkers' Fight Ignorance," *The Christian Science Monitor*, September 22, 1989, 14.

54. Herb Walters, "Contras," *Rural Southern Voice for Peace* 38, May/June 1988, 1–5, 4.

55. John Elkington, Julia Hailes, and Joel Makower, *The Green Consumer Guide* (New York: Penguin Books, 1990).

56. Joel Makower, "The Green Revolution," *Vis-a-Vis*, April 1990, 48–54, 48.

57. Donella H. Meadows, *The Global Citizen* (Washington, D.C.: Island Press, 1991).

CHAPTER 10

Creating the Future

Putting all the foregoing social processes together, what would a single caring institution look like? We might consider any single social institution or organization—educational, religious, family, medical, or social service—but prefer to focus on business, not only because it is such a dominating societal influence, but also because it is generally presumed to be incompatible with care. Our question thus becomes: What would a caring business look like? We sketch the answer here in broad terms; the details and examples are more amply provided in the chapters dealing with each of the processes below.

A caring business would bond its employees by attending to their basic biological and emotional needs. The physical environment would be comfortable without being lavish, its major purpose to serve as the setting in which health and emotional needs can be met. Managers would encourage play and playfulness of thought and spirit (as apparently is the case at Ben & Jerry's Homemade, for example), and find means, both spontaneous and ritualized, through which all members could share their achievements and losses (as described by John Witte at SI), express their griefs (as Terrence Deal did for Pacific Bell managers after the AT&T divestiture), and be initiated into new statuses and roles. The business would provide concrete services to employees and their families in times of particular stress (serious illnesses or severe personal and family tensions), as well as under more routine circumstances (such as accommodating schedules so that employees could fulfill their responsibilities as parents or as the children of aged parents, or providing socializing opportunities for single people). While it would attend to the special needs of people, it would try to do so by focusing on the commonalities they share with others. Most important, managers would avoid rituals of degradation and exclusion. But even as they attempt to build group cohesiveness and a sense of belonging to the group, managers would also encourage autonomy and independence of thought, supporting innovation and experimentation without the threat that failure might mean expulsion.

A caring business would help employees empathize with others by encouraging them to first know themselves—exploring their own thoughts and feelings—and to simultaneously understand others' perspectives and needs through appropriate questioning, role playing, and simulations. Since success at these endeavors depends on a trusting climate, managers would seek to create conditions conducive to trust building. Empathy would not preclude high expectations of others but instead lead to realistic expectations based on understanding rather than arbitrary determinations. So as to avoid the excesses of insulation and isolation, employees would be encouraged to interact with each other and the community (as did Steven Simpson at Sun Ship) and become sensitive to needs around them by a continuous education program which would keep them informed without overwhelming them.

Business leaders would make clear that they were committed to caring norms by saying so frequently, orally and in writing (as do Johnson and Johnson and the Norton Company of Massachusetts, for example). The norms themselves would be included in a code of conduct which would revolve around social responsibility to those within the organization and outside it, and quality products increasingly developed to be commensurate with sustainable development needs. Employees would have ample opportunities to discuss how these norms would apply in specific contexts, and to consider how current norms might be revised in light of expanded understandings. Managers would not tolerate serious normative transgressions, using their powers of punishment and reward as necessary. Above all, they would encourage internalization of norms through inductive reasoning, the use of appropriate language and labeling and by recounting stories of heroes who exemplify them in the business culture (Jim Treybig of Tandem might serve as an example).

Employees would have opportunities to practice care and assume personal responsibility for doing so. They would come to understand that taking care of others may be necessary at times but that practices which empower others to take care of themselves and others are generally preferable. Participants would be listened to and would learn to be active and supportive listeners. They would help colleagues develop a sense of personal responsibility and potency by encouraging them to solve problems on their own, and teaching them skills (such as persuasion, effective teaching techniques, and preparation for potential risks) whereby they could recruit others in such projects. Participants would also be given opportunities to engage in other caring routines, such as mentoring new recruits, being available for consultation as needed, or peer counseling. So as to further promote their sense of personal responsibility, employees would act as partners with management to fashion corporate policies (as occurred under the leadership of John Morrison at Norwest) and be encouraged to call attention to policy violations through an internal whistleblowing process aimed at improvement rather than punishment. So as to be better prepared to cope with the realities of multiple responsibilities, participants would need to accept the fact that not all their behaviors or decisions will be optimally caring or just (as personnel manager Evelyn Grant discovered, for example).

A caring business would facilitate employee contacts with diverse groups within the organization and with multiple groups outside it, including varied community interest groups, for the purpose of mutual understanding. Managers would promote this based on the conviction that such groups have a legitimate interest in what the company does, that diverse relationships can stimulate new ideas potentially beneficial for the enhancement of the company and broaden conceptions of available choices in making decisions. Commensurate with the spirit of understanding, company participants would be encouraged to appreciate cultural differences, whether rooted in economic class, specialized jobs, or ethnicity, and to avoid cultural misunderstandings when dealing with others. They would be given opportunities to examine their own biases and inclinations toward "us/them" thinking, with the intent of learning to monitor them internally and to talk about them objectively. So as to avoid group stereotyping, participants would have experiences that promote their recognition of variability within groups (such as those provided by the Perkins Project with respect to the visually impaired). Such experiences would be deliberately chosen to show groups acting contrary to expectations and could include information about variations within groups, direct observations of others in their own social contexts, and "dialoguing." Company participants would learn dialoguing skills (as did executives at Cummins Engine Company of Columbus, Indiana, in interacting with varied community groups), including techniques to elicit others' stories, particularly in relation to their most intense concerns, and avoid patronizing, derogatory comparisons, and expressions of self-righteous indignation.

Networking would be a routine orientation in a caring business, based on the conviction that enlightened self-interest and community welfare are mutually enhancing and desirable goals. Management and other employees would be encouraged to search for new social linkages so as to expand the business's resources in developing and implementing common goals and solving problems. Networking would occur both with primary stakeholders—the company's first line of concern—and with secondary stakeholders, all of whom would be recognized as necessary for the company's survival and having a legitimate interest and rightful expectations about company policy and performance. Participants would learn how to work with stakeholders in developing common superordinate goals around which they could cooperate, jointly planning and sharing information, predicated on the assumption that relationships would be long-term rather than temporary (as did Digital when changing its policy) and that reciprocity and partnership are the best ways to promote positive relationships (e.g., voluntary disclosure policies as adopted by BankAmerica Corporation). While specific individuals might be trained or recruited for playing boundary-spanner roles linking diverse groups together (see, for example, the roles played by Steve Coulter and Michael Erikesen at Pacific Bell), all people in the business—whether technicians or supervisors, line workers or management—would learn to think holistically rather than narrowly in solving problems. Businesses in other words would become "open systems," working cooperatively with other social institutions—families, schools, other businesses, community groups, and particularly urban centers—to overcome "rotten outcomes," strengthen societal cohesion, and improve the quality of life for all.

Conflicts would be an integral part of a caring business, but rather than suppressing or avoiding them, managers would strive to make them productive. Rather than depending on top-down or external solutions to conflict, managers would aim to regulate and resolve it. Regulation means keeping it at a level which is neither too high nor too low, using techniques such as surfacing and discussing problems, not presuming that everyone shares common feelings or interests, disseminating information that reveals problems, debunking notions of the exceptional virtue of a particular group or modifying the organizational structure to compel cooperation. Resolution requires that parties to the conflict themselves work out solutions, with management providing the resources to make this possible (as occurred in the laboratory at South Side Hospital, for example). All participants in the business would learn conflict resolution strategies and would come to appreciate the potential benefits of conflict in creating needed change. They would also come to appreciate the fact that order, stability, and peaceful relationships are largely the consequence of an ongoing process for resolving conflicts. But even as they would recognize that conflict resolution strategies can promote a sense of care because they concentrate on relationships among people, they would also acknowledge that resolutions may not always be just.

Business participants would come to see themselves as personally related to and responsible for global welfare. Committed to principles of stewardship and restoration, their values would include a deep respect for natural and diverse life forms, a sense of human equality, a particular appreciation for those attributes that can visualize and create a more humane and balanced future, and a recognition that peace is essential for the foregoing to occur (examples of small businesses adhering to some or all of these values include Michael Helm of Urban Ore, Don Hayden of "The Undaunted Recycler," Anita Roddick of The Body Shop, and Ben & Jerry's Homemade). The business community would be encouraged to think globally by talking globally and to act locally. This is different from the type of local action which is mere accommodation to others' points of view, for local action in this context does not mean simply surrendering and abandoning evaluation of others' behaviors. Management would encourage "mindful" opportunism—that is, taking quick advantage of new products and processes which can reduce environmental degradation (e.g., recycling industrial chemicals in-house as done by 3-M Corporation, and AT&T's internal paper recycling program) and promoting development of products and processes with this goal in mind. Rather than simply reacting to presumed consumer demands, they would also work toward creating reflective consumer demands commensurate with a sustainable economic future. They would cooperate with grassroots restoration efforts locally and internationally and network with national and international groups to develop and implement environmental codes. As they work in international contexts, they would see themselves as citizen diplomats as much as economic entrepreneurs, seeking to promote positive relationships among people in various nations through such efforts as supporting groups providing humanitarian aid, seeking to mitigate international hostilities (through such projects as Track II diplomacy and grass-roots reconciliatory dialogues), and promoting personally warm interactions among nationals.

The above, we have argued, would help root business participants in caring relationships with those in their immediate vicinity, their local and national communities as well as the globe. Business participants would thus avoid the limitations of parochial attachments that pit the welfare of their business concerns against all outsiders and would instead consider its welfare intimately connected with society as a whole. Business managers would similarly reject ruthless pursuit of even presumably benevolent global gains— such as replacement of polluting technologies or investment transfers to countries needing to develop greater self-sufficiency—without regard for potentially damaging consequences to people within their organization, but rather would work toward alleviating such negative effects.

How would caring families, educational institutions, or religious institutions differ from businesses? Like businesses, they would have to attend to the same processes: bonding groups, promoting empathy and caring norms, and providing opportunities for participants to practice care and assume personal responsibility for doing so. So as to widen their circles of care, they too would need to encourage diversifying, networking, resolving conflicts, and making global connections. As we have attempted to demonstrate, the conditions and competencies associated with these processes become salient even under extreme circumstances, such as those relating to rescue activities during the Holocaust. Many rescuers were strongly bonded people, capable of empathic understanding, who had internalized caring norms and practiced them, had experiences with diverse people, and had networking skills. Yet to suggest that caring institutions need to attend to these same processes does not mean that each would do so identically. Families, for example, would be more intimately and intensively concerned about emotional and health issues than businesses. Religious institutions would continue to elicit their norms and rituals from their traditions and their sense of the sacred. Schools would spend more time helping youngsters find their interests and exposing them to a wide variety of learning opportunities than either businesses or religious institutions. And networking possibilities would likely be much greater in the business sector and schools than in families. But despite these variations, the caring functions of families, education, religious institutions, and work would overlap considerably, each one contributing substantially to the other and each accepting the view that no single social institution can bear the exclusive responsibility for promoting care.

No single process of itself—whether bonding or empathizing, diversifying or networking—can be sufficient for the task of creating this type of care. We view the processes we have identified as mutually reinforcing, each one strengthening the other and capitalizing on the particular strengths of each. We also view them as occurring concurrently—that is, not in a sequenced order, with one following the other as though in a developmental pattern that requires mastery of one before the other can be undertaken, but rather synchronously. In this manner, participants would have the opportunity to apprehend and activate their caring impulses according to their particular styles. Some people might be more responsive to empathic considerations while others might be more influenced by considered norms; some people might be very gifted at perceiving networking possibilities while others' styles might incline them to serve exceptionally well as conflict resolution facilitators. Whatever the particular individual preferred mode might be, the net effect of institutional support for all these processes should communicate the message that care is a valued goal.

Working from "within" in this fashion would inevitably produce structural changes; bureaucracy would give way to decentralization, hierarchy to partnerships, rigidity to flexibility, standardization to empowerment, closed systems to open systems, and unchanged reproductive systems to evolving and productive systems.

This view of change from "within" depends primarily on the internal resources of the institution rather than external agents (such as government or pressure groups) or imposed economic or political structures. This does not mean that outside forces would have no role to play, but rather that their activities would be primarily supportive. Care, it seems to us, is more likely to occur when core participants within institutions assume responsibility for it and help shape it. In this view, an institutional structure supporting care comes only after an internal culture supports it; that is, after caring impulses are integrated and incorporated into the heart of institutional life.[1]

Is there reason to believe such changes can occur? As we have suggested, the processes we've proposed are being promoted among educators, psychologists, peace advocates, and management theorists, including business management theorists. As we have demonstrated, they are actually occurring in some form in varied social contexts, including the most enlightened and profitable business ventures. What motivates them may be partially care—real concern about the welfare of others—but it is also enlightened self-interest.

But just as enlightened self-interest need not be purged from caring contexts, neither does it require the elimination of competition, individualism, authority, rational and utilitarian principles, or reciprocity. Not unlike Alan Fiske, who proposes that societies everywhere demonstrate four of what he calls "elementary relational models," we would argue that such forms of relating are functional, fulfilling basic human and societal needs and ultimately helping to integrate societies.[2] Humans apparently have a strong motivation to achieve and to assert their autonomy, to separate themselves from others and also to submerge themselves, to relate to others in terms of considered reasons, logic, and cost-benefit analyses, and to expect fair exchanges with others and to express altruism. Expecting them to act on the basis of care alone would require a radical transformation of human nature. The danger arises only when such relationships are out of balance: that is, when one type of relationship dominates all others, either weakening others excessively or excluding them. As Fiske among others has noted, our society is out of balance.[3]

What constitutes an appropriate "balance" for society? No quantitative measure has yet been proposed by which to assess it. What does seem clear is that the tensions and violence which characterize so much of contemporary life suggest the absence of a caring ethic and practice. And unlike the view of care that relegates it to the private domain, we believe balance can only be achieved when care penetrates all our social institutions, including public institutions.

For some people, given more to activism and large visions, care may be manifested in large-scale political engagements. We owe a great deal to such individuals, for they assume much of the leadership role in instituting change and preparing the way for cultural change.

For others, temperamentally more modest and withdrawn, it may be expressed in what Kim Chernin calls "the politics of the small,"[4] limited and intermittent acts of concern. Rather than viewing these as of little issue or inconsequential, we are reminded that the rescuers we studied largely belonged to this category. Ordinary people, concerned about self and survival, many risked their lives to help Jews survive because they had integrated small acts of kindness into their daily routines.

The schematic framework we have proposed here might be considered "the politics of the middle." Not dependent on large-scale political action, yet going beyond the limited acts of personal responsibility expressed by single individuals, the scheme seeks to deliberately infuse care within institutional life by creating conditions and developing competencies that encourage its widespread materialization.

We believe our proposed scheme can be useful as a lens or assessment tool by which individuals can examine practices within the social contexts in which they routinely operate and that the specifics we have provided can help them consider how to strengthen caring behaviors within them. Since its processes are already to be found in some form in many social institutions and are often compatible with and sometimes encouraging of other institutional goals, they do not require a radical change in either social arrangements or human nature. In that sense, our effort could be considered a contribution toward what Elise Boulding might call "practical Utopia building,"[5] an attempt to intensify caring behaviors by consciously broadening the nurturant cracks that may already exist and initiating them where they are conspicuously absent.

NOTES

1. Political scientist Benjamin Barber made this same point with reference to the democratization process. Democracy, he said, can only be ensured by conscious political will and that cannot occur from the bottom up any more than from the top down, but rather from the inside out. What this means is that the institutional superstructure comes last, after indigenous democratic impulses are cultivated, incorporated, and integrated in the heart of cultural life (Benjamin R. Barber, "Jihad Vs. McWorld," *The Atlantic* 269:3, March 1992, 53–63).

2. More precisely, Alan Fiske claims that societies everywhere demonstrate four basic (elementary) forms of human relations, each with its own form of making moral judgments: *communal sharing*, which makes moral judgments on the basis of care, altruism, and selflessness in the interest of group solidarity; *equality matching*, which makes moral judgments on the basis of justice, balanced reciprocity, fairness, and equal treatment; *authority ranking*, which looks to leaders and tradition (divine or secular) for guidance; and *market pricing*, which depends on rational and utilitarian principles. Most societies, says Fiske, use of all of these models extensively and infers from this that each is functional in providing a means for people to act in an integrated and concerted fashion with others.

3. As Fiske puts it, each of the basic human relations he identifies also has a dysfunctional potential to destroy societal coherence and break societies apart if carried to excess. American society, he says, is out of balance because it is dominated by market relations (Alan Page Fiske, *Structures of Social Life: The Four Elementary Forms of Human Relations* [New York: Free Press, 1991]). Others who have similarly argued that our society is out of balance include Robert Bellah et al. (*The Good Society* [New York: Alfred A. Knopf, 1991]); Herman E. Daly and John B. Cobb, Jr. (*For the Common Good: Redirecting the Economy toward Community, the Environment, and a Sustainable Future* [Boston: Beacon Press, 1989]); and Christopher Lasch,

(*The True and Only Heaven: Progress and its Critics* [New York: W. W. Norton, 1991]).

4. Kim Chernin, "The Politics of the Small," *Tikkun* 8:5, September/October 1993, 15–18.

5. Elise Boulding, "Women's Visions of the Future," in *Visions of Desirable Societies,* ed. Eleanora Masini (Oxford: Pergamon Press, 1983), 9–24.

Bibliography

Abbott, Susan. "Letters exchanged between Susan Abbott and her mother Miriam, 1980." In *Between Ourselves: Letters Between Mothers and Daughters, 1950–1982.* Ed. Karen Payne. Boston: Houghton Mifflin, 1983, 310–322.

Abdennur, Alexander. *The Conflict Resolution Syndrome: Volunteerism, Violence, and Beyond.* Ottawa, Ont.: University of Ottawa Press, 1987.

Abrahams, Barbara, Shirley S. Feldman, and Sharon C. Nash. "Sex-role Self-concept and Sex Role Attitudes: Enduring Personality Characteristics or Adaptations to Changing Life Situations?" *Developmental Psychology* 14 (1978): 393–400.

Ackerman, Diane. *A Natural History of the Senses.* New York: Random House, 1990.

Ahlgren, Andrew, and David W. Johnson. "Sex Differences in Cooperative and Competitive Attitudes from the 2nd Year Through the 12th Grades." *Developmental Psychology* 15 (1979): 45–49.

Ainsworth, Mary D. S. "Infant-Mother Attachment." *American Psychologist* 34 (1979): 932–937.

Allen, Jon G., and Dorothy M. Haccoun. "Sex Differences in Emotionality: A Multi-Dimensional Approach." *Human Relations* 29 (1976): 711–720.

Allport, Gordon W. *The Nature of Prejudice.* Reading, Mass.: Addison-Wesley, 1954.

Amir, Yehuda. "The Role of Intergroup Contact in Change of Prejudice and Ethnic Relations." In *Towards the Elimination of Racism.* Ed. Phyllis A. Katz. New York: Pergamon, 1976, 245–308.

Anderson, Julia. "How Technology Brings Blind People into the Workplace." *Harvard Business Review* (March–April 1989): 36–38.

Ansoff, Igor. *Corporate Strategy.* New York: McGraw-Hill, 1965.

Anthony, E. James, and Cyrille Koupernik, eds. *The Child in His Family.* New York: John Wiley & Sons, 1970.

Anti-Defamation League. *Audit of Anti-Semitic Incidents: 1993.* New York, N.Y.: Anti-Defamation League, 1994.

Antonucci, Toni C., and James S. Jackson. "The Role of Reciprocity in Social Support." In *Social Support: An Interactional View*. Eds. Barbara R. Sarason, Irwin G. Sarason, and Gregory R. Pierce. New York: John Wiley & Sons, 1990, 173–198.

Arco, Christina M. B., and Kathleen A. McCluskey. "A Change of Pace: An Investigation of the Salience of Maternal Temporal Style in Mother-Infant Play." *Child Development* 52 (1981): 941–949.

Aronfreed, Justin M. *Conduct and Conscience: The Socialization of Internalized Control Over Behavior*. New York: Academic Press, 1968.

Asher, Steven R., John M. Gottman, and Sheri L. Oden. "Children's Friendships in School Settings." In *Contemporary Readings in Child Psychology*. Eds. E. Mavis Hetherington and Ross D. Parke. New York: McGraw-Hill, 1977.

AtKisson, Alan. "Living Restoration: An Interview with Savitra." *In Context* 22 (Summer 1989): 48–53.

———. "The Utility of Global Thinking." *In Context* 25 (Late Spring 1990): 55–57.

Babbie, Earl. *You Can Make a Difference*. Anaheim Hills, Calif.: Opening Books, 1985.

Bakan, David. *The Duality of Human Existence*. Boston: Beacon Press, 1966.

Baker, Russell W. "Citizen Diplomats: 'Peace Walkers' Fight Ignorance." *The Christian Science Monitor*, September 22, 1989, 14.

———. *Growing Up*. New York: Congdon & Weed, 1982.

Bandura, Albert. *Social Learning Theory*. Englewood Cliffs, N.J.: Prentice-Hall, 1977.

———. *Principles of Behavior Modification*. New York: Holt, Rinehart and Winston, 1969.

———. "Social Learning Theory of Identificatory Processes." In *Handbook of Socialization Theory and Research*. Ed. David A. Goslin. Chicago: Rand McNally, 1969.

Banks, James A. "The Canon Debate, Knowledge Construction, and Multicultural Education." *Educational Researcher* 22:5 (June–July 1993): 4–14.

———. *Teaching Strategies for Ethnic Studies*. New York: Allyn & Bacon, 1987.

Banks, Michael. "Four Conceptions of Peace." In *Conflict Management and Problem Solving: Interpersonal to International Applications*. Eds. Dennis J. D. Sandole and Ingrid Sandole-Staroste. New York: New York University Press, 1987, 259–274.

Barber, Benjamin R. "Jihad Vs. McWorld." *The Atlantic* 269:3, March 1992, 53–63.

Barnett, Chris. "Earth Day 1990." *Vis-a-Vis*, April 1990, 38–44.

Barrett, David E., and Marion R. Yarrow. "Prosocial Behavior, Social Inferential Ability, and Assertiveness in Young Children." *Child Development* 48 (1977): 475–481.

Bar-Tal, Daniel, and Arie W. Kruglanski, eds. *The Social Psychology of Knowledge*. Cambridge, England: Cambridge University Press, 1988.

Bartolomé, Fernando. "Nobody Trusts the Boss Completely—Now What?" *Harvard Business Review* (March–April 1989): 138.

Bates, Percy. "Desegregation: Can We Get There From Here?" *Phi Delta Kappan* (September 1990): 8–17.

Bateson, Gregory. *Steps To an Ecology of Mind*. New York: Ballantine Books, 1972.

———. "A Theory of Play and Fantasy." In *Steps To an Ecology of Mind.* Gregory Bateson. New York: Ballantine Books, 1972.

Batson, C. Daniel. *The Altruism Question: Toward a Social-Psychological Answer.* Hillsdale, N.J.: Lawrence Erlbaum, 1991.

———. "Prosocial Motivation: Is it Ever Truly Altruistic?" In *Advances in Experimental Social Psychology.* Ed. L. Berkowitz. New York: Academic Press, 1987, 65–122.

Battistich, Victor, Daniel Solomon, Marilyn Watson, Judith Solomon, and Eric Schaps. "Effects of an Elementary School Program to Enhance Prosocial Behavior on Children's Cognitive-Social Problem Solving Skills and Strategies." *Journal of Applied Development Psychology* 10 (1989): 147–169.

Baumgartner, M. P. *The Moral Order of a Suburb.* New York: Oxford University Press, 1988.

Baumrind, Diana. "Sex-related Socialization Effects." Paper presented at the biennial meeting of the Society for Research in Child Development, San Francisco, March 1979.

———. "Current Patterns of Parental Authority." *Developmental Psychology Monographs* 4 (1971): 1–103.

Beaman, Arthur L., C. Cole, M. Preston, B. Klentz, and N. M. Steblay. "Fifteen Years of Foot-in-the-door Research." *Personality and Social Psychology* 9 (1983): 181–196.

Beck, Evelyn Torton. "The Politics of Jewish Invisibility." *NWSA Journal* 1:1 (1988): 93–102.

Beer, Jennifer E. *Peacemaking in Your Neighborhood: Reflections on an Experiment in Community Mediation.* Philadelphia, Pa.: New Society, 1986.

Bellah, Robert, Richard Madsen, William N. Sullivan, Ann Swidler, and Steven M. Tipton. *The Good Society.* New York: Alfred A. Knopf, 1991.

———. *Habits of the Heart: Individualism and Commitment in American Life.* Berkeley: University of California Press, 1985.

Belsky, Jay. "Mother-Father-Infant Interaction: A Naturalistic Observational Study." *Developmental Psychology* 15 (1979): 601–607.

Bem, Daryl J. "Self-perception Theory." In *Advances in Experimental Social Psychology.* Vol. 6. Ed. Leonard Berkowitz. New York: Academic Press, 1972, 1–62.

Bergler, E. *Parents Not Guilty of Their Children's Neuroses.* New York: Liveright, 1964.

Berkowitz, Bill. *Local Heroes: The Rebirth of Heroism in America.* Lexington, Mass.: Lexington Books, 1987.

Berkowitz, Leonard, ed. *Advances in Experimental Social Psychology.* Vol. 10. New York: Academic Press, 1977.

Berman, Phyllis M., Lori C. Monda, and Rodney P. Myerscough. "Sex Differences in Young Children's Responses to an Infant: An Observation Within a Daycare Setting." *Child Development* 48 (1977): 711–715.

Bernstein, Ellen, and Honey Vizer. *Greening the Holidays* (Shomrei Adamah). Wyncote, Pa.: Reconstructionist Rabbinical College, 1990.

Bernstein, Irving. *A Caring Society: The New Deal, the Worker, and the Great Depression.* Boston: Houghton Mifflin, 1985.

Berry, Wendell. "The Futility of Global Thinking." *Harper's* 279, September 1989, 16–22.

Berscheid, Ellen, David Boye, and John M. Darley. "Effect of Forced Association Upon Voluntary Choice to Associate." *Journal of Personality and Social Psychology* 8 (1968): 13–19.

Biennial Report of the United States Institute of Peace, 1989. Washington, D.C.: United States Institute of Peace, December 1989.

Billig, Otto. "The Lawyer Terrorist and His Comrades." *Political Psychology* 6:1 (1985): 29–46.

Binur, Yoram. *My Enemy, My Self.* New York: Doubleday, 1989.

Blake, Robert R., and Jane S. Moutin. "The Intergroup Dynamics of Win-Lose Conflict and Problem-Solving Collaboration in Union-Management Relations." In *Intergroup Relations and Leadership.* Ed. Muzafer Sherif. New York: John Wiley & Sons, 1962, 94–140.

―――. "Reactions to Intergroup Competition Under Win-Lose Conditions." *Management Science* 7 (1961): 420–435.

Blanck, Peter D., R. Rosenthal, S. E. Snodgrass, B. M. DePaulo, and M. Zuckerman. "Sex Differences in Eavesdropping on Nonverbal Clues: Development Changes." *Journal of Personality and Social Psychology* 41 (1981): 391–396.

Blau, Joel. *The Visible Poor: Homelessness in the United States.* New York: Oxford University Press, 1992.

Blau, Peter. *Exchange and Power in Social Life.* New York: John Wiley & Sons, 1964.

Blauner, Robert. *Black Lives, White Lives: Three Decades of Race Relations in America.* Berkeley: University of California Press, 1989.

Block, Jeanne H. "Conceptions of Sex Role: Some Cross-cultural and Longitudinal Perspectives." *American Psychologist* 28 (1973): 512–26.

Bok, Sissela. *A Strategy for Peace.* New York: Pantheon Books, 1989.

Bosk, Beth Robinson, interviewer. "Michael Helm of City/Country Miner and Urban Ore, *The New Settler Interview* 29, mid-March–mid-April 1988, 35–54.

Boulding, Elise. "Foreward." In *Peacemaking in Your Neighborhood: Reflections on an Experiment in Community Mediation.* Jennifer E. Beer. Philadelphia, Pa.: New Society, 1986, iii–vi.

―――. "Women's Visions of the Future." In *Visions of Desirable Societies.* Ed. Eleanora Masini. Oxford: Pergamon Press, 1983, 9–24.

Bowlby, John. *Attachment and Loss.* Vol. 1. New York: Basic Books, 1969.

―――. *Maternal Care and Mental Health: A Report for the World Health Organization.* Geneva: World Health Organization, 1952.

Boyte, Harry C. "People Power Transforms a St. Louis Housing Project." *Utne Reader,* July/August 1989, 46–47.

Brabeck, Mary B., ed. *Who Cares: Theory, Research, and Educational Implications of the Ethic of Care.* New York: Praeger, 1989.

Bradshaw, Thornton, and David Vogel, eds. *Corporations and Their Critics: Issues and Answers to the Problems of Corporate Social Responsibility.* New York: McGraw-Hill, 1981.

Bragaw, Donald H. "New York's Experiment: Participation in Government." *Social Education* (October 1989): 364+.

Bridges: Promising Programs for the Education of Immigrant Children. San Francisco: California Tomorrow, 1989.

Brody, Leslie R. "Gender Differences in Emotional Development: A Review of Theories and Research." *Journal of Personality* 53 (1985): 102–149.

———. "Children's Emotional Attributions to Themselves and Others: A Measure of Children's Defensiveness." Paper presented at the annual convention of the American Psychological Association, Anaheim, California, August 1983.

Broverman, Inge K., S. R. Vogel, D. M. Broverman, F. E. Clarkson, and P. S. Rosenkrantz. "Sex Role Stereotypes: A Current Appraisal." *Journal of Social Issues* 28:2 (1972): 59–79.

Brown, L. David. *Managing Conflict at Organizational Interfaces*. Reading, Mass.: Addison-Wesley, 1983.

Bryan, James H. "Model Affect and Children's Imitative Behavior." *Child Development* 42 (1971): 2061–2065.

Burr, Wesley R. *Theory Construction and the Sociology of the Family*. New York: John Wiley & Sons, 1973.

Burton, John W. *Conflict and Communication: The Use of Controlled Communication in International Relations*. New York: Free Press, 1969.

———. *Resolving Deep-Rooted Conflict: A Handbook*. New York: University Press of America, 1987.

Butterfield, Fox. "Arab-Americans Report Increase in Death Threats and Harrassment." *The New York Times National*. August 8, 1990, IV, 24.

Cairns, Robert B. "Meaning and Attention as Determinants of Social Reinforcer Effectiveness." *Child Development* 41 (1970): 1067–1082.

Caldwell, Bettye M. "The Effects of Infant Care." In *Review of Child Development Research*. Vol. 1. Eds. Martin L. Hoffman and Lois Wladis Hoffman. New York: Russell Sage Foundation, 1964.

Campbell, Joseph. *Myths to Live By*. New York: Viking Press, 1972.

———. *The Hero with a Thousand Faces*. New York: Pantheon Books, 1949.

Carlson, Don, and Craig Comstock, eds. *Citizen Summitry: Keeping the Peace When it Matters Too Much to be Left to Politicians*. Lafayette, Calif.: Ark Communications Institute, 1986.

Carp, Teresa. "Wastebuster," *In Business*, Summer 1989, 28–29.

Carpenter, Betsy. "The Greening of the Church." *U.S. News & World Report*, Nov. 27, 1989, 66+.

Carroll, Raymonde. *Cultural Misunderstandings: The French-American Experience*. Chicago: The University of Chicago Press, 1987.

Chandler, Michael. "Egocentrism and Antisocial Behavior: The Assessment and Training of Social Perspective-taking Skills." *Development Psychology* 9, 1973: 326–332.

Chernin, Kim. "The Politics of the Small." *Tikkun* 8:5, September/October 1993, 15–18.

Chin, Steven A. "Minority Lawyers Quitting in Droves." *San Francisco Examiner*, September 30, 1990, A–7.

Chodorow, Nancy. *The Reproduction of Mothering: Psychoanalysis and the Sociology of Gender*. Berkeley: University of California Press, 1978.

Clark, Christopher M. "The Teacher and the Taught: Moral Transactions in the Classroom." In *The Moral Dimensions of Teaching*. Eds. John I. Goodlad, Roger Soder, and Kenneth A. Sirotnik. San Francisco: Jossey-Bass, 1990, 251–265.

Clark, M. S., and H. T. Reis. "Interpersonal Processes in Close Relationships." In

Annual Review of Psychology 39. Eds. Mark R. Rosenzweig and Lyman W. Porter, 1988, 609–672.

Clark, Todd. "Youth Community Service." *Social Education* (October 1989).

Clarke-Stewart, K. Alison. "And Daddy Makes Three: The Father's Impact on Mother and Young Child." *Child Development* 49 (1978): 466–478.

Clausen, A. W. "Voluntary Disclosure: An Idea Whose Time Has Come." In *Corporations and Their Critics: Issues and Answers to the Problems of Corporate Social Responsibility.* Eds. Thornton Bradshaw and David Vogel. New York: McGraw-Hill, 1981, 61–70.

Cohen, Elizabeth G. "The Effects of Desegregation on Race Relations." *Law and Contemporary Problems* 39 (1975): 271–99.

Coles, Robert. *The Moral Life of Children.* Boston: The Atlantic Monthly Press, 1986.

Collins, W. A., ed. *Minnesota Symposia on Child Psychology.* Vol. 14. Minneapolis: University of Minnesota Press, 1981.

Comstock, Craig. "Going Beyond War." In *Citizen Summitry: Keeping the Peace When It Matters Too Much to be Left to Politicians.* Eds. Don Carlson and Craig Comstock. Lafayette, Calif: Ark Communications Institute, 1986, 8–13.

Connell, James P., and Richard M. Ryan. "A Developmental Theory of Motivation in the Classroom." *Teacher Education Quarterly* 11 (1984): 64–77.

Cook, Stuart W. "Motives in a Conceptual Analysis of Attitude-Related Behavior." In *Nebraska Symposium on Motivation.* Vol. 17. Eds. William J. Arnold and David Levine. Lincoln: University of Nebraska Press, 1969, 179–235.

Cooley, Charles H. *Human Nature and the Social Order.* New York: Schocken, 1964. Originally published in 1902.

Cornbleth, Catherine, and Dexter Waugh. *The Great Speckled Bird: Multicultural Politics and Education Policymaking.* New York: St. Martin's Press, 1994.

Cortese, Anthony. *Ethnic Ethics: The Restructuring of Moral Theory.* Albany: State University of New York Press, 1990.

Cortright, David. *Peace Works: The Citizen's Role in Ending the Cold War.* Boulder: Westview Press, 1993.

Coser, Lewis. *The Functions of Social Conflict.* Glencoe, Ill.: Free Press, 1956.

Crain, Robert L., Rita E. Mahard, and Ruth E. Narot. *Making Desegregation Work: How Schools Create Social Climate.* Cambridge, Mass.: Ballinger, 1982.

Crow Dog, Mary, with Richard Erdoes. *Lakota Woman.* New York: Grove Weidenfeld, 1990, 174–175.

Daly, Herman E., and John B. Cobb, Jr. with contributions by Clifford W. Cobb. *For the Common Good: Redirecting the Economy toward Community, the Environment, and a Sustainable Future.* Boston: Beacon Press, 1989.

Damon, William. *The Chronicle of Higher Education,* May 3, 1989, B1.

Dass, Ram, and Paul Gorman. *How Can I Help?* New York: Alfred A. Knopf, 1988.

Davis, Allison. *Leadership, Love and Aggression.* San Diego: Harcourt, Brace, Jovanovich, 1983.

Deal, Terrence E. "Cultural Change: Opportunity, Silent Killer, or Metamorphosis." In *Gaining Control of the Corporate Culture.* Eds. Ralph H. Kilmann, Mary J. Saxton, Roy Serpa and Associates. San Francisco: Jossey-Bass, 1985, 292–331.

Deal, Terrence E., and Allan A. Kennedy. *Corporate Cultures: The Rites and Rituals of Corporate Life.* Reading, Mass.: Addison-Wesley, 1982.

Denham, Susanne A. "Social Cognition, Prosocial Behavior, and Emotion in Preschoolers: Contextual Validation." *Child Development* 57 (1986): 94–201.

Derman-Sparks, Louise, and the ABC Task Force. *Anti-Bias Curriculum: Tools for Empowering Young Children.* Washington, D.C.: The National Association for the Education of Young Children, 1989.

Dertouzos, Michael L., Richard K. Lester, Robert M. Solo, and The MIT Commission on Industrial Productivity. *Made in America: Regaining the Productive Edge.* Cambridge, Mass.: The MIT Press, 1989.

Deutsch, Francine. "Observational and Sociometric Measures of Peer Popularity and their Relationship to Egocentric Communication in Female Preschoolers." *Developmental Psychology* 10 (1974): 745–747.

Deutsch, Helene. *The Psychology of Women: A Psychoanalytic Interpretation.* Vols. 1 & 2. New York: Grune and Stratton, 1944, 1945.

Deutsch, Morton. *The Resolution of Conflict: Constructive and Destructive Processes.* New Haven: Yale University Press, 1973.

Deutsch, Morton, and Mary Evans Collins. *Interracial Housing: A Psychological Evaluation of a Social Experiment.* Minneapolis: University of Minnesota Press, 1951.

Devall, Bill, and George Sessions. *Deep Ecology: Living as if Nature Mattered.* Salt Lake City: Peregrine Smith, 1985.

Devine, Patricia G. "Stereotypes and Prejudice: Their Automatic and Controlled Components." *Journal of Personality and Social Psychology* 56:1 (1989): 5–18.

Dewey, John. *Democracy and Education.* New York: Macmillan, 1916.

———. "Ethical Principles Underlying Education." *The Third Yearbook of the National Herbart Society.* Chicago: National Herbart Society, 1897.

Dewit, Jan, and Willard W. Hartup, eds. *Determinants and Origins of Aggressive Behavior.* The Hague, Netherlands: Mouton, 1975.

Diamond, Randy. "In Brooklyn, Bigotry Yields to Basketball." *San Francisco Examiner*, April 5, 1990, A8.

Dillon, D. R. "Showing Them that I Want Them to Learn and that I Care About Who They Are: A Microethnography of the Social Organization of a Secondary Low-track English Reading Classroom." *American Education Research Journal* 26:2 (Summer 1989): 227–259.

Doll, Ronald C. *Curriculum Improvement: Decision Making and Process.* 8th ed. Boston: Allyn and Bacon, 1992.

Doob, Leonard W. *Resolving Conflict in Africa: The Fermeda Workshop.* New Haven: Yale University Press, 1970.

Durning, Alan B. "Grass-roots Groups Are Our Best Hope for Global Prosperity and Ecology." *Utne Reader*, July/August 1989, 40–49.

Dusky, Lorraine. "Mommy Tracks that Lead Somewhere Good." *Working Woman* 14:11, November 1989, 132–134.

Eagly, Alice H., and Linda L. Carli. "Sex of Researchers and Sex-typed Communications as Determinants of Sex Differences in Influenceability: A Meta-analysis of Social Influence Studies." *Psychological Bulletin* 90 (1981): 1–20.

Edelstein, Wolfgang, and Thomas E. Wren, eds. *Morality and the Self.* Boston: The MIT Press, in press.

Edgerton, Russell. "Editorial: Filling the Void." *Change* 19:5 (September/October 1987): 6.

Ehrenreich, Barbara. "You Lived Through the 80's and Forgot to Get Rich." Review of *The Imperial Middle: Why Americans Can't Think Straight About Class,* by Benjamin De Mott. *The New York Times Book Review,* October 14, 1990, VII, 9.

Eisenberg, Nancy. *The Caring Child.* Cambridge: Harvard University Press, 1992.

————. *Altruistic Emotion, Cognition and Behavior.* Hillsdale, N.J.: Lawrence Erlbaum, 1986.

Eisenberg, Nancy, ed. *The Development of Prosocial Behavior.* New York: Academic Press, 1982.

Eisenberg, Nancy, and Paul Mussen. *The Roots of Prosocial Behavior in Children.* New York: Cambridge University Press, 1989.

Eisenberg, Nancy, and Janet Strayer, eds. *Empathy and its Development.* New York: Cambridge University Press, 1987.

Eisenberg, Nancy, Jeanette F. Pasternack, Ellen Cameron, and Kelly Tryon. "The Relations of Quantity and Mode of Prosocial Behavior to Moral Cognitions and Social Style." *Child Development* 55 (1984): 1479–1485.

Eisenberg, Nancy, and Randy Lennon. "Sex Differences in Empathy and Related Capacities." *Psychological Bulletin* 94:1 (1983): 100–131.

Eisenberg, Nancy, Ellen Cameron, Kelly Tryon and Renee Dodez. "Socialization of Prosocial Behavior in the Preschool Classroom." *Developmental Psychology* 17 (1981): 773–782.

Eisenberg-Berg, Nancy. "Relationship of Prosocial Moral Reasoning to Altruism, Political Liberalism, and Intelligence." *Developmental Psychology* 15 (1979): 354–355.

Elkington, John, Julia Hailes, and Joel Makower. *The Green Consumer Guide.* New York: Penguin Books, 1990.

"Emet ve'Emunah." Statement issued by the Jewish Theological Seminary of America in 1988.

Erickson, Peter. "Multiculturalism and the Problem of Liberalism." *Reconstruction* 2:1 (1992): 97–101.

Erikson, Erik H. "The Human Life Cycle." In *A Way of Looking at Things: Selected Papers from 1930–1980, Erik H. Erikson.* Ed. Stephen Schlein. New York: W. W. Norton, 1987, 595–610.

Erkut, Sumru, Daniel S. Jaquette, and Ervin Staub. "Moral Judgment-situation Interaction as a Basis for Predicting Prosocial Behavior." *Journal of Personality* 49 (1981): 1–14.

Ermann, M. Davis. "How Managers Unintentionally Encourage Corporate Crime." *Business and Society Review* 59 (Fall 1986): 30.

Evaluation of the Child Development Project: Summary of Findings to Date. San Ramon, Calif.: Child Development Project, April 1990.

Feather, Frank, ed. *Through the '80s: Thinking Globally, Acting Locally.* Washington, D.C., 1980.

Feldman, Shirley S., Zeynep C. Biringen, and Sharon C. Nash. "Fluctuations of Sex-related Self-attributions as a Function of Stage of Family Life Cycle." *Developmental Psychology* 17 (1981): 24–25.

Feldman, Shirley S., and Sharon C. Nash. "Interest in Babies During Young Adulthood." *Child Development* 49 (1978): 617–622.

Feldman, Shirley S., Sharon C. Nash, and Carolyn Cutrona. "The Influence of Age and Sex on Responsiveness to Babies." *Developmental Psychology* 13 (1977): 675–676.

Ferraro, Barbara, and Patricia Hussey. *No Turning Back: Two Nuns' Battle with the Vatican over Women's Right to Choose.* New York: Poseidon, 1990.

Feshbach, Norma, D. "Sex Differences in Empathy and Social Behavior in Children." In *The Development of Prosocial Behavior.* Ed. Nancy Eisenberg. New York: Academic Press, 1982, 315–358.

———. "Empathy Training: A Field Study in Affective Education." In *Aggression and Behavior Change: Biological and Social Processes.* Eds. Seymour Feshbach and Adam Fraczek. New York: Praeger, 1979, 234–249.

———. "The Relationships of Child-Rearing Factors to Children's Aggression, Empathy, and Related Positive and Negative Social Behaviors." In *Determinants and Origins of Aggressive Behavior.* Eds. Jan Dewit and Willard W. Hartup. The Hague, Netherlands: Mouton, 1975.

Feshbach, Norma D., and Seymour Feshbach. "Empathy Training and the Regulation of Aggression: Potentialities and Limitations." *Academic Psychological Bulletin* 4 (1982): 399–413.

Feshbach, Norma D., Seymour Feshbach, Mary Fauvre, and Michael Ballard-Campbell. *Learning to Care: Classroom Activities for Social and Affective Development.* Glenview, Ill.: Scott, Foresman, 1983.

Feshbach, Seymour, and Adam Fraczek, eds. *Aggression and Behavior Change: Biological and Social Processes.* New York: Praeger, 1979.

Festinger, Leon, Stanley Schacter, and Kurt Back. *Social Pressures in Informal Groups: A Study of Human Factors in Housing.* New York: Harper & Bros., 1950.

Fisher, J. D., A. Nadler, and S. Whitcher-Alagna. "Recipient Reactions to Aid." *Psychological Bulletin* 91, 1982, 27–34.

Fisher, Roger, and William Ury, with Bruce Patton, eds. *Getting to Yes: Negotiating Agreement Without Giving In.* Boston: Houghton Mifflin, 1981.

Fisher, Ronald. *The Social Psychology of Intergroup and International Conflict Resolution.* New York: Springer-Verlag, 1990.

Fiske, Alan Page. *Structures of Social Life: The Four Elementary Forms of Human Relations.* New York: Free Press, 1991.

Foster, C. D., Mark A. Siegel and Nancy R. Jacobs, eds. *Women's Changing Roles.* Wylie, Tex.: Information Aids, 1988.

Freedman, Jonathan L., and Scott C. Fraser. "Compliance Without Pressure: The Foot-in-the-door Technique." *Journal of Personality and Social Psychology* 4 (1966): 195–202.

Freeman, Edith M., and Marianne Pennekamp. *Social Work Practice: Toward a Child, Family, School, Community Perspective.* Springfield, Ill.: Charles C. Thomas, 1988.

Freeman, R. Edward. *Strategic Management: A Stakeholder Approach.* Boston: Pitman, 1984.

Freudberg, David. *The Corporate Conscience: Money, Power, and Responsible Business.* New York: AMACOM (American Management Association), 1986.

Freudberg, David, and Janet Dudrow. "Norwest Bank: Developing an Approach." In *The Corporate Conscience: Money, Power and Responsible Business.* David Freudberg. New York: AMACOM (American Management Association), 1986, 114–122.

Friedman, Milton. "The Social Responsibility of Business is to Increase its Profits." *The New York Times Magazine,* September 13, 1970, 32+.

Friedman, Richard C., Ralph M. Richart, and Raymond L. Vande Wiele, eds. *Sex Differences in Behavior.* New York: John Wiley & Sons, 1974.

Frieze, Irene H., Jacquelynne E. Parsons, Paula B. Johnson, Diane N. Ruble, and Gail L. Zellman. *Women and Sex Roles: A Social Psychological Perspective.* New York: W. W. Norton, 1978.

Geffré, Claude. "Christian Faith and Religious Pluralism." *TD* 38:1 (Spring 1991): 15–18.

Gentile, Mary C., Kenneth E. Goodpaster, and Thomas R. Piper, eds. *Managerial Decision Making and Ethical Values: Instructor's Manual.* Boston: Harvard Business School, 1989, Section 8.

Gergen, Kenneth, Martin S. Greenberg, and Richard H. Willis, eds. *Social Exchange: Advances in Theory and Research.* New York: Plenum, 1980.

Gilligan, Carol. *In a Different Voice: Psychological Theory and Women's Development.* Cambridge: Harvard University Press, 1982.

Gilman, Robert. "Gaian Leadership: An Interview with David Gershon." *In Context* 22 (Summer 1989): 54–55.

Glass, David C. "Changes in Liking as a Means of Reducing Cognitive Discrepancies Between Self-esteem and Aggression." *Journal of Personality* 32 (1964): 531–549.

Goffman, Erving. *Stigma: Notes on the Management of Spoiled Identity.* Englewood Cliffs, N.J.: Prentice-Hall, 1965.

———. *Relations in Public: Microstudies of the Public Order.* New York: Harper & Row, 1971.

Goldstein, Jerome. "The Bank with the Welcoming Environment." *In Business,* September/October 1989, 18–19.

———. *The Least is the Best Pesticide Strategy.* Emmaus, Pa.: J. G. Press, 1978.

Goldstein, Nora. "The New Reality." *In Business,* Summer 1989, 17–19.

Good, Thomas L., and Jere E. Brophy. *Looking in Classrooms.* New York: Harper & Row, 1987.

Goodlad, John I., Roger Soder, and Kenneth A. Sirotnik, eds. *The Moral Dimensions of Teaching.* San Francisco: Jossey-Bass, 1990.

Goodpaster, Kenneth E., and John B. Matthews, Jr. "Can a Corporation Have a Conscience?" *Harvard Business Review* (January–February 1982): 132+.

Gordis, Robert. "Judaism and the Environment." *Congress Monthly,* September/October 1990, 7–10. Originally published in slightly different form in *Congress Bi-Weekly,* April 2, 1971, 8.

Goslin, David A., ed. *Handbook of Socialization Theory and Research.* Chicago: Rand McNally, 1969.

Gottman, John, Jonni Gonson, and Brian Rasmussen. "Social Interaction, Social Competence, and Friendship in Children." *Child Development* 46 (1975): 709–718.

Gouldner, Alvin W. "The Norm of Reciprocity: A Preliminary Statement." *American Sociological Review* 25 (April 1960): 161–178.

Grant, Carl, ed. *Review of Research in Education* 17. Washington, D.C.: American Education Research Association, 1991.

Grant, Gerald. *The World We Created at Hamilton High.* Cambridge: Harvard University Press, 1988.

Greenberg, Martin S. "A Theory of Indebtedness." In *Social Exchange: Advances in Theory and Research.* Eds. Kenneth Gergen, Martin S. Greenberg, and Richard H. Willis. New York: Plenum, 1980.

Grolnick, Wendy S., and Richard M. Ryan. "Autonomy in Children's Learning: An Experimental and Individual Difference Investigation." *Journal of Personality and Social Psychology* 51 (1987): 890–898.

Grusec, Joan E., and R. Mills. "The Acquisition of Self-control." In *Psychological Developmental in the Elementary Years.* Ed. Judith Worell. San Francisco: Academic Press, 1982.

Grusec, Joan E., and Erica Redler. "Attribution, Reinforcement, and Altruism: A Developmental Analysis." *Developmental Psychology* 16 (1980): 525–534.

Hacker, Andrew. *US: A Statistical Portrait of the American People.* New York: Viking, 1993.

Halabisky, Heather. "Hosting a Home Environmental Party." *In Context* 25 (Late Spring 1990): 8.

Halil, William E. *The New Capitalism.* New York: John Wiley & Sons, 1986.

Hall, Judith A. "Gender Effects in Decoding Nonverbal Clues." *Psychological Bulletin* 41:1 (1978): 845–875.

Harding, Sandra. "The Curious Coincidence of Feminine and African Moralities: Challenges for Feminist Theory." In *Women and Moral Theory.* Eds. Eva Feder Kittay and Diana T. Mayers. Totowa, N.J.: Rowman and Littlefield, 1987, 296–315.

Harman, Willis, and John Hormann. *Creative Work: The Constructive Role of Business in a Transforming Society.* Munich: Schweisfurth Foundation, 1990.

Harrison, Roger. "Quality of Service: A New Frontier for Integrity in Organizations." In *Executive Integrity: The Search for High Human Values in Organizational Life.* Eds. Suresh Srivastva and Associates. San Francisco: Jossey-Bass, 1988, 45–67.

Hartshorne, Hugh, and Mark May. *Studies in the Nature of Character.* 3 vols. New York: Macmillan, 1928–1930.

———. "A Summary of the Work of the Character Education Inquiry." *Religious Education* 25 (September 1930): 607–619, (October 1930): 754–762.

Hass, Robert M. "Spotlight on Alumni: An Advocate for Women and Minorities." *Educator* 4:3 (Fall 1990): 42–44.

Havel, Vaclev. "The Art of the Impossible." *The Spectator,* January 27, 1990, 11+.

Hawken, Paul. "Entrepreneurs: The Real Cultural Revolutionaries." *Utne Reader,* January/February 1989, 72–73. Excerpted from a speech given to the Commonwealth Club of California, October 23, 1987.

Heath, Robert L., and Associates. *Strategic Issues Management: How Organizations Influence and Respond to Public Interests and Policies.* San Francisco: Jossey-Bass, 1988.

Hetherington, E. Mavis. "Divorce: A Child's Perspective." *American Psychologist* 34 (1979): 851–858.

Hetherington, E. Mavis, Martha Cox, and Roger Cox. "Stress and Coping in Divorce: A Focus on Women." In *Psychology and Women: In Transition.* Ed. Jeanne E. Gullahorn. Washington, D.C.: V. H. Winston and Sons, 1979, 95–130.

Hetherington, E. Mavis, and Ross D. Parke, eds. *Contemporary Readings in Child Psychology.* New York: McGraw-Hill, 1977.

Hill, David, interviewer. "Tracy Kidder," *Teacher Magazine,* September/October 1989, 74–80.

Hochschild, Arlie Russell. *The Managed Heart: Commercialization of Human Feeling.* Berkeley: University of California Press, 1983.

Hoffman, Martin L. "The Contribution of Empathy to Justice and Moral Judgment." In *Empathy and Its Development.* Eds. Nancy Eisenberg and Janet Strayer. Cambridge, Eng.: Cambridge University Press, 1987.

———. "Sex Differences in Empathy and Related Behaviors." *Psychological Bulletin* 64 (1977): 712–722.

———. "Moral Internalization: Current Theory and Research." In *Advances in Experimental Social Psychology.* Vol. 10. Ed. L. Berkowitz. New York: Academic Press, 1977.

Hoffman, Martin L., and Lois Wladis Hoffman, eds. *Review of Child Development Research.* Vol. 1. New York: Russell Sage Foundation, 1964.

Horowitz, Frances D., ed. *Review of Child Development Research.* Vol. 4. Chicago: University of Chicago Press, 1975.

Hume, David. "Morality, Self-Love, and Benevolence." In *Egoism and Altruism.* Ed. Ronald D. Milo. Belmont, Calif.: Wadsworth, 1973. Originally published in 1751.

Hyde, Janet S. "How Large are Cognitive Gender Differences?" *American Psychologist* 36 (1981): 892–901.

Ianni, Francis A. J. *The Search for Structure: A Report on American Youth Today.* New York: The Free Press, 1989.

Institute for Social Research. *ISR Newsletter* 7:1 (Winter, 1979).

Jandt, Fred Edmund, with the assistance of Paul Gillette. *Win-Win Negotiating: Turning Conflict into Agreement.* New York: John Wiley & Sons, 1985.

Janeway, Elizabeth. *Man's World, Woman's Place.* New York: William Morrow, 1971.

Jarvis, Bob. Interview with the Altruistic and Prosocial Behavior Institute, Humboldt State University, November 13, 1985.

Jarymowicz, Maria. "Self, We, and Other(s): Schemata, Distinctiveness, and Altruism." In *Embracing the Other: Philosophical, Psychological and Historical Perspectives on Altruism.* Eds. Pearl M. Oliner, Samuel P. Oliner, Lawrence Baron, Lawrence A. Blum, Dennis L. Krebs, and M. Zuzanna Smolenska. New York: New York University Press, 1992, 194–212.

Jensen, Roger E., and Shirley G. Moore. "The Effect of Attribute Statements on Cooperativeness and Competitiveness in School-age Boys." *Child Development* 48 (1977): 305–307.

Johnson, David W., and Roger T. Johnson. *Cooperation and Competition: Theory and Research.* Edina, Minn.: Interaction, 1989.

Johnson, David W., Roger T. Johnson, E. Holubec, and P. Roy. *Circles of Learning: Cooperation in the Classroom.* Alexandria, Va.: Association for Supervision and Curriculum Development, 1984.

Johnson, Huey D., and Peggy Lauer. "Let's Develop a Marshall Plan for U.S. Environmental Quality." *San Francisco Examiner*, January 19, 1992, A–13.

Jones, Edward E., Stephen L. Hester, Amerigo Farina, and Keith E. Davis. "Reactions to Unfavorable Personal Evaluations as a Function of the Evaluator's Perceived Adjustment." *Journal of Abnormal Social Psychology* 59 (November 1959): 363–370.

Kanter, Rosabeth M. *When Giants Learn to Dance: Mastering the Challenge of Strategy, Management, and Careers in the 1990's.* New York: Simon & Schuster, 1989.

————. *The Change Masters: Innovations for Productivity in the American Corporation.* New York: Simon & Schuster, 1983.

Katz, Alvin M., and Reuben Hill. "Residential Propinquity and Marital Selection: A Review of Theory, Method, and Fact." *Marriage and Family Living* 20 (1958): 237–335.

Katz, Phyllis A., ed. *Towards the Elimination of Racism.* New York: Pergamon, 1976.

Kegan, Robert. *The Evolving Self: Problems and Process in Human Development.* Cambridge: Harvard University Press, 1982.

Keller, Evelyn Fox. *A Feeling for the Organism: The Life and Work of Barbara McClintock.* San Francisco: W. H. Freeman, 1983.

Kelly, Marjorie. "Revolution in the Marketplace." *Utne Reader*, January/February 1989, 54–62.

————. "At the Frontlines." *Utne Reader*, January/February 1989, 76.

Kelman, Herbert. "The Problem-Solving Workshop in Conflict Resolution." In *Communication in International Politics.* Ed. Richard L. Merritt. Urbana: University of Illinois Press, 1972, 168–204.

Kephart, William M. *Extra-ordinary Groups: Sociology of Unconventional Lifestyles.* New York: St. Martin's Press, 1982.

Kidder, Tracy. *Among Schoolchildren.* New York: Houghton Mifflin, 1989.

Kilmann, Ralph H., Mary J. Saxton, Roy Serpa and Associates, eds. *Gaining Control of the Corporate Culture.* San Francisco: Jossey-Bass, 1985.

Kindsvatter, Richard, William Wilen, and Margaret Ishler. *Dynamics of Effective Teaching.* 2d ed. White Plains, N.Y.: Longman, 1992.

King, Joyce Elaine. "Dysconscious Racism: Ideology, Identity, and the Miseducation of Teachers." *Journal of Negro Education* 60:2 (Spring 1991): 133–146.

Kirp, David L. "Uncommon Decency: Pacific Bell Responds to AIDS." *Harvard Business Review* (May–June 1989): 140–151.

Kittay, Eva Feder, and Diana T. Mayers, eds. *Women and Moral Theory.* Totowa, N.J.: Rowman and Littlefield, 1987.

Klaus, Marshall H., and John H. Kennell. *Maternal-infant Bonding.* St. Louis: C. V. Mosby, 1976.

Kluckhohn, Clyde. *Mirror for Man.* New York: Whittlesey House, 1949.

Knight, George P., and Spencer Kagan. "Apparent Sex Differences in Cooperation-Competition: A Function of Individualism." *Developmental Psychology* 17 (1981): 783–790.

Koestner, Richard, Carol Franz, and Joel Weinberger. "The Family Origins of Empathic Concern: A 26-year Longitudinal Study." *Journal of Personality and Social Psychology* 58 (1990): 709–717.

Kogan, Michael S. "Jews and Christians: Taking the Next Step." *Journal of Ecumenical Studies* 26:4 (Fall 1989): 703–713.

Kohlberg, Lawrence. *Collected Papers on Moral Development and Moral Education*. Cambridge: Laboratory of Human Development, Harvard University, 1973.

Kohn, Alfie. *The Brighter Side of Human Nature*. New York: Basic Books, 1990.

Kozol, Jonathan. *Savage Inequalities: Children in America's Schools*. New York: Crown, 1991.

Krebs, Dennis, and Alli Rosenwald. "Moral Reasoning and Moral Behavior in Conventional Adults." *Merrill Palmer Quarterly* 23 (1977): 77–87.

Kriesberg, Louis, Terrell A. Northrup, and Stuart J. Thorson, eds. *Intractable Conflicts and Their Transformation*. Syracuse, N.Y.: Syracuse University Press, 1989.

Küng, Hans, and Karl-Josef Kuschel, eds. *A Global Ethic*. New York: Continuum, 1993.

Lamb, M. Elissa. "Paternal Influences and the Father's Role." *American Psychologist* 34 (1979): 938–943.

———. "Twelve-month Olds and their Parents: Interaction in a Laboratory Playroom." *Developmental Psychology* 12 (1978): 237–244.

———. "Father-Infant and Mother-Infant Interaction in the First Year of Life." *Child Development* 48 (1977): 167–181.

Lamb, Michael E., and Ann L. Brown, eds. *Advances in Developmental Psychology*. Vol. 2. Hillsdale, N.J.: Lawrence Erlbaum, 1982.

Lamb, Michael E., and Carl-Philip Hwang. "Maternal Attachment and Mother-neonate Bonding: A Critical Review." In *Advances in Developmental Psychology*. Vol. 2. Eds. Michael E. Lamb and Ann L. Brown. Hillsdale, N.J.: Lawrence Erlbaum, 1982, 1–40.

Lappé, Frances Moore. *Rediscovering America's Values*. New York: Ballantine Books, 1989.

Larrieu, Julie, and Paul Mussen. "Some Personality and Motivational Correlates of Children's Prosocial Behavior." *Journal of Genetic Psychology* 147 (1986): 529–542.

Larson, Erik. "I Scream, You Scream . . ." *Utne Reader*, January/February 1989: 64–75.

Lasch, Christopher. *The True and Only Heaven: Progress and its Critics*. New York: W. W. Norton, 1991.

Laue, James. "The Emergence and Institutionalization of Third Party Roles in Conflict." In *Conflict Management and Problem Solving: Interpersonal to International Applications*. Eds. Dennis J. D. Sandole and Ingrid Sandole-Staroste. New York: New York University Press, 1987, 17–29.

Lepper, Mark R. "Intrinsic and Extrinsic Motivation in Children: Detrimental Effects of Superfluous Social Controls." In *Minnesota Symposia on Child Psychology*. Vol. 14. Ed. W. A. Collins. Minneapolis: University of Minnesota Press, 1981.

Lepper, Mark R., and David Greene. *The Hidden Costs of Reward*. New York: John Wiley & Sons, 1978.

Lerner, Michael. "Looking Forward to the Nineties." *Tikkun*, November/December 1989, 39–41.

Lester, Julius. *Lovesong: Becoming a Jew*. New York: Henry Holt, 1988.

LeVine, Robert A. "Properties of Culture: An Ethnographic View." In *Culture Theory: Essays on Mind, Self, and Emotion*. Eds. Richard A. Shweder and Robert A. LeVine. New York: Cambridge University Press, 1984, 67–88.

Lickona, Thomas, ed. *Moral Development and Behavior*. New York: Holt, Rinehart and Winston, 1976.

Lieberman, Alicia F. "Preschoolers' Competence with a Peer: Relations with Attachment and Peer Experience." *Child Development* 48 (1977): 1277–1287.

Lieberman, Seymour. "The Effects of Changes in Roles on the Attitudes of Role Occupants." *Human Relations* 9 (1956): 385–402.

Lightfoot, Sara Lawrence. *The Good High School: Portraits of Character and Culture*. New York: Basic Books, 1983.

Limerick, Patricia Nelson. "Some Advice to Liberals on Coping With Their Conservative Critics." *The Chronicle of Higher Education*, May 4, 1994, B1–B2.

Lips, Hilary M. *Sex and Gender: An Introduction*. Mountain View, Calif.: Mayfield, 1988.

Longstreth, Langdon E. "Revisiting Skeels' Final Study: A Critique." *Developmental Psychology* 17 (1981): 620–625.

Looft, William R. "Egocentrism and Social Interaction Across the Life Span." *Psychological Bulletin* 78 (1972): 73–92.

Lott, Bernice. "Behavioral Concordance with Sex Role Ideology Related to Play Areas, Creativity and Parental Sex Typing." *Journal of Personality and Social Psychology* 36 (1978): 1087–1100.

Ludeman, Kate. *The Work Ethic: How to Profit from the Changing Values of the New Work Force*. New York: E. P. Dutton, 1989.

Lyons, Nona Plessner. "Two Perspectives: On Self, Relationships, and Morality." *Harvard Educational Review* 53 (1983): 125–145.

Maccoby, Eleanor E. *Psychological Growth and the Parent-child Relationship*. New York: Harcourt, Brace, Jovanovich, 1980.

———. *Social Development*. New York: Harcourt, Brace, Jovanovich, 1980.

Maccoby, Eleanor E., and Carol N. Jacklin. "Sex Differences in Aggression: A Rejoinder and Reprise." *Child Development* 51 (1980): 964–980.

———. *The Psychology of Sex Differences*. Stanford: Stanford University Press, 1974.

Mackey, Sandra. *Lebanon: Death of a Nation*. New York: Congdon and Weed, 1989.

Main, Mary, and Donna R. Weston. "The Quality of the Toddler's Relationship to Mother and to Father: Related to Conflict Behavior and the Readiness to Establish New Relationships." *Child Development* 52 (1981): 932–940.

Makower, Joel. "The Green Revolution." *Vis-a-Vis*, April 1990, 48–54.

"Management for the 1990's." *Business Week*, April 1989.

Mansnerus, Laura. "Worlds Apart: Schools Take Time Out for Lessons in Tolerance." *The New York Times: Education Life*, August 5, 1990, 4A, 28.

March, James G., and Herbert A. Simon. *Organizations*. New York: John Wiley & Sons, 1958.

Marin, Peter. "Helping and Hating the Homeless." *Harper's Magazine*, January 1987.

Martin, Barclay. "Parent-child Relations." In *Review of Child Development Research*. Vol. 4. Ed. Frances D. Horowitz. Chicago: University of Chicago Press, 1975.

Martin, John A. "A Longitudinal Study of the Consequences of Early Mother-Infant

Interaction: A Microanalytic Approach." *Monographs of the Society for Research in Child Development,* 1981, 46.

Marty, Martin E., and R. Scott Appleby. *The Glory and the Power: The Fundamentalist Challenge to the Modern World.* Boston: Beacon Press, 1992.

"Mary Gonzales." In *Second Thoughts on the American Dream.* Studs Terkel. New York: Pantheon Books, 1988, 74–78.

Masini, Eleanora, ed. *Visions of Desirable Societies.* Oxford: Pergamon Press, 1983.

Masnick, George, and Mary Jo Bane. *The Nation's Families: 1960–1990.* Cambridge, Mass.: Joint Center for Urban Studies, 1980.

Mathews, M. Cash. *Strategic Intervention in Organizations: Resolving Ethical Dilemmas.* Sage Library of Social Research, Vol. 169. Newbury Park, Calif.: Sage Publications, 1988.

McGuffey, William H. "The Bird's Nest." *McGuffey's Revised Eclectic First Reader, 1879.* In *The Annotated McGuffey: Selections from the McGuffey Eclectic Readers: 1836–1920.* Ed. Stanley W. Lindberg. New York: Van Nostrand Reinhold 1976, 19–21.

McNamara, Robert S. *Out of the Cold: New Thinking for American Foreign and Defense Policy in the 21st Century.* New York: Simon & Schuster, 1989.

Meadows, Donella H. *The Global Citizen.* Washington, D.C.: Island Press, 1991.

Merritt, Richard L., ed. *Communication in International Politics.* Urbana: University of Illinois Press, 1972.

Milgram, Stanley. "Some Conditions of Obedience and Disobedience to Authority." *Human Relations* 18 (1965): 57–76.

———. *Obedience to Authority.* New York: Harper & Row, 1974.

Miller, Arthur. *Timebends: A Life.* New York: Harper & Row, 1987, 23–26.

Miller, Jean Baker. *Toward a New Psychology of Women.* Boston: Beacon Press, 1976.

Miller, John W. "Birdmen of Harlem." *The New York Times Magazine,* November 19, 1989, 49+.

Milosz, Czeslaw. *The Captive Mind.* Trans. J. Zielonks. New York: Alfred A. Knopf, 1951.

Minnich, Harvey C. "William Holmes McGuffey and the Peerless Readers." *Miami University Bulletin* (1928).

———. *William Holmes McGuffey and His Readers.* New York: American Book Co., 1936.

Morrison, Delmont, Michael Siegal, and Robin Francis. "Control, Autonomy, and the Development of Moral Behavior: A Social-Cognitive Perspective." *Imagination, Cognition, and Personality* 3 (1984): 337–351.

Morrison, Toni. *Playing in the Dark.* Cambridge: Harvard University Press, 1992.

Morse, David. "About Men: Gray Wolf's Choice." *The New York Times Magazine,* January 21, 1990, 12–13.

Mosier, Richard. *Making the American Mind: Social and Moral Ideas in the McGuffey Readers.* New York: Russell & Russell, 1965.

Moss, Howard A. "Early Sex Differences and Mother-Infant Interaction." In *Sex Differences in Behavior.* Eds. Richard C. Friedman, Ralph M. Richart, and Raymond L. Vande Wiele. New York: John Wiley & Sons, 1974, 149–164.

Mueller, Robert K. "Criteria for the Appraisal of Directors." *Harvard Business Review* (May/June 1979): 48+.

Newsom, David D. "The Limits of Citizen Diplomacy." *Christian Science Monitor*, October 12, 1990, 18.

Niven, Anne Newkirk. "Recycled Paper: A Printer's Story." *In Context* 22 (Summer 1989): 7.

Noddings, Nel. *Caring: A Feminine Approach to Ethics and Moral Education.* Berkeley: University of California Press, 1984.

Norwood, J. L. *The Male-Female Earnings Gap: A Review of Employment and Earnings Issues.* U.S. Department of Labor, Bureau of Labor Statistics, Report 673, September 1982.

Oliner, Pearl M., Samuel P. Oliner, Lawrence Baron, Lawrence A. Blum, Dennis L. Krebs, and M. Zuzanna Smolenska, eds. *Embracing the Other: Philosophical, Psychological and Historical Perspectives on Altruism.* New York: New York University Press, 1992.

Oliner, Pearl M., Samuel P. Oliner, and Mary B. Gruber. "Altruism and Peace: Some Propositions Based on Gender and Cross-Cultural Comparisons." *International Journal on World Peace* VIII:1 (March 1991): 35–44.

Oliner, Samuel P., and Pearl M. Oliner. *The Altruistic Personality: Rescuers of Jews in Nazi Europe.* New York: Free Press, 1988.

Oreffice, Paul F. "Social Responsibility at Dow Chemical." In *Corporations and Their Critical Issues and Answers to the Problems of Corporate Social Responsibility.* Eds. Thornton Bradshaw and David Vogel. New York: McGraw-Hill, 1981, 199–207.

Orlich, Donald C., Robert J. Harder, Richard C. Callahan, Donald P. Kauchak, and Harry W. Gibson. *Teaching Strategies: A Guide to Better Instruction.* 4th ed. Lexington, Mass.: D.C. Heath, 1994.

Osofsky, Joy D. ed. *Handbook of Infancy.* New York: John Wiley & Sons, 1978.

Palmer, Parker J. "Community, Conflict, and Ways of Knowing: Ways to Deepen Our Educational Agenda." *Change* 19:5 (September/October 1987): 20–25.

Palmieri, Victor H. "Corporate Responsibility and the Competent Board." *Harvard Business Review* (May/June 1979): 46–48.

Paris, Scott G., and Robert B. Cairns. "An Experimental and Ethological Analysis of Social Reinforcement with Retarded Children." *Child Development* 43 (1972): 717–729.

Parke, Ross D. "Perspectives on Father-Infant Interaction." In *Handbook of Infancy.* Ed. Joy D. Osofsky. New York: John Wiley & Sons, 1978.

Parsons, Talcott, and Robert F. Bales. *Family, Socialization, and Interaction Processes.* New York: Academic Press, 1955.

Patterson, G. R., and J. A. Cobb. "A Dyadic Analysis of 'Aggressive' Behaviors." In *Minnesota Symposium on Child Psychology*, Vol. 5. Ed. J. P. Hill. Minneapolis: University of Minnesota Press, 1971.

Payne, Karen, ed. *Between Ourselves: Letters Between Mothers and Daughters, 1950–1982.* Boston: Houghton Mifflin, 1983.

Perry, David G., Kay Bussey, and Kathryn Freiberg. "Impact of Adults: Appeals for Sharing on the Development of Altruistic Dispositions in Children." *Journal of Experimental Child Psychology* 32 (1981): 127–138.

Peters, Lynn H. "The Essential Values of Business." In *Management and Society.* Compiler, Lynn H. Peters. Belmont, Calif.: Dickenson Publishing, 1968, 53–59.

Peters, Lynn H., comp. *Management and Society*. Belmont, Calif.: Dickenson, 1968.

Peters, Thomas J. *Thriving on Chaos: Handbook for a Management Revolution*. New York: Alfred A. Knopf, 1988.

Peters, Thomas J., and Robert H. Waterman, Jr. *In Search of Excellence: Lessons from America's Best-Run Companies*. New York: Harper & Row, 1982.

Pliner, Patricia, Heather Hart, Joanne Kohl, and Dory Saari. "Compliance Without Pressure: Some Further Data on the Foot-in-the-door Technique." *Journal of Experimental Social Psychology* 10 (1974): 17–22.

Pompa, Gilbert G. "The Community Relations Service." In *Conflict Management and Problem Solving: Interpersonal to International Applications*. Eds. Dennis J. D. Sandole and Ingrid Sandole-Staroste. New York: New York University Press, 1987, 130–142.

Porter, Judith. *Black Child, White Child: The Development of Racial Attitudes*. Cambridge: Harvard University Press, 1971.

Prutzman, Priscilla, Lee Stern, M. Leonard Burger, and Gretchen Bodenhamer. *The Friendly Classroom for a Small Planet: A Handbook on Creative Approaches to Living and Problem Solving for Children*. Philadelphia, Pa. and Santa Cruz, Calif.: New Society Publishers, 1988.

Quattrone, George A. "On the Perception of a Group's Variability." In *Psychology of Intergroup Relations*. 2d ed. Eds. Stephen Worchel and William G. Austin. Chicago: Nelson-Hall, 1986, 25–48.

Quindlen, Anna. "The Nuns' Story." *The New York Times*, November 9, 1990, E23.

Rajashekar, J. Paul. "Dialogue with People of Other Faiths and Ecumenical Theology." *The Ecumenical Review* 39:4 (October 1987): 455–461.

Rapoport, Anatol Ray. *Fights, Games, and Debates*. Ann Arbor: University of Michigan Press, 1960.

Raths, Louis E., Merrill Harmin, and Sidney B. Simon. *Values and Teaching*. 2d ed. Columbus, Oh.: Merrilll, 1978.

Reardon, Betty. *Comprehensive Peace Education: Educating for Global Responsibility*. New York: Teachers College Press, 1988.

Reykowski, Janusz. "Resolving Large Scale Political Conflict: The Case of the Round Table Negotiations in Poland." Paper presented at the 1990 Texas A&M Symposium on Group Conflict. College Station, Texas, April 1990.

Rheingold, Harriet L. "Little Children's Participation in the Work of Adults, a Nascent Prosocial Behavior." *Child Development* 53 (1982): 114–125.

Rich, Adrienne. *Of Woman Born: Motherhood as Experience and Institution*. New York: W. W. Norton, 1977.

Rodriguez, Richard. *Hunger of Memory: The Education of Richard Rodriguez: An Autobiography*. Boston: David R. Godine, 1981.

Rohner, Ronald P. "Sex Differences in Aggression: Phylogenetic and Enculturation Perspectives." *Ethos* 4 (1976): 57–72.

Roper, Roy, and R. Hinde. "Social Behavior in a Play Group: Consistency and Complexity." *Child Development* 49 (1978): 570–579.

Rosenhan, David L. "On Being Sane in Insane Places." *Science* 173 (1973): 250–258.

Rosenthal, A. M. "On My Mind: On Black Anti-Semitism." *The New York Times*, January 11, 1994, A, 21.

———. "On My Mind: Germany: Hidden Words." *The New York Times*, February 4, 1990, E, 23.

Rosenthal, Robert, D. Archer, M. R. DiMatteo, J. H. Kowumaki, and P. O. Rogers. "Body Talk and Tone of Voice: The Language Without Words." *Psychology Today* 8 (1974): 64–68.

Rosenzweig, Mark R., and Lyman W. Porter. *Annual Review of Psychology* 39, 1988.

Rothkop, Sonja. "Mixed Heritage Jews Share Stories About their 'Double Lives'." *Jewish Bulletin*, April 1, 1994, 27+.

Rousseau, Jean Jacques. "A Discourse on the Origin of Inequality." In *The Social Contract and Discourses.* Trans. G.D.H. Cole. New York: E. P. Dutton, 1950. "Preface," paragraph 11. Originally published in 1755.

Rubin, Kenneth H. "Relationship Between Egocentric Communication and Popularity among Peers." *Developmental Psychology* 7 (1972): 364.

Rubin, Kenneth H., and Frank W. Schneider. "The Relationship Between Moral Judgment, Egocentrism and Altruistic Behavior." *Child Development* 44 (1973): 661–665.

Ruble, Thomas L. "Sex Stereotypes: Issues of Change in the 1970's." *Sex Roles* 9 (1983): 397–402.

Rushton, J. Philippe. "Genetic Similarity, Human Altruism, and Group Selection." *Behavioral and Brain Sciences* 12 (1989): 503–553.

Rutter, Michael. "Maternal Deprivation, 1972–1978: New Findings, New Concepts, New Approaches." *Child Development* 50 (1979): 283–305.

———. "Sex Differences in Children's Response to Family Stress." In *The Child in His Family.* Eds. E. James Anthony and Cyrille Koupernik. New York: John Wiley & Sons, 1970, 165–196.

Rytina, N. F. "Earnings of Men and Women: A Look at Specific Occupations." *Monthly Labor Review*, April 1982, 251–71.

Sadker, Myrna, David Sadker and Susan Klein. "The Issue of Gender in Elementary and Secondary Education." In *Review of Research in Education* 17. Ed. Carl Grant. Washington, D.C.: American Education Research Association, 1991.

Sagan, Carl. "To Avert a Common Danger." *Parade*, March 1, 1992, 10–14.

Sagi, Abraham, and Martin L. Hoffman. "Empathic Distress in the Newborn." *Developmental Psychology* 12 (1976): 175–176.

Sandole, Dennis J. D., and Ingrid Sandole-Staroste, eds. *Conflict Management and Problem Solving: Interpersonal to International Applications.* New York: New York University Press, 1987.

Sarason, Barbara R., Irwin G. Sarason, Gregory R. Pierce, eds. *Social Support: An Interactional View.* New York: John Wiley & Sons, 1990.

Schacht, Henry B., and Charles W. Powers. "Business Responsibility and the Public Policy Process." In *Corporations and Their Critics: Issues and Answers to the Problems of Corporate Social Responsibility.* Eds. Thornton Bradshaw and David Vogel. New York: McGraw-Hill, 1981, 23–32.

Schelling, Thomas C. *The Strategy of Conflict.* Cambridge: Harvard University Press, 1960.

Schiller, Herbert. *Culture, Inc: The Corporate Takeover of Public Expression.* New York: Oxford University Press, 1989.

Schlesinger, Arthur, Jr. Review of *The Opening of the American Mind*, by Alan Bloom. *The New York Times Book Review*, July 23, 1989, 1+.

Schmidt, Fran, and Alice Friedman. *Creative Conflict Solving for Kids: Grades 4–9.* Miami Beach, Fla.: Grace Contrino Abrams Peace Education Foundation, 1983.

Schmidt, Peter. " 'Hate Crimes' Are Called 'Serious Problem' in L.A." *Education Week,* November 15, 1989, 7.

Schofield, Janet Ward. *Black and White in School: Trust, Tension or Tolerance?* New York: Teachers College Press, 1989.

Schorr, Lisbeth B., with Daniel Schorr. *Within Our Reach: Breaking the Cycle of Disadvantage.* New York: Doubleday, 1988.

Schwartz, Richard D. "Arab-Jewish Dialogue in the United States: Toward Track II Tractability." In *Intractable Conflicts and Their Transformation.* Ed. Louis Kriesberg, Terrell A. Northrup, and Stuart Thorson. Syracuse, N.Y.: Syracuse University Press, 1986, 180–209.

Seigfried, Charlene Haddock. "Pragmatism, Feminism, and Sensitivity to Context." In *Who Cares: Theory, Research, and Educational Implications of the Ethic of Care.* Ed. Mary B. Brabeck. New York: Praeger, 1989, 63–83.

Seligson, Tom. "To Survive, We Must Trust." *Parade,* October 8, 1989, 10–12.

Selman, Robert L. *The Growth of Interpersonal Understanding: Developmental and Clinical Analyses.* New York: Academic Press, 1980.

———. "Social-Cognitive Understanding: A Guide to Educational and Clinical Practice." In *Moral Development and Behavior.* Ed. Thomas Lickona. New York: Holt, Rinehart and Winston, 1976, 299–316.

Shanker, Albert. "Where We Stand: The Sobol Report." Advertisement under the auspices of the New York State United Teachers and the American Federation of Teachers. *The New York Times,* January 28, 1990, E7.

Sherif, Muzafer. *Group Conflict and Co-operation.* London: Routledge and Kegan-Paul, 1967.

Sherif, Muzafer, ed. *Intergroup Relations and Leadership.* New York: John Wiley & Sons, 1962.

Sherif, Muzafer, and Carolyn W. Sherif. *Social Psychology.* New York: Harper & Row, 1969.

———. "In-Group and Intergroup Relations: Experimental Analysis." In *Social Psychology.* Muzafer Sherif and Carolyn W. Sherif. New York: Harper & Row, 1969, 221–288.

Shipler, David K. *Russia: Broken Idols, Solemn Dreams.* New York: Penguin Books, 1986.

Shweder, Richard A., and Robert A. LeVine, eds. *Culture Theory: Essays on Mind, Self, and Emotion.* New York: Cambridge University Press, 1984.

Silverstein, Michael. "The Joys of Environmental Employment." *In Business,* Summer 1989, 29–31.

Simmel, Georg. *Conflict.* Trans. Kurt H. Wolff. Glencoe, Ill.: Free Press, 1955.

Simner, Martin L. "Newborn's Response to the Cry of Another Infant." *Developmental Psychology* 5 (1971): 136–150.

Simon, Sidney B., Leland W. Howe, and Howard Kirschenbaum. *Values Clarification: A Handbook of Practical Strategies for Teachers and Students.* New York: Hart, 1972, 219–220.

Simon-McWilliam, Ethel, ed. *Resegregation of Public Schools: The Third Generation.* Portland, Ore.: Network of Regional Desegregation Assistance Centers and

Northwest Regional Educational Laboratory, 1989.

"Singing to Save the Earth." *In Business,* September/October 1989, 10.

Slavin, Robert E. *Cooperative Learning: Theory, Research, and Practice.* Englewood Cliffs, N.J.: Prentice-Hall, 1990.

Sleeter, Christine E. "Staff Development for Desegregated Schooling." *Phi Delta Kappan* (September 1990): 33–40.

Smith, Adam. *The Theory of Moral Sentiments.* Richmond, Va.: Ibis Publications, 1986. Originally published in 1759.

Smith, Brian H. *More Than Altruism: The Politics of Private Foreign Aid.* Princeton: Princeton University Press, 1990.

Smith, Wendy K., under the supervision of Richard S. Tedlow. "James Burke: A Career in American Business." In *Managerial Decision Making and Ethical Values: Instructor's Manual.* Eds. Mary C. Gentile, Kenneth E. Goodpaster, and Thomas R. Piper. Boston: Harvard Business School, 1989, Section 8.

Sobol, Thomas. "Understanding Diversity," *Educational Leadership* 48 (November 3, 1990): 27–30.

Solomon, Daniel, Marilyn Watson, K. Delucchi, Eric Schaps, and Victor Battistich. "Enhancing Children's Prosocial Behavior in the Classroom." *American Educational Research Journal* 25 (1988): 527–554.

Spence, Janet T. "Verbal Reinforcement Combinations and Concept-Identification Learning: The Role of Nonreinforcement." *Journal of Experimental Psychology* 85 (1970): 321–329.

Spence, Janet T., Robert L. Helmreich, and Joy Stapp. "Ratings of Self and Peers on Sex Role Attributes and their Relation to Self-esteem and Conceptions of Masculinity and Femininity." *Journal of Personality and Social Psychology* 32 (1975): 29–39.

Spring, Joel. *The American School: 1642–1985 Varieties of Historical Interpretation of the Foundations and Development of American Education.* New York: Longman, 1986.

Srivastva, Suresh, and David L. Cooperrider. "Introduction: The Urgency for Executive Integrity." In *Executive Integrity: The Search for High Human Values in Organizational Life.* Eds. Suresh Srivastva and Associates. San Francisco: Jossey-Bass, 1988, 1–28.

Sroufe, L. Alan. "The Coherence of Individual Development: Early Care, Attachment, and Subsequent Developmental Issues." *American Psychologist* 34 (1979): 834–841.

Staff of the Child Development Project. *A Program to Promote Interpersonal Consideration and Cooperation in Children.* San Ramon, Calif.: The Child Development Project, October 1982.

Staub, Ervin. "Individual and Group Selves, Motivation and Morality." In *Morality and the Self.* Eds. Wolfgang Edelstein and Thomas E. Wren. Boston: The MIT Press, in press.

———. *Positive Social Behavior and Morality: Socialization and Development.* Vol. 2. New York: Academic Press, 1979.

Stone, Pat. "Christian Ecology: A Growing Force in the Environmental Movement." *Mother Earth News,* January/February 1989, excerpted in *Utne Reader* 36, November/December 1989, 78–79.

Stone, Robin, Gail Lee Cafferata, and Judith Sangl. "Caregivers of the Frail Elderly: A National Profile." *The Gerontologist* 27:5 (1987): 616–626.

Strong, Maurice F. "Preface: A Time for Action." In *Through the '80s: Thinking Globally, Acting Locally.* Ed. Frank Feather. Washington, D.C., 1980, 3–4.

Suresh Srivastva and Associates, eds. *Executive Integrity: The Search for High Human Values in Organizational Life.* San Francisco: Jossey-Bass, 1988.

Susskind, Lawrence, and Jeffrey Cruikshank. *Breaking the Impasse: Consensual Approaches to Resolving Public Disputes.* New York: Basic Books, 1987.

Swidler, Leonard. "Toward a Universal Declaration of a Global Ethic." June 14, 1993 revision.

Takooshian, Harold, Sandra Haber, and David J. Lucido. "Who Wouldn't Help a Lost Child?" *Psychology Today,* February 1977, 67–68.

Tannen, Deborah. *You Just Don't Understand: Women and Men in Conversation.* New York: William Morrow, 1990.

Tenth Yearbook of the Department of Superintendence. *Character Education.* Washington, D.C.: National Education Association of the United States, 1932.

Terkel, Studs. *Second Thoughts on the American Dream.* New York: Pantheon Books, 1988.

Thomas, Laurence. *Living Morally: A Psychology of Moral Character.* Philadelphia, Pa.: Temple University Press, 1989.

Thomas, Lewis. *The Youngest Science: Notes of a Medicine-Watcher.* Toronto: Bantam Books, 1983.

Toffler, Barbara Ley. *Tough Choices: Managers Talk Ethics.* New York: John Wiley & Sons, 1986.

Trice, Harrison M., and Janice M. Beyer. "Using Six Organizational Rites to Change Culture." In *Gaining Control of the Corporate Culture.* Eds. Ralph H. Kilmann, Mary J. Saxton, Roy Serpa and Associates. San Francisco: Jossey-Bass, 1985, 370–395.

Tuller, David. "The Latest Job Benefit—Care for Elderly Relatives." *San Francisco Chronicle,* August 7, 1989, 136+.

Tunstall, W. Brooke. "Breakup of the Bell System: A Case Study in Cultural Transformation." In *Gaining Control of the Corporate Culture.* Eds. Ralph H. Kilmann, Mary J. Saxton, Roy Serpa and Associates. San Francisco: Jossey-Bass, 1985, 44–65.

"Vietnam Veteram Arthur E. 'Gene' Woodley, Jr., Combat Paratrooper, 5th Special Forces Group, 173rd Airborne Division, U.S. Army, An Khe, November 1968–December 1969." In *Bloods: An Oral History of the Vietnam War by Black Veterans.* Terry Wallace. New York: Random House, 1984, 243–265.

Volkan, Vamik. *The Need to Have Enemies and Allies: From Clinical Practice to International Relations.* Northvale, N.J.: Jason Aronson, 1988.

Waldrop, Judith, and Thomas Exter. "The Legacy of the 1980s." *American Demographics* (March 1991): 32–38.

Waldrop, Mary F., and Charles F. Halverson, Jr. "Intensive and Extensive Peer Behavior: Longitudinal and Cross-sectional Analyses." *Child Development* 46 (1975): 19–26.

Wallace, Terry. *Bloods: An Oral History of the Vietnam War by Black Veterans.* New York: Random House, 1984.

Walters, Herb. "Contras." *Rural Southern Voice for Peace* 38, May/June 1988, 1–5.

Walton, Anthony. "Willie Horton and Me." *The New York Times Magazine*, August 30, 1989, 52+.

Waters, Everett, Judith Wippman, and L. Alan Sroufe, "Attachment, Positive Affect, and Competence in the Peer Group: Two Studies in Construct Validation." *Child Development* 50 (1979): 821–890.

Weber, James A. "Case: Corporate Codes of Conduct." In *Business and Society*. Ed. Donna J. Wood. Glenview, Ill.: Scott, Foresman/Little, Brown Higher Education, 1990, 284–287.

Weick, Karl E. *The Social Psychology of Organizing*. 2d ed. Reading, Mass.: Addison-Wesley, 1979.

———. "Educational Organizations as Loosely Coupled Systems." *Administrative Science Quarterly* 21 (1976): 1–19.

Weiss, Edith Brown. "Global Environmental Change and International Law: The Introductory Framework." In *Environmental Change and International Law: New Challenges and Dimensions*. Ed. Edith Brown Weiss. Tokyo, Japan: United Nations University Press, 1992, 3–38.

Weiss, Edith Brown, ed. *Environmental Change and International Law: New Challenges and Dimensions*. Tokyo, Japan: United Nations University Press, 1992.

White, Lynn, Jr. "The Historical Roots of Our Ecological Crisis." *Science*, 1967.

Whiting, Beatrice B., and John W. M. Whiting. *Children of Six Cultures: A Psychocultural Analysis*. Cambridge: Harvard University Press, 1975.

Wichert, Susanne. *Keeping the Peace: Practicing Cooperation and Conflict Resolution with Preschoolers*. Philadelphia, Pa.: New Society Publishers, 1989.

Wiesel, Elie. "Are We Afraid of Peace?" *Parade*, March 19, 1989, 8.

Wilder, David A. "Social Categorization: Implications for Creation and Reduction of Inter-Group Bias." In *Advances in Experimental Social Psychology*. Vol. 19. Ed. Leonard Berkowitz. New York: Academic Press, 1986, 293–356.

———. "Predictions of Belief Homogeneity and Similarity Following Social Categorization." *British Journal of Social Psychology* 23 (1984): 323–333.

Wilkes, Paul. "The Hands That Would Shape Our Souls." *The Atlantic* 266:6, December 1990, 59–88.

Williams, Juan. "Integration Turns 40: The New Segregation." *Modern Maturity*, April-May 1994, 24–34.

———. *Eyes on the Prize: America's Civil Rights Years 1954–1965*. New York: Viking, 1987.

Williamson, Roger. "Why is Religion Still a Factor in Armed Conflict," *Bulletin of Peace Proposals* 21:3 (1990): 243–253.

Willis, S. "Coop Learning Shows Staying Power." *Association for Supervision and Curriculum Development Update*, March 1992, 34, 1–2.

Winkler, Karen J. "Scholars Say Issues of Diversity Have 'Revolutionalized' Field of Chicano Studies." *The Chronicle of Higher Education*, September 26, 1990, A-4+.

Wispé, Lauren. "The Distinction Between Sympathy and Empathy: To Call Forth a Concept, a Word is Needed." *Journal of Personality and Social Psychology* 50: 2 (1986): 314–321.

Witte, John F. *Democracy, Authority, and Alienation in Work: Workers' Participation in an American Corporation*. Chicago: University of Chicago Press, 1980.

Wood, Donna J. *Business and Society.* Glenview, Ill.: Scott, Foresman/Little, Brown Higher Education, 1990.

Worchel, Stephen, and William G. Austin, eds. *Psychology of Intergroup Relations.* 2d ed. Chicago: Nelson-Hall, 1986.

Worell, Judith, ed. *Psychological Development in the Elementary Years.* San Francisco: Academic Press, 1982.

Wormser, Richard. *Transcript for "Fighting Ministers,"* 31, p. 3. Shown on POV (Point of View), PBS, in Arcata, California, September 5, 1989, 10:00–11:00 P.M.

Wynn, Ruth L. "Custody Disputes and the Victims." In *Intractable Conflicts and Their Transformation.* Eds. Louis Kriesberg, Terrell A. Northrup, and Stuart J. Thorson. Syracuse, N.Y.: Syracuse University Press, 1989, 83–92.

Zablocki, Benjamin. *Alienation and Charisma: A Study of Contemporary American Communes.* New York: Free Press, 1980.

Zanna, Mark, and John K. Rempel. "Attitudes: A New Look." In *The Social Psychology of Knowledge.* Eds. Daniel Bar-Tal and Arie W. Kruglanski. Cambridge, England: Cambridge University Press, 1988, 315–334.

Zongren, Liu. *Two Years in the Melting Pot.* San Francisco: China Books, 1984.

Index

About the Authors

PEARL M. OLINER is Professor of Education at Humboldt State University in California and research director for the Altruistic Personality and Prosocial Behavior Institute.

SAMUEL P. OLINER is Professor of Sociology at Humboldt State University and project director for the Altruistic Personality and Prosocial Behavior Institute.

ISBN 0-275-95198-7

EAN

9 780275 951986

HARDCOVER BAR CODE